Here's wha' other authors, speakers and
professionals say about

FIRED UP!
by Snowden McFall

"This is a truly great book. Chock full of great hands-on tools and techniques for realizing your dreams. Real-life stories show how anyone can live their dreams, when they're FIRED UP! and take action. I highly recommend it."

> **- Jack Canfield, CSP**
> **President, Self-Esteem Seminars**
> Bestselling Author of *Chicken Soup for the Soul*

"FIRED UP! is one of the most exciting books I have ever enjoyed reading. What tremendous stories of doers, dreamers, achievers on every page. If you think you are tired or discouraged, forget aspirin. Open this book at any chapter and become FIRED UP! for life. I love it and highly recommend it."

> **- Dottie Walters**
> **President, Walters International Speakers Bureau**
> Author of *Speak and Grow Rich*

"Those who read FIRED UP! will help themselves to great success keys. Obviously, Snowden has not only 'researched' her topic – she has <u>lived</u> it. Many people who teach about success can only tell <u>their</u> story, but Snowden has broken her steps towards success into an easy-to-follow path. She has shown how success can be duplicated by anyone who stays FIRED UP!"

> **- Dr. Robert Rohm**
> **Personality Consultant/ Speaker**
> Bestselling Author of *Positive Personality Profiles*

"What an extraordinary book. With its inspirational true life stories, practical hands-on tools and techniques and foolproof action plan, FIRED UP! is sure to help you ignite the fire of your dream and achieve success."

- Cavett Robert
Founder and Chairman Emeritus
of the National Speaker's Association

"If FIRED UP! doesn't fire you up or rekindle your fire, you are dead or soon will be!"

- Charlie "Tremendous" Jones, CPAE
Speaker and Owner, Executive Books
Bestselling Author of *Life is Tremendous*

"First you need a dream. Then you need to FIRE UP! that dream. Snowden's book shows you how to do both."

- **W. Mitchell**
"The Man Who Would Not be Defeated"
Speaker and Author

"Snowden has written a terrific book. FIRED UP! is destined to become a motivational classic."

- **Michael Jeffreys**
Speaker
Author of *Success Secrets of the Motivational Superstars*

"Whoever you are and whatever your dreams, FIRED UP! can help you make them come true. With easy to use tools and activities, FIRED UP! shows you how to take action and overcome obstacles. No matter what your fears have been in the past, FIRED UP! can help you succeed and live your dreams. It's awesome!"

- **Ed Gerety**
Gerety Presentations
Youth Motivational Speaker

FIRED UP!

How To Succeed By Making Your Dreams Come True

Snowden McFall

SUCCESS PUBLISHERS
Hummelstown, Pennsylvania

FIRED UP!
How To Succeed By
Making Your Dreams Come True
Snowden McFall

Copyright © 1997 by Snowden McFall

Published by **SUCCESS PUBLISHERS,**
One Oakglade Circle, Hummelstown, PA 17036 USA. 717-566-0468

All possible care has been taken to trace the ownership of every selection included and to make full acknowledgement for its use. If any errors have occurred, they will be corrected in subsequent editions provided notification is sent to the publisher.

Publisher's Cataloging in Publication
(Prepared by Quality Books Inc.)

McFall, A. Snowden.
    Fired up! : how to succeed by making your dreams come true / A. Snowden McFall. - 1st ed.
    p. cm. --(Personal development series; 3)
    Includes bibliographical references.
    Preassigned LCCN: 96-077532
    ISBN 0-938716-31-X
    1. Success. 2. Motivation (Psychology) I. Title
BF637.S8M34 1997   158
                                      QBI96-40277

Dedication

To my greatest love
and biggest cheerleader,
my husband Spencer.
You continually keep me
"FIRED UP!"
about my life.
I love you!

*"You are the sunshine that lights my days
and the fire that warms my nights.
You are the dance partner
that glides me through life
and lifts me into the heavens.
You are my champion and friend,
my protector and lover,
my playmate and spiritual partner
I honor the radiance of your being,
the tenderness of your soul
and the courage of your heart."*

Acknowledgements

I am grateful to so very many people who helped me make my dream come true. From the very beginning, Cindy Hubbard, you have given me love and encouragement and complete acceptance for who I am. You are such an angel in my life. Thank you.

I want to thank my staff at Brightwork Advertising and Training, Inc., especially Jason. He labored many long hours with me for over a year, designing covers and formatting and typesetting the book. He bent over backwards to make everything look great, always with a cheerful attitude. He never once complained, and his solid, grounded nature and excellent design and computer skills made my life so much easier. Thank you, Jay, for the great work. And thank you, Jan, for your excellent proofreading and consistent encouragement.

My book mentor, Tom Anastasi, gave me invaluable advice about approaching publishers and marketing my book. His guidance and experience as a bestselling author, coupled with his upbeat attitude, helped a great deal.

I also wish to extend my appreciation to a very special group of friends I lovingly call "readers." In the early days, Frank Clark, Stawn Barber, Corky Newcomb, Mark Molinoff, Bill Cummings and Mary Ann Somerville read the first chapters and gave me great feedback. As we grew closer to publication, a whole other group joined in. All of you contributed so much in terms of constructive feedback, careful proofreading and insightful suggestions. Your input was inestimable, as was your ongoing belief in me. Thank you so very much, Stawn Barber,

Jan Gallagher, Jon Choate, Sally Garrett, and my dear husband, Spencer. I love you all and am so grateful to have you in my life.

I also greatly appreciate all the people who have taken my "Making A Difference in the World" trainings over the years. Many of your experiences are in this book, in the great stories. Special thanks to the marvelous assistants who volunteered through the years, especially Patti D'Addieco, Lisa Boone, Terry Stevens, Stawn Barber, Ed Boufford, Mark Molinoff, Will Skaskiw and Grace Fairbairn. Special kudos to Greg Saccardo and Carolyn Cardella for being willing to share your dream collages and personal sagas with the readers.

Several of my clients have been particularly kind and supportive of my effort. Jeanne Pepper and Susan Elliott of Langdon Place of Nashua, thank you for your kind generosity of hosting a champagne booksigning party. John Merva, Marcel Laflamme and Valerie Arguin of Northeast Robotics, thanks for listening to my stories and cheering my progress. Frank Clark of Lewis and Clark, thanks for your advice and guidance about expansion for the future. Henry Huntington and everyone at Pleasant View Gardens, thanks for listening and encouraging. Amy and Brian Sanders of Ultrablend Systems, you have been terrific cheerleaders for me – thank you. Ed Gerety, of Gerety Presentations, you have always shared the fire of your enthusiasm for my dream.

And Corky Newcomb, of C.N. Is Believing, thank you for your considerable help and effort in marketing and selling my book all over the United States. Your infinite creativity, unstoppable, resilient nature and ceaseless, loving optimism have meant so much to me through the years.

One of the greatest gifts in my life is my wonderful group of friends, many of whom have already been mentioned. You all know who you are and I so much appreciate your love, patience, enthusiasm and support throughout this process. It has been very much like giving birth, and I could not have done it without you.

To my dear friends and publishers, thank you for all your love, support and expertise as we refined and improved "FIRED UP!" I appreciate all your brilliant creativity, insightful editing and willingness to honor my message and my integrity. Your belief in the value of this book and its ability to help others has sustained us all through the process. It is a delight to know you and I am so glad we were able to do this together.

Michelle Taylor, your love, dynamism and belief in me have been such gifts. Thank you for your editorial insights and for the NSA Convention. Your generosity of spirit and eagerness to share the people and profession you love mean so much.

Oprah Winfrey, for a long time, you have been a guiding light and role model. Your courage and willingness to share your fears and vulnerability, and your determination to live life on your terms demonstrate the magnificence of who you are. You impact and uplift millions of men and women worldwide.

Jack Canfield, you have inspired and educated me for over a decade. You are such a wonderful, kind human being and your willingness to assist me with my book has meant the world to me. You touch so many hearts, especially mine with your wisdom and loving, your generosity and hard work.

Les Brown, you are another soul who helped to ignite the flame of "FIRED UP!" Your message and charisma, warmth and power, vulnerability and humor have delighted and motivated me more than you know. You are a caring, passionate man who makes a big difference in the world. Thank you.

W. Mitchell, you are amazing! Your heart is as big as your courage and your graciousness towards me at NSA and then about the book have meant so much.

To Dottie Walters, Rosita Perez, Nido Qubein, Greg Godek, Margot Robinson, Michael Jeffreys, Glenna Salsbury, Jeff Fleming, Dan Poynter and Jim Hennig, your enthusiastic welcoming of me to NSA and to the world of publishing have been bright lights for me as I embark on this journey. Thank you for your encouragement and love, your wisdom and insights.

And to everyone at the National Speaker's Association, the 1996 Annual Convention was a pinnacle experience for me. I have never felt such love, kindness and mutual support amongst 2000 professionals in one setting. The workshops, general sessions, events and celebrations all helped me stay "FIRED UP!" about my dream of helping others.

To my wonderful, loving husband Spencer – you are the best. You have believed in my dreams, cheered at every victory and buoyed me up at every challenge. You are my best friend and the love of my life. Thank you for the phenomenal gift of you.

And finally, I wish to thank God, for all the learnings and lessons, blessings and miracles, grace and gifts.

"FIRED UP!" Acronym

How to Succeed by Making Your Dreams Come True!

Fire up your life by living your dreams.

Inside of you is everything you need to do what you love.

Receive guidance and assistance from others.

Enthusiasm radiates out from you when you live your dreams.

Dreams <u>do</u> come true, when you get "FIRED UP!" and take action.

Use every experience as an opportunity to learn and grow.

Pursue your dream with passion, persistence and a positive vision of the outcome.

"FIRED UP!"

CONTENTS

Prologue

The Fire Starts Inside You
Experiencing the Fire Within

"Success isn't a result of spontaneous combustion.
You must set yourself on fire."
Arnold Glascow

The twelve foot strip of sizzling hot coals lit up the inky black night. Flaming orange embers and blazing sparks flew up in the frigid winter chill and hissed in the darkness. The people huddled together around the strip of fire, singing, praying and clutching each other in their fear and elation. Some looked very peaceful, some were overjoyed; but most looked terrified. One by one, each who felt it was time stepped forward, leaving the circle of song and walking to the strip of smoldering coals.

At last it was her turn. Something inside her shifted. She felt a sense of protection, alignment and purpose guide her. Her fear magically transmuted into courage as she stepped to the edge of the coals. Her bare pink feet emerged from the warmth of her heavy winter boots. She lifted her left foot first and gingerly placed it onto the 1200 degree coals. "This is hot," she thought and then she relaxed and continued the walk, feeling nothing but calm.

Quickly, she checked her feet and they were not hurt, except for a tiny red spot. In that split second, she realized with amazement what she had done. She had tread on smoldering hot coals and emerged unharmed. Yes, she had a tiny sore, but most people would expect their feet to be completely burned and blistered. She had transcended the laws of nature and been lifted into a higher experience. *Victorious, glowing and infinitely triumphant, she turned around and grinned broadly at her companions. "I did it!" she exclaimed, "I did it!" She was quite simply, "FIRED UP!"*

That woman was *me* in 1988, participating in a weekend seminar in Iowa called *Overcoming Fear and Limitation.* The firewalk was the culminating exercise of a weekend filled with many wonderful lessons. I found the firewalk to be an incredible reference point that proved I could, in fact, transcend previous limitations, step forward and express the deepest part of who I am. The firewalk enabled me to confront much of my pain and confusion about my childhood. It helped me to forgive and let go of the negative self-talk and patterns ingrained inside me.

It was also an experience of expanding my self-definition. In preparing for the firewalk, Michael, the leader, who has taken thousands of people safely through firewalks, shared the nature of fear and how adrenaline affects our bodies. I learned that during a firewalk, a burst of adrenaline shifts from fear to power, allowing us to overcome traditional limitations. There are tribes in Africa who roll their entire bodies through fire to rid themselves of disease. And many of us have read stories about mothers who miraculously lift cars off their children. All of this showed me the power of the heart, coupled with purpose and God's help. It demonstrated the phenomenal value of being "FIRED UP!"

Have there been times in your life when you have broken free from the bonds of the past and succeeded even when it seemed nearly impossible? Many people have such experiences during athletic events, where they're able to set new records or exceed their personal best. If you've ever been in sales, do you remember what it was like to make your first sale? It felt great, right? Or you may have created a surprise birthday party for someone you love. These would all be examples of being "FIRED UP!" about life.

● Now, I'm going to share a story of someone who made his dream come true and is still "FIRED UP!" about his life – my husband, Spencer. Spencer's mission in life and his real joy is to work full-time with children. He grew up with four brothers and sisters and now thoroughly enjoys his thirteen nieces and nephews. Spencer dreamed of taking his sales training expertise and people skills and using them to work with young children. He regularly volunteered at community children's events, but he had no teaching credentials. All his professional experience had been in business, not education. He kept focused on his dream, though, visualized living it fully and continually took action toward it.

A few months later, he made a key contact. At a Rotary meeting, he met the Associate Director of a new YMCA, who needed a Family Services Director. She was impressed with Spencer's dedication and enthusiasm, his people skills and his drive. She encouraged him to apply for the job. In spite of stiff competition (200 other applicants) and several rounds of interviews, he got the job! Spencer now runs an after-school daycare center, a kindergarten and child care services for over 120 children daily. His favorite part of the job is interacting with the kids, listening and encouraging, playing and teaching. He is doing what he loves.

When you are "FIRED UP!" miracles can take place. You can do more than you ever thought you could and excel in ways you might never have thought possible before. This book can help you get "FIRED UP!" about your life and help you overcome obstacles you may have let stop you in the past. It has tools, techniques and real life stories of people just like you and me who made their dreams come tue. Their experiences are shared here, to inspire and assist you in achieving your dreams. If you've been looking for ways to have more success, happiness, love and prosperity in your life, then continue reading. *Your future begins today.* You *can* do what you love and live your dream. It's just a decision away.

Introduction

As a child, did you ever dream *big* dreams? Were you excited about life? Did you feel you were really going to make a difference in the world? What happened when you grew up? Did you bring those dreams to life and share your fire with the world? Are you "FIRED UP!" about life, and making your dreams come true?

Inside you are all the gifts and talents to make your dreams come true. You have unique gifts to share with the world and only *you* can offer them.

Little kids have great big dreams which seem totally attainable when they are young, open and idealistic. For most young children, the sky's the limit. But sometimes their fire and enthusiasm gets doused or at least dampened by the challenges and traumas of childhood and adolescence. When that happens, dreams are often forgotten. The child grows up, leads a day-to-day existence, just "getting by."

Crises Can Be Our Teachers

Some people wait until they experience a crisis before they stop and look at their lives. All of a sudden, they "wake up" and realize something's missing and that their life needs more meaning and purpose.

In many respects, the firewalk was the perfect analogy for much of my life. Throughout a difficult and painful childhood, I walked across the "hot coals" of crisis after crisis, and emerged stronger and wiser from the lessons.

My mother became seriously ill when I was six; she was in and out of the hospital for the next fifteen years until she finally died. Alcoholism was a constant presence in the family, and like most children from that environment, I grew up insecure and scared. When I was in my late twenties, I nearly married an alcoholic. Fortunately, I learned from these experiences, got help through therapy, personal growth workshops and recovery support groups. Stepping off the coals, I was able to break free of the barriers of my past. I know now that those crises were blessings in disguise, for they taught me compassion and understanding, strength and courage, perseverance and faith. And much like the firewalk, there has been exultation in burning away the negativity and stepping forward into my dreams. My dreams were what kept me going all along, and they are still a very important part of my life.

As a child, my dreams were to be a teacher and help other people and to be happily married. As I grew older and wanted to do even more, from opening my own business to writing books, my dreams have helped sustain me.

So What About Your Dreams?

How about those dreams you had when you were a little kid? Are you living them? Do you still want them? Or, do you now have other dreams that are equally important to you, but you're not sure where to start?

Don't worry. You *can* make your dreams come true and start living a more fulfilling and satisfying life. Many of the answers about how you can do that are in this book.

Making a Difference in the World

You can also make a difference in the world – big or small. You are the only person who can share your dream and touch the lives of others. In fact, you're already making a difference in ways that you may be unaware of.

The foundation of this book is my *Making a Difference in the World* seminar, a weekend training dedicated to helping people do what they love, take action on their dreams and make a positive difference in the world. Many of the seminar's tools and techniques came from my own "stress survival tool kit." For example, I encourage people to pair up with "dreambuddies" and form "Inspiration Circles" to stay "FIRED UP!" as they work on their dreams. These techniques will work for you, too.

For the last four years, I have led this training and have seen amazing results. When people believe in themselves, get "FIRED UP!" and start moving on their dreams, miracles can happen. I have witnessed case after case of people transcending previous limitations, going for their dreams and succeeding against all odds.

That can happen for you, too. You have the power and ability to make every one of your dreams come true. With the tools in this book, you can start taking action, transcending previous barriers and get moving on what is most dear to your heart.

The Birth of "FIRED UP!"

The *Making a Difference* seminar led me to my next dream, which you are actively participating in now. Watching each person in the training move on their dreams was so inspiring. Each one of these people was like a match striking against kindling. The fire inside of me was set ablaze. I learned that my deepest fulfillment comes from helping others take action on their dreams and make them come true. That's why I have written *FIRED UP!*

FIRED UP! is the first in a series of several books I have wanted to write since I was a child. Even though I've kept a journal since I was ten, this is the first time I have shared my heart on paper. It has been a journey in and of itself.

I created this book for *you*, to help you make *your* dreams come true. Through the years, I have discovered that while almost everyone has a dream, very few people actually *live* their dreams. Since there is no training for it in school, most people don't know *how* to make their dreams come true, *how* to take action and *how* to complete and succeed.

That's what this book is all about. It's filled with useful techniques and tips for overcoming obstacles and moving forward.

There are fun and interesting activities and real life stories of people like you and me (many from actual seminar participants) meeting their challenges and achieving their dreams. All of these are meant to assist, educate and inspire you and most of all, get you "FIRED UP!"

Thank you for sharing in my dream by reading this. I thank God every day for the lessons He has shared with me in the creation of this book and for the blessings of my life. I am very grateful.

May you have a life of joy, love and fulfillment and may all your dreams come true!

With love to you all,

Snowden

*"Winning
starts with
Beginning."*

Robert H. Schuller

DREAMS

*"The future belongs
to those
who believe
in the beauty
of their dreams."*
Eleanor Roosevelt

*"Dreams are what
everything
is about."*
Michael Jordan

*"If you can dream it,
you can do it."*
Walt Disney

Graphics Key

These graphics appear throughout the book, and are designed to make it easy for you to find what most interests you. Most are symbols representing the theme of fire. The flame logo above signifies the start of a new chapter.

 Diamonds are key bullet points. Diamonds result when intense heat and pressure compact coal into brilliant stones.

 The single flame graphic means that a story follows in the text. Most are real accounts of people going for their dreams or enjoying their lives.

 These candles appear at the end of every chapter and signify the closing of a chapter. They increase in quantity depending on the chapter number.

TIP 1   These boxes are key tips or action options, usually in resource chapters.

"FIRED UP!" Principles

#1 Choose and Commit to Success

#2 Do What You Love Often

#3 Doing What You Love Makes a Difference in the World Around You

#4 Get Clear About What You Want

#5 Use Your Imagination

#6 Uncover Your Myths

#7 Identify Role Models

#8 Use Motivational Tapes and Seminars

#9 "Act As If"

#10 Take Action and Keep Moving

#11 Have A Plan

#12 Capture Your Creativity on Paper

#13 Tap Into Your Resources

#14 Connect with the Right People

The Fire Inside You

Inside of you is the fire of life. That fire is your passion, your life purpose, your mission and your fulfillment. It ignites and burns brightly inside of you when you do what you love and live your dreams. When you're "FIRED UP!" your fire warms others, igniting their flames and creating enthusiasm, joy and a desire to join you in your quest to make your dreams come true. When you're "FIRED UP!" you feel strong, vibrantly alive and invincible. You can overcome any obstacle, and meet any challenge head-on and win. You can succeed in ways you never before thought possible. You can have more love, more joy, more abundance and more peace than you ever imagined. It all starts inside of you – with your fire and your dreams. The choice is always yours. The time to live the life of your dreams is now. So let's get started. Let's get "FIRED UP!"

"Whatever you can do
Or dream you can,
Begin it.
Boldness has genius,
power and magic in it.
BEGIN IT NOW. "
Goethe

Chapter 1

Your Dreams Create Your Life

Your Belief Is Your Fuel

"When you learn to believe that what you want is possible, your belief will be your fuel. And when you release the passion inside of you to accomplish your dreams, then the fire inside of you will burn brightly enough to accomplish all that you desire and nothing will stand in your way."
Jack Canfield and Mark Victor Hansen

There's A Fire Inside You

There is nobody else just like you, and you uniquely reflect your enthusiasm to the world when you are "FIRED UP!" about your life. You have the ability to touch the lives of others and live a life of happiness and success. Whatever you have done up until now is in the past. The rest of your life begins today, right now, in the present moment. And the *present* is a gift you give yourself.

Dreams keep the fire inside you alive. As you anticipate and develop your dreams and make them come true, your life takes on new meaning and value. You enjoy greater success and prosperity; you feel empowered and energized about your life. You are also more attractive to others.

When you do what you love and love what you do, your enthusiasm radiates out to others and automatically lifts them. Your joy and excitement are contagious, and spark other people into action. The fire ignites and spreads from you to others, and every aspect of your life becomes more fulfilling than you ever believed possible.

We've all had experiences in our lives when we've been "FIRED UP!" or we've seen someone else who was "FIRED UP!" Think about Olympic speed skater Dan Jansen at the 1994 Winter Olympics. People were excited that he finally won after all his disappointing losses. He persevered and triumphed! He won the gold medal and demonstrated that persistence and a positive attitude pay off.

Perhaps you've seen the movie *Dances with Wolves*, which portrays how the United States military uprooted Native Americans from their homes, treating them like animals. Kevin Costner directed and produced this movie against all odds, with very little support from Hollywood. A masterpiece that stirred the hearts of those who watched it, that film went on to receive great acclaim. It brought in millions of dollars at the box office and was culturally recognized. He pursued his dream with passion and excellence, producing a movie that reflected his enthusiasm. As people watched the film, they got "FIRED UP!" too.

Jansen and Costner are but two examples of people who were "FIRED UP!" about their lives and went on to achieve their dreams. You, too, can have exciting experiences. You can make your dreams come true, step-by-step. You can be revved-up about life, doing more of what you love every day.

Why Aren't More People "FIRED UP!"?

If it's true that every one of us has a fire inside as well as unique talents and gifts, why aren't more people living the lives they've dreamed about? Part of the answer is *lack of a positive, proactive education.*

Similar in some respects to the classroom scenes of the popular movie *Dangerous Minds*, I taught English and history to junior high students in the mid-1970's. I saw many youngsters negatively labeled, as they were placed in classes according to their "intelligence." While teaching English to a class of "low level academic" boys in the ninth grade, I witnessed how destructive labels really are. Those boys, ranging in age from 13-16, didn't believe in themselves and thought they were failures.

When I spoke to them the first day, I wiped their "slates clean." I told them that every student in the class could make an A, *if they worked for it*. Most of them didn't trust me – at first. Then, as we spent more time together, they understood that I really did believe in them and was willing to work with them to help them learn.

Little by little, small miracles occurred. One boy, who hated reading, began regularly volunteering to read aloud to the class. Two others immediately saw their work pay off in the form of B's on the first test. They were stunned. By the end of the year, there were many B's, several C's and only one D. No one failed that class! In addition to discovering they could read, write and communicate effectively, these boys learned they were intelligent and capable, even though labeled otherwise. Up until that time, they had not had that experience. They had believed their label and their behavior reflected this. They needed someone to encourage them to achieve, like we all do.

That happens to many people. Sometimes they allow their negative self-talk and childhood programming to stop them from growing. *They have negative experiences where they are labeled as failures and they give up on themselves.* Most contemporary schooling does not teach you how to succeed and achieve your dreams. While many people have dreams, *few have the tools, confidence and support* to move on them and turn them into reality. Most education does not teach you how to take action, step-by-step and follow-through to create the life you truly want, doing what you believe you are meant to do.

That's exactly what this book is all about. *It's a step-by-step handbook for defining and achieving your dreams.* The tools and techniques in this guide can be applied to any goal, dream or mission. They have been used effectively by thousands to create the lives they've always wanted. I'll be sharing some of these true stories later on, so you'll know you can do it too – become "FIRED UP!" and make your dreams come true.

Did You Know?

Sandra Day O'Connor could not get a job as a lawyer when she graduated from law school in 1952. Instead, she chose to enter public service, and served as county deputy attorney before opening her own law firm. In 1981 she became the first woman Justice of the United States Supreme Court.

🔥 When Henry Ford wanted to create the V-8 engine, he was told repeatedly that it was impossible. He sent his staff back to work and told them to stay on the job until they did what he asked. After a year, there was no success. He told them to keep at it. He knew persistence would pay off. Eventually they did it and the V-8 became a huge success. It helped Ford and his motor company outstrip the competition and take the lead in the automotive market. He refused to believe "It's impossible."

🔥 Amy Grant, the popular Grammy winner who has multiple gold and platinum albums, launched her recording career with a colossal flop. While on her first tour, she was due to sign autographs and sing for an hour at a record store in Southern California. Twelve hundred invitations had gone out and everyone was expecting a huge crowd. *Not one person showed up* – not even one out of the twelve hundred invited! Although she seriously considered quitting music at that point, she persevered and learned to never take her fans for granted.

How It Feels To Be "FIRED UP!"

🔥 Don Shula, famous football coach and author of *Everyone's a Coach*, describes what it feels like for him to be "FIRED UP!" He writes, "You want to know what motivates me? When the stadium's full, the crowd is yelling and the referee raises his hand to signal the start of the game, I can feel adrenaline rush through my body. I wouldn't want to be anywhere else in the world." That attitude led Don to break George Halas's all-time coaching record of 324 wins.

🔥 Bonnie Blair, Olympic speed skater and five time gold medalist, epitomizes someone who is completely "FIRED UP!" about her life and her dream. Every time she was interviewed on television during the 1994 Olympics, she enthusiastically exclaimed, "I love to skate!"

For me, there's nothing quite like the energy and excitement of being "FIRED UP!" When I step in front of a crowd to give a motivational talk, or lead a seminar of people working on their dreams, a powerful and unmistakable physical reaction washes over me. I get goosebumps from the top of my scalp to the tips of my toes, and I am usually very moved emotionally.

I feel joy, anticipation and tremendous gratitude to be able to be living my life, doing what I enjoy the most. It is one of the most amazing experiences in the world, and I love it.

I actively work to live more and more of my life in a state of being "FIRED UP!" It doesn't take much to make it happen. One heartfelt contact with another human being can bring it on. Picturing an opportunity to help other people also works. Remembering the times when I have triumphed over obstacles does it. *Whatever does it for you, start getting yourself "FIRED UP!" The flame inside of you is ready to ignite. Light the fire today and start living your dreams!*

"It's never too late to be what you might have been."
George Eliot

Remember These Key Points

◆ You have a unique fire inside. That fire is your passion and purpose.
◆ Your dreams keep your fire alive.
◆ Your fire is contagious – it radiates out to others and gets them excited too.
◆ By using the tools that are in this book, you will learn how to discover your dreams, take action and make them come true.

Now Take These "FIRED UP!" Action Steps

◆ Pay attention to the other people in your life and what fires them up. Notice what excites them and let yourself get "FIRED UP!" by their positive energy.

◆ Look back over your life and recall any times when you were truly "FIRED UP!" Maybe it was before a championship softball game, a music recital or business presentation. Perhaps you worked all summer to earn the money to buy a car. Maybe you took a life-saving course and survived a kicking, screaming 200 pound victim struggling with you in the water. Perhaps you ran for office in a school election or acted a major role in a school play. Whatever the events were, remember them and let the feelings of triumph and satisfaction take over. Start becoming more and more familiar with the excitement of being "FIRED UP!"

"Dreams
put to work
create the miracle."
Jim Rohn

Chapter 2

Negativity Can Douse Your Fire
Keeping the Embers Alive

"Argue for your limitations and sure enough, they're yours."
Richard Bach

Negative Thoughts are "Dreamstealers"

Why do some people achieve their dreams, while many don't? *The greatest "dreamstealers" are often the doubts people have.* In many cases, people allow the limiting beliefs they learned during childhood or even later in life to stop them from taking that extra step. False beliefs often keep them from extending themselves and taking risks to make their dreams come true. They buy into false statements or myths which take on a life of their own, and frequently have power over their subconscious. As Robert H. Schuller said in his book *Power Thoughts*, *"To discover your potential, reject the negative programming all of us are exposed to."* Here are some examples of people who let negativity steal their dream.

7

Mary Lets Negativity Rule

🔥 Mary sees an ad in the paper for the job she's always yearned for. Instead of going after it and sharing her dynamism and excellent work skills with the people at that company, she doesn't even bother applying for the job. Why? She thinks people need to have a degree to do that kind of job; all she has is experience. She undermines herself with negative self-talk and quits before she starts. She gives up on her dream and then feels cheated and depressed.

Tom's Misperceptions Get in the Way

🔥 Tom reads a story about a local community center that needs volunteers to work with troubled youth. He's excited because he remembers how much an older man helped him when he was a struggling adolescent. But before he even meets anyone at the center, he lets his negative self-talk take over. Perceiving that he doesn't have enough training in child psychology, he fears he won't know how to handle every kind of problem he'd encounter. He thinks he needs to be earning lots of money to be a good role model. Then his wife tells him that those kids might be dangerous, and he considers that possibility. The result is he doesn't take action; he stays immobilized by his doubts and fears and feels empty and unfulfilled.

Doubt Steals Jim and Linda's Dream

🔥 Jim and Linda's life is one of mundane survival. They were given an opportunity to generate some additional income in a part-time business and take ongoing motivational seminars for personal growth. Even though they know they're "in a rut," they continue to let their fear of the unknown stop them. They cover up their fear by using the *excuse* that they don't have time. They remain frustrated and bored while doing nothing to change their circumstances.

> *"Insanity is doing the same things while expecting different results."*   Author Unknown

Just in these three examples, it's evident how strong a hold negativity and myths can have. Even though these people let their false beliefs stop them, that doesn't mean you need to let yours stop you. *With your enthusiasm, passion and talents, you can make your dreams come true.* Right now, at this very moment, you can start making changes in your life and begin doing more of what you love. You'll find that what you love to do reflects what your talents are. Once you know that, you can start evaluating where you are and where you want to be. You'll start getting more and more "FIRED UP!" about your life.

As you begin taking steps toward living the life you've always wanted, you'll discover that you can give up the grind of something you don't enjoy – sooner than you might have thought. You may want to quit your job or dramatically change your life. However, you'll need to make sure your new dream is securely in place before you do so. The best way to make that happen is to take action and prepare yourself for your new life. Do your homework, lay the foundation and "stack the deck" in your favor. *You deserve it and you can have it – when you get "FIRED UP!" and make it happen!*

Perhaps these stories remind you of someone you know. Do they sound familiar? Later, you'll learn more about the doubts and fears that stop people from having the kind of life they would like to have. *Everyone has some kind of voice that tries to hold them back. Replace that voice with positive self-talk and take action anyway, no matter what the negative voice says.* Feel your fear and go for your dreams in spite of the fear. When you make up your mind and start moving, amazing things can happen in extraordinary ways. Here are a few examples.

Walt Disney went bankrupt several times before he actually succeeded. His vision of what was possible kept him going. He never quit, not ever. Now his creations, cartoons, movies and theme parks touch millions of lives every year. As he once said, *"All of our dreams can come true when we have the courage to pursue them."*

Abraham Lincoln experienced many defeats before he became one of this country's greatest Presidents. Born poor, he lost his job, failed in business twice and failed to get elected in eight campaigns prior to becoming senator. He went bankrupt and later had a nervous breakdown. He never quit; he persisted in following his dreams. What would this country be like if he had allowed his lack of formal childhood education and political success hold him back from running for President?

After Michael Worsley relocated to Manchester, New Hampshire, he discovered he was one of only a few black males in the area. Instead of dwelling on the isolation and developing a negative attitude, he put his skills to use. He channeled his energies into the Webster House, where he nurtures neglected children from broken homes with self-esteem, love and encouragement. He regularly receives feedback from area professionals about the positive impact of his work on these children. He makes a big difference in their lives, which, in turn, affects their behavior with others. [1]

Is Fire and Enthusiasm Enough?

Success takes much more than fire and enthusiasm – it takes determination, planning, follow-through, clarity and above all, *action.* It also requires genuine awareness of what your dreams are, what blocks have held you back until now and what action steps will lead you to success. *The more information you have about what drives and inspires you,* the better you can determine your destiny in a purposeful, focused way. The more you are aware of what in-grained myths operate in your life, the sooner you can let them go and replace them with new beliefs and behaviors which support your dreams.

The more you use the "FIRED UP!" Action Plan and tools, the sooner you can be living your dreams and sharing your joy, triumph and enthusiasm with others. Once you achieve your first dream, you can use the same approach over and over again to achieve your other dreams. Or you can use it to make your current dream even bigger. You can be doing the things you love to do, and consistently experiencing greater satisfaction, prosperity and happiness.

"FIRED UP!" PRINCIPLE # 1 – Choose and Commit to Success

Did you know that choice and commitment are very powerful? Every great achievement came as a result of choice and commitment. Olympic athletes *choose* to spend hours and hours every day training for an event that comes once every four years. After they have made that choice and committed to it, the actions they take and the attitude they carry naturally fall into line. When you make a choice and commit to it, you are saying "yes" to your future. You are actively setting into motion a *willingness* to succeed and openness to opportunity and magic. You are instilling the attitude of "do whatever it takes." You are freeing up all the levels of your being to search and find creative sparks to help you achieve your dream. Such choice and commitment are deliberate and intentional; they clarify your direction and align your life with your focus.

So What About Your Dream?

The choice is yours. You can live the same life you've always lived – which may be just fine. But you're probably reading this because you want more out of life, and because you know, deep down inside, that *you deserve more.* Whether it's a better job, more money, a bigger home, freedom from the job, more time with your family, a new business, a way to touch the lives of others or more happiness and love, you *can* have it. To begin, all you need to do is *choose, commit,* start moving and let your dreams show you the way. Once you know the "why," you'll figure out the "how." It only takes a tiny spark to light a huge fire. And you have hundreds of sparks inside you. Start discovering them now and let them get you "FIRED UP!"

"To change one's life:
* *Start immediately*
* *Do it flamboyantly*
* *No exceptions."*
William James

Remember These Key Points

◆ Negative self-talk, labels and myths can stop you from going for your dreams before you start.
◆ Stories of other people's victories can help you get "FIRED UP!"
◆ Success requires determination, planning, follow-through, clarity and action, plus fire and enthusiasm for your dream.
◆ Get moving; start doing and taking action on your dreams.
◆ Choice and commitment are very powerful; they set into motion a great many things to help align you more with your dream. Choose and commit to succeed; the choice and commitment will support you in ways you can't even imagine.

Now Take These "FIRED UP!" Action Steps

◆ Read inspirational books, like *Chicken Soup for the Soul* by Jack Canfield and Mark Victor Hansen, *Live Your Dreams* by Les Brown and *Storms of Perfection* by Andy Andrews.

◆ If you like uplifting movies, watch *Field of Dreams, Rudy* or *Working Girl.*

◆ Actively choose your success. On a 3"x 5" card, write the "I,___(your name)___, choose and commit to succeed in life and in making my dreams come true." Carry this card with you in your wallet and look at it every day. If you know what your dream is, write that down too. For example – "I, Mary Smith, choose and commit to succeed in life and in making my dream of being a top executive come true."

"To win or lose,
To love or hate,
To try or quit,
To risk or withdraw,
To accelerate or hesitate,
To dream or stagnate,
To open or close,
To succeed or fail,
To live or die.
Everyone of these
starts with a
CHOICE."

Snowden McFall

Chapter 3

Discovering Your Dream
Locating the Spark Inside

"The indispensible first step to getting the things you want out of life is this: decide what you want."
Ben Stein

Where Do You Begin?

Have you ever known anyone with enthusiasm and a sincere desire to change, but who didn't know where to begin or even what their dream might be? This is quite common. Many people have little or no idea how to best use their talents. They don't know how they can make their rough ideas take shape and become something much bigger. While many people have interest, commitment and curiosity, they often need to gain clarity about what they really want. So where do you start? It's really very simple. *Start with what you enjoy doing in your life.*

"FIRED UP!" PRINCIPLE # 2 – Do What You Love Often

The people who are the happiest in their lives, who are consistently successful and "FIRED UP!"about their lives, regularly schedule what they love to do – into every day, every week or every month, depending on the activity. They manifest their dreams by regularly focusing on them and taking action to support them.

How Greg's Dream Changed Him

Greg is normally a shy, good-natured young man who works for a Fixed Base Operator at a local airport. His dream is to become a commercial pilot. My husband and I went flying with Greg in a small Cessna. The change in him astonished us! It was as though he had grown three inches. He was confident, powerful and in charge. He took time to go through a meticulous safety check; he paid attention to every detail. From the time he started the engine and lifted the airplane off the runway, his entire being took on a sense of self-assurance and strength. It was clear that Greg loved to fly and he became a better person because of it. He was "FIRED UP!" That's the power of doing what you love; it can transform you in all ways – physically, mentally and emotionally.

Peter Loves Sharing His Products

Peter works from home, marketing quality products to others. Watching him in action when he meets with customers is exciting. His whole persona changes; he believes he is bringing something of value to people. The caring he has for people shows in the way he listens and asks questions. His enthusiasm for his products bubbles forth as he speaks faster and with more intensity. His eyes light up as he realizes he can solve a problem for his customer. It's obvious he loves working with people and helping them. He is "FIRED UP!" when he connects with others.

Often the best way to understand something is to experience it. *To know the feeling of being "FIRED UP!" that comes from sharing what you love, do this next brief activity.* You'll also get the opportunity to practice effective listening. It only takes six minutes and it's a lot of fun. You'll need one other person that can sit with you for a few minutes, plus a stopwatch, clock or timer. That's all you need. Try it right now.

Sharing and Listening

Set a timer for three minutes. Sit down with someone and take turns playing the roles of sharer and listener. The sharer talks for three minutes about the various activities they love to do. They go into detail about each one, describing what specifically they love about the activity and keep talking until the time is up. If there are periods of silence, that's fine. The role of the listener is to actively listen; that means giving full attention to the sharer and not saying a word; just listening during those three minutes, even if there is silence. The listener has complete eye contact with the sharer and gives full attention to that person. Author M. Scott Peck, in *The Road Less Traveled*, says, *"True listening, total concentration on the other, is always a manifestation of love."* To be truly listened to is a rare experience in our world. It is a gift of great value. Savor it. Then, after three minutes, switch roles. Reset the timer. Now the first person listens attentively, silently, while their "partner" shares about what they love to do. The listener observes the body language of their "partner" to see how animated they become. The listener looks into their eyes for the sparkle. Often laughter and joy are present.

After both people have shared, have a brief conversation about what you've each experienced. Notice how you feel and what your voice sounds like. Most people become highly energized during this process, with lots of gesturing, fast talking and laughter. It's fun to hear others share what they love to do. It's exciting to share what you love doing. It's invigorating to do what you love. *You're meant to do what you love, to live your dreams and share them with others.* You're meant to be "FIRED UP!" and enthusiastic about life.

"FIRED UP!" PRINCIPLE # 3 – Doing What You Love Makes A Difference in the World Around You

When you're in touch with what you love and live your dreams, you automatically make a positive difference in the world. Your happiness and excitement attract and inspire others to join you. It's like striking a match to a pile of dry sticks. One ignites and sparks the next and the next until a blaze is burning bright.

This listening activity can give you a great deal of insight into yourself and others. *The most effective business people know that the best way to create relationships is to discover what your customers love and always bring that up when you see them.* Eventually, your customers start associating you with the thing they enjoy, and they automatically have a positive feeling when you arrive. That means the relationship grows stronger and more positive; your customer will then be more receptive to what you say.

Does Your Family Really Know You?

Family members also need to share what they love with each other. How many of you believe your family really knows what you love to do? If your family is among the small number who do share what they're passionate about doing, consider yourself fortunate.

How many unsuitable birthday presents you have received from people you thought knew you? If you want to develop stronger bonds with those you care about, find out what gets them "FIRED UP!" Learn about their passions, what they love to do and make a point of asking about these things frequently, whether or not you share their interests. Your attention will demonstrate to your loved ones that what matters to them, matters to you. It will help you be a better partner, parent, sibling, son or daughter or friend.

Your Fire Radiates to Others

Did you know that you radiate joy and natural well-being when you are working towards your dreams? It's true. Just like when you share what you love, your enthusiasm for life shines out from you to others. My banker often comments that I always sound so upbeat and positive when I talk to him on the phone. That's because I am working on my dreams, doing what I love. I look forward to getting up in the morning. I'm "FIRED UP!"

Can you imagine what the world would be like if more and more people did what they most enjoyed in life on a regular basis? The U.S. statistics from Gallup polls say that nearly two-thirds of all people hate getting up and going to work. More heart attacks occur on Monday mornings before 9 A.M. than any other time. What if two-thirds of the people loved what they were doing because they were living their dreams? What if they were enthusiastic and energetic and couldn't wait to get out of bed to start their days? This would be a different world. It would be pretty amazing! You can start living your life that way right now, by learning about what you want the most in your life.

"FIRED UP!" PRINCIPLE #4 – Get Clear About What You Want

You need to know what your dream is before you can focus on it. And you probably won't know what your dream is until you look at what you want in your life.

In *Technologies for Creating*, a course developed by Robert Fritz, there's an activity which helps you clarify what you want. It goes like this. On a piece of paper, make two columns like those shown below, one on the left and one on the right. Number each from one to ten. On the left, list ten things you have in your life right now *which you don't want*. On the right, write the opposite of that thing you don't want – what you want instead.

Don't Want	Do Want
1. debt	1. abundance and wealth
2. a broken down car	2. a car that runs well
3. a boring job	3. a stimulating job

Next, draw an X through all the don't wants. Put your energy into what you *do* want.

Ask yourself this test question with each of the items in the right hand column: "If I could have this right now, would I take it?" If the answer is anything but an absolute "yes" – cross it off. Put your attention on what you're sure you want. Clarity is key.

I personally know how well this works. In 1986 I took the course and did this activity. One item was "a beautiful sunny home on the water," which at that time I had pictured as an ocean front villa off in the future. One night, I was sitting at home, and the idea of buying a house came to me. I checked the Sunday paper, and sure enough, there was an ad whose headline read "Live on the Water." I spent the entire afternoon walking around the advertised property, which sat on a river bank. It was easy to imagine living there – it was peaceful and lovely. I bought the property the next day and they began building my new home. I visited every week and watched it take shape. Now my husband and I live in that beautiful sunny home on the water! You can live in your dream house, too. Get "FIRED UP!" today and start creating the life you want.

"I never worked a day in my life
...it was all fun."
Thomas Edison

Remember These Key Points

◆ The people who are the happiest, consistently successful and effective, regularly schedule what they love to do – into every day, every week or every month, depending on the activity.

◆ Being "FIRED UP!" about what you do can change your entire personality and even make you look healthier and more alive.

◆ Be an excellent listener because it is very rare to be listened to in this world. By listening, you increase the value you give others.

◆ Two-thirds of all people hate going to work in the morning. More heart attacks occur on Monday morning before 9 A.M. than any other time. So be sure you're doing what you love.

Now Take These "FIRED UP!" Action Steps

◆ Take time to listen to your family and friends. Find out what they love to do and bring it up in your conversations often. Show genuine curiosity about them and their interests.

◆ Next time you go to meet with a client or business associate, find out what they love to do for fun and talk about it.

◆ Invite your closest friends to lunch this week, on separate days. Notice how it feels to spend time with people you enjoy.

Chapter 4

What Do You Love to Do?

Stirring the Inner Sparks

"I would rather fail at what I love than succeed at what I hate."
George Burns

Do What You Love

One of the best ways to learn about your dreams is to consider what you love doing. It's amazing the kind of information you can discover about yourself when you take a few minutes to list your favorite activities and how often you do them. If you want to have some fun and learn more about yourself, take ten minutes now to do a little creative detective work and complete the list called "My Favorite Activities." *Completing this is very worthwhile, because you are gaining some valuable personal information.*

Many people learn that the things they love to do don't cost much money. Sometimes they are free! Others realize that it has been a long time since they did these fun things. They need to schedule them more often. Some learn to understand how important other people are to them. They actively develop their skills to become better friends, spouses and parents, as well as more effective and caring co-workers with their business associates.

People who are the happiest and most at peace in their lives regularly schedule what they enjoy doing. They spend more of their time being "FIRED UP!" and that joy shines through all areas of their lives. They have acknowledged their goals and dreams and are doing whatever it takes to accomplish them. They no longer make excuses why they "can't" do it. Instead, they look for reasons why they can. They may delay gratification on certain activities if they would interfere with progress on their dream. They know that taking action will keep them "FIRED UP!"

Your Favorite Activities

On a piece of paper, list 15 favorite things you enjoy doing for fun. Just allow yourself to randomly jot down ideas. If you come up with more than 15, that's great. Here's an example.

My Favorite Activities		
	Last Done	Do with Others/Alone
1. go sailing		
2. share with people		
3. learn new things		
4. face new challenges		
5. travel overseas		
6. go to comedy clubs		
7. host a dinner party		

Once you have made your list, review it and ask yourself two questions: When did you last do this activity and do you need other people to do it? [2] Write down the answers next to the list. You might also consider whether these activities require advance planning, whether they support you mentally or physically, whether they are structured or unstructured. Like a good detective, take the time to really learn about yourself and study your personal preferences. All of this information is really quite useful when determining your dreams, because identifying your favorite activities gives you significant clues about what you find meaningful and enjoyable.

My Favorite Activities

	Last Done	Do With Others/Alone
1. go sailing	5 months	with others
2. read books	yesterday	alone
3. learn new things	last week	alone
4. face new challenges	4 months	with others
5. travel overseas	7 months	with others
6. go to comedy clubs	1 month	with others
7. host a dinner party	1 month	either

Learning About Yourself

As you review your list, you'll probably see a pattern emerge. Often the things you love to do may require little to no planning. That means when you arrive home from work, you could spontaneously do many of the things that get you "FIRED UP!"

Chances are that if most all of your favorite activities require advance planning, you probably prefer a highly organized lifestyle. You are less likely to do things spontaneously and more likely to plan your life carefully. If physical risk is involved in most of your favorite activities, you probably prefer excitement over security, freedom over structure and creativity over analysis. If most of your favorites are about your physical health, that is a key priority for you and something you value highly. Many of your life choices will be based on whether something is good for you physically, and keeping yourself fit is probably a primary goal in your life.

The value in studying this list is that you learn things about yourself which you might not have known. Your favorite activities provide valuable clues as to what gets you "FIRED UP!" They say a great deal about your personality and values. Later we'll discuss how they fit with your life purpose.

One thing you'll need to consider when you look at this list is how long it's been since you did the things you love. If you regularly do things which get you "FIRED UP!" it's likely that you are often content, happy and peaceful. If you have not done your favorite things recently, you might want to schedule them in your calendar right away. Picture how great this coming week will be as you spend time doing something you're excited about every day. Imagine how terrific your life will be when every day you are living your dreams, "FIRED UP!" about your life!

"Success is how you collect your minutes.
You spend millions of minutes to reach one triumph,
one moment,
then you spend maybe a thousand minutes
enjoying it.
If you are unhappy through those millions of minutes,
what good are the thousands of minutes of triumph?
It doesn't equate.
Life is made up of small pleasures,
Happiness is made up of those tiny successes.
The big ones come too infrequently.
If you don't have all those
zillions of tiny successes,
the big ones don't mean anything."

Norman Lear

Remember These Key Points

◆ Discovering your favorite activities can help you learn more about your life and your dreams.
◆ It is often true that many things which get you "FIRED UP!" cost little or no money.
◆ If many of your favorite activities require little to no planning, you can do them anytime, including right now.
◆ Some people wait until their vacations to do their favorite activities, when they could do many of them now, at home. Is that true of you? What do you enjoy most on vacation? Could you could do it at home, sometime soon? Schedule it into your life.
◆ People who are the happiest and most "FIRED UP!" about their lives regularly participate in their favorite activities.

Now Take These "FIRED UP!" Action Steps

◆ If you have not done it already, complete the "My Favorite Activities" list.
◆ Read over your list and learn more about yourself.
◆ Schedule in two of your favorite activities for later this week.
◆ Make a plan for next month. Schedule in all your favorite activities in that month.

INSPIRATION

*"When you are inspired
by some great purpose,
some extraordinary project,
all your thoughts break their bonds.
Your mind transcends limitations,
your consciousness expands
in every direction,
and you find yourself
in a new great wonderful world...
You discover yourself to be
a greater person
by far
than you ever dreamed
yourself to be."*
Patanjali

Chapter 5

Use Imagination To Fuel Your Dream

Fueling the Spark Inside

"Your potential is unlimited. Aspire to a high place. Believe in your abilities, in your taste, in your own judgment. Image and perceive that which you wish to be. Back your image with enthusiasm and courage. Feel the reality of your new self; live in the expectancy of greater things and your subconscious will actualize them."
Brian Adams

The Fire of Life is Inside You

You can have the life you've always wanted. Since you've gotten this far, it's likely you really do want to make your dreams come true. But maybe you still aren't quite sure what your dreams are. In this book, there are tools and techniques to help you discover your dreams, develop a high-powered action plan and make them come true. You'll read about other people like you who have gone on to live their dreams every day. Your discovery process can often be easy and fun, and you'll be amazed at how much progress you make in such a short time. So relax and let yourself enjoy the process; it's all for you!

"FIRED UP!" PRINCIPLE # 5 – Use Your Imagination

Your imagination is a powerful tool. It can help you resolve tough situations and fuel your dreams. Famous Olympic athletes from all over the world have used visualization for decades to picture the success they want. One statistic from the 1980's showed that the East German and Russian Olympic athletes spent 75% of their training time doing visualization. That meant they were only on the field doing the actual physical training 25% of the time! Today, many professional athletes in basketball, tennis and golf swear by visualization; they mentally see themselves winning and they do. They trigger that part of their brain that knows how to succeed and they do. You can too.

🔥 Dan O'Brien, 1996 U.S. Decathlon champion, practiced every day for years to go to the Olympics. In 1992 he had faced the heartbreak of not qualifying at the Olympic trials; he was determined not to let that happen again. At home, he jogged every day, visualizing himself running through the Olympic stadium, triumphant. He imagined himself wearing the gold medal and people chanting his name as he earned the title, "The world's greatest athlete." He called himself that every day, affirming it to himself. With the heart and mind of an Olympian, Dan got "FIRED UP!" for the 1996 Olympics. All of his dreams came true as he won the Decathlon gold medal and reclaimed it for the United States for the first time in 20 years.

The Clearer You Are, The Easier It Is

The clearer you are about what you want, the easier it is to create it. It's essential to clearly define your dreams in vivid detail. However, if your dreams are still fuzzy or even a complete mystery, take heart. You're going have a chance right now to learn more about your dreams.

One of the best ways to gain more information is to *visualize* each of your dreams fully realized in all its glory. Thomas Edison spent a great deal of time visualizing and dreaming about his life. To stay refreshed and keep his creative energy flowing, he often took naps and encouraged his employees to do the same. He got some of his best ideas either daydreaming or visualizing. That's why it's smart for you to use this process. It'll help you access the creative part of your brain and gain valuable insight about how your life could be. It will help you get "FIRED UP!"

Visualize What You Want

Take ten minutes by yourself in a private, quiet space. Get a notebook and a couple of pens. If you have a tape recorder, you might want that nearby, too. Perhaps you'll want to play a piece of soft instrumental music in the background. Turn the phone off and make sure you won't be disturbed. You can either read this to yourself and then do the creative imagery or read it aloud to your tape recorder and play it back for yourself.

If you've ever done visualization before, you know how simple and relaxing it can be. If this is new to you, you'll find it's much like a lovely daydream. It's easy to do; just let your imagination run wild. Tell yourself that you are easily and clearly picturing your future and that this will be a totally safe and positive experience for your greatest benefit. Trust the process; you have a treasure chest of great ideas inside you and it's up to you to decide what to do with them.

Now picture yourself walking in a beautiful natural setting that is totally safe. The temperature is perfect and you can feel a gentle breeze against your skin. You smell the rich aromas of the trees and flowers nearby, or perhaps it's a fresh sea scent. Notice the brilliant colors of nature around you. Feel the textures of the ground and the earth under your feet. You may feel cool grass or warm sand. Perhaps you hear birds nearby, the wind as it rustles through the trees or waves splashing against the shore. Wherever you are, it's ideal, safe and private.

As you continue walking, you feel more and more peaceful and relaxed. There's a strong feeling of positive well-being inside you and a sense of wonder and childlike anticipation. Straight ahead, you come to a beautiful scenic clearing, a wide open space with a bench in your favorite color. In this totally protected and safe place, you gently sit down on the bench. You notice a large white movie screen directly in front of you. You look at the dial and you turn on the movie of your ideal life *one year from now.*

Magically and fully, you're living your dream. You are doing exactly what your heart most desires and you are "FIRED UP!" Notice what you're doing and how you're living your life. See yourself smiling and rejoicing. Observe the direction your life is taking.

How are you spending your time? Where are you living and who is in your life? Notice how abundant your life is and how healthy and energized you feel. How does it feel to be doing what you love? What are others saying to you? What are you saying to others? Hear their voices and hear your own voice. Listen to the joy and commitment there; feel the passion and sense of purpose. You know your contribution is valuable and meaningful.

What does your life look like? What is happening? Listen to how wise and caring your voice sounds. *What work are you doing and how are you playing? Oh yes, they seem like one and the same, don't they?* You're having so much fun all the time, it's hard to believe that this is how you earn your living. What does the world look like to you from this perspective? See it very clearly. Feel your joy and satisfaction.

Take your time and experience only good things; see all the positive aspects of your life and feel your own passion and vitality. Allow your creative imagination to paint a vivid picture; make it real with sounds and smells and colors. Observe the people and feel the emotions. *Let the images get you "FIRED UP!" See it all perfectly as totally fulfilling.*

Write Down Your Feelings

After dreaming for several minutes, make some notes on your experience. This can be done on paper or just dictated into a tape recorder. (Did you know that what you wind into a tape recorder, you wind into your subconscious? Wouldn't it be powerful to wind success and happiness onto your internal tapes?) Perhaps you found yourself doing something you never even considered; that often happens during this activity. Note your feelings, actions, companions and lifestyle, even if some of it seems foreign to you. All of this is important information as you gain greater clarity about igniting your internal fire. You may not understand the exact nature of what you were doing, but it just felt right. That's perfectly normal. *There is a part of you that has much more wisdom than you think. All it takes is the courage to start exploring and trusting yourself.*

 One woman who did this visualization got such clear information about her life's work (which was dramatically different from her job at the time) that she completely changed her life in six months. She envisioned herself doing her new job in complete detail. After the process, she researched this field, then moved across the country to San Francisco. She got a new job and apartment, and begin taking courses in this field. She didn't understand the nature of the work fully until she researched it. As she learned more, she discovered that she had been doing it perfectly in her imagination.

Patti was another person who did this exercise, even though at the time, she was enjoying her work. Through visualization, she discovered that her great love was children, and that she wanted to be working with them directly. While her previous job had been mentally stimulating, working with children was deeply satisfying and much more heartfelt. Within nine months, she changed jobs and began working for a children's wing of an area hospital. She is now a mother, and plans on writing children's books, using some of the skills she had developed from her previous work.

Now congratulate yourself on your progress so far, and take a break. Acknowledge yourself for doing these exercises and putting energy into your life. You're worth it! Enjoy the dream experience; savor it like a new flavor. Let it sink in and get richer. It's too new to expose to possible critics, so don't share it with others yet. Let it blossom under your tender care. You may find that more information comes to you in your sleep. Be sure to keep a notebook by the bed for just that reason, and write down what shows up. And again, keep it to yourself.

Remind yourself of all the successes you have had in your life until now. *You have rare gifts and unique talents to share with others. Remember your greatness.* Let it get you "FIRED UP!" Pat yourself on the back for your progress in this book and your new awareness. You're moving on and taking action. Bravo!

"With visualization, you begin to tell yourself visual truths."
John-Roger

Remember These Key Points

◆ Your imagination is a powerful tool for discovering and fueling your dreams.

◆ Visualization is a very useful and effective technique for creating success. In the 1970's East German and Russian athletes in the Olympics spent 75% of their training time visualizing their success.

◆ The clearer you are about what you want, the easier it is to create it.

◆ There is a part of you that has much more wisdom than you may think and you can access it through your imagination.

◆ What you record into a tape player also gets recorded into your subconscious.

◆ Visualizing your life exactly the way you want it to be gets you "FIRED UP!"

Now Take These "FIRED UP!" Action Steps

◆ If you have not done so already, do the visualization exercise in this chapter.

◆ Review your notes or listen to your tape from this experience; let it become real inside you.

◆ Spend some time daydreaming about how you picture your life to be when you're "FIRED UP!" about it.

◆ Create a success journal (a notebook) of all the major accomplishments you've had in your life until now. Include major childhood learnings like how to ride a bike or confronting the neighborhood bully. Give yourself credit for all that you have accomplished.

Chapter 6

What are Your Myths?

Dousing the Sparks

"Our doubts are traitors, and make us lose
the good we oft might win, by fearing to attempt."
William Shakespeare

Negative Self-Talk is a "Dreamstealer"

Did you know that we have between 40,000 and 50,000 thoughts a day? Research has shown that 75-85% of those thoughts are negative in most people. That's why becoming aware of our myths and negative self-talk is so important. *Two reasons why more and more people are not living their dreams is that they allow negative self-talk and limiting belief systems to stop them from taking action on their dreams.* Frequently, they have learned negative myths which restrict their thinking and hold them back— these are "dreamstealers."

"FIRED UP!" PRINCIPLE # 6 – Uncover Your Myths

Often, people learn myths through childhood or some unpleasant life experiences. Sometimes parents unintentionally pass along incorrect information like: *"If you don't get a good education, you'll never amount to anything,"* or *"Keep your nose to the grindstone and your shoulder to the wheel." "If you want to get ahead in this world, you have to make lots of money."* Your parents weren't intentionally trying to set up blocks for you. Most of the time, they believed they were motivating you with what they thought was true. But you may have subconsciously perceived all of these as threats, fear or negativity.

If people don't have a positive influencer in their lives to show them that challenges are just part of learning and growing, they often develop myths that limit their belief in themselves and steal their dreams. Instead of viewing each obstacle as a necessary step in the overall process of success, when people stumble, they may label themselves failures, and believe they're losers. They may have no one to encourage them over the hurdles.

During adolescence, they may have learned other destructive myths like: *"I'm not good enough," "I can't have what I want"* or *"Nobody likes me or my ideas."* While these myths may seem to provide some protection or consolation during youth, they're rarely constructive in adulthood. *Sometimes myths become deeply ingrained in the subconscious, where they are most dangerous. They cause people to sabotage their successes and give up on their dreams. They then turn into excuses.*

Many popular authors have written about how negative self-talk can harm your health. Barbara Levine, in her book, *Your Body Believes Every Word You Say*, demonstrates that even a simple statement like "So and so is a pain in the neck" can create genuine neck pain. Discover what your negative self-talk is and replace it with positive affirmations so you can succeed. You'll be happier and healthier, as well. (We'll discuss affirmations in Chapter 18. You'll learn how to phrase your affirmations so they work best for you, and how to put them into action.)

Awareness of myths is the key to releasing them. You'll be amazed to learn what untruths sleep in your subconscious. Take the time now to investigate and you can learn to laugh at your myths and release their negative hold on you. *Here are three action options to help you learn more about your own false beliefs.* Each one is short and fun, and can help you be more successful. Choose the activity that appeals to you most and do it now.

Step 1/Action Option A – Talk with a Friend

Pick a friend who will be neutral, supportive and a good listener. A family member is usually too close to be neutral, so pick someone else to talk with. Sit down with that friend and just talk about your dream and what is stopping you from living it right now, today, in this very moment. Record the myths that show up while you talk. Make a list, or have your friend make the list and keep going. Continue talking until you believe you have covered all the possible blocks to your success. Then copy the list if your friend wrote it, so it's in your handwriting. Now go to Step 2 on page 34.

Step 1/Action Option B – Review Your Personal History

Find a nice quiet place, turn on some soft soothing music and be sure you won't be disturbed. You have already been a success in many areas of your life. But right now, you need to look at your disappointments. Think back over your life and look at the goals and dreams you have not yet achieved. *Pay attention to the limiting beliefs or myths that may have held you back. Decide if those beliefs still have power over you.* (One way to do this is to say the myth out loud and see if you are a little nauseous or tense. If so, you're still letting it have power over you. If you just laugh or have no reaction, then it no longer affects you.) Make a written list of the ones that you still find painful to think about. Now go to Step 2 on page 34.

Step 1/Action Option C – The "Dreamstealer" Checklist

Listed below are several common dreamstealing thoughts which can stop people from living their dreams. Read over the list and check off which ones you believe are true to you. Write down those that you have allowed to have power over you and add any new ones. Now go to Step 2 on page 34.

Checklist: Check those that ring true for you.
____ People who live their dreams have to be rich.
____ People who live their dreams must be well-educated and have degrees.

___ People who live their dreams have to be well-connected.

___ People who live their dreams are selfish.

___ People who live their dreams have to be healthy and fit.

___ People who live their dreams have lots of free time.

___ People who live their dreams have to be 100% confident at all times.

___ People who live their dreams have to be well-organized.

___ People who live their dreams have loads of energy.

___ People who live their dreams are unusually talented.

___ People who live their dreams must be fearless.

___ People who live their dreams must take big risks.

___ People who live their dreams are always good-looking.

___ People who live their dreams must be young (or old).

___ People who live their dreams must have independent sources of income.

___ People who live their dreams don't have time for their families.

___ People who live their dreams have to be totally unique.

___ People who live their dreams must have their "act together" (always know exactly what they are doing).

___ People who live their dreams have to be a certain race or sex.

___ People who live their dreams are _____. (Fill in the blank.)

___ _____

___ _____

Once you have completed one of the action options, are you ready to laugh about your dreamstealing beliefs? Do you realize how untrue they really are?

Step 2 – Laugh a Little

Someone once said, "Laughter is the best medicine." It can help you get a new perspective on the myths you have allowed to hurt you up until now. Look over your list and notice how silly some of these beliefs are. Some of them even contradict each other. Some make no sense at all. *Without exception, I can give you examples of real-life people who prove every one of these myths is false.* So relax and laugh a little at the words. Soon they'll have no power over you because you will have let them go, eliminating their hold on you.

Step 3 – Release the Myths

Whichever action option you picked, you need to have a piece of paper with the myths written on it that you have allowed to affect you. *Here are two of the many ways you can release the myths.*

#1 For each myth you have written, write a positive statement in its place that invalidates it.

Myth – People need to be well-educated and have degrees to live their dreams.

Positive statement – People of any education level can live their dreams.

After you have done this for *each* myth, go to #2.

#2 With a pen and draw a big "X" through the list of myths.

Or if you prefer, individually cross each myth out. Do whichever will give you the greatest satisfaction. *Next, tear up that piece of paper into tiny pieces while saying out loud* "I permanently release these limiting beliefs. I am now free to make my dreams come true." If you like, you can also burn those pieces of paper, symbolically destroying those myths. While this may sound a little trite and simple, *it works!* It can be very powerful. Feel the relief that comes with no longer carrying that emotional garbage. Let it all go, and get on with the joy and magic of your life.

"FIRED UP!" PRINCIPLE # 7 – Identify Role Models

To succeed in life, we all need positive programming and excellent role models – people who beat the odds and won. They show us that if they can make it, so can we. These people need not be big, famous heroes; it could be the child with a mental or physical challenge who finally got on the baseball team. Or it could be the criminal who became a full-fledged civil rights activist. Or it could be the bus driver who called you by your name every morning and told you that you were special.

Take a minute now to think about the inspirational role models in your life. Who are they? Are they famous people or are they people like your teacher, your grandmother or your next door neighbor? What did they do for you? How did they touch your life? Often, you discover that it was all the little actions through the years that made a difference, not one big gesture. When you are working on your dream, it helps to contact those people who inspire you. Tell them why they inspire you and how they touched your life. Everyone, no matter how famous, loves to hear sincere feedback about how they made a difference in the lives of others. If you share with them from your heart, the odds are they will encourage you.

From my early years on, my grandmother McClamroch was a tremendous role model for me. Her parents were killed in a car accident when she was 12, and she went to live with an aunt and uncle. That hardship and the financial strain taught her to be self-reliant. She went to Goucher College and later married a college professor from another university. While her husband was in the Army during World Wars I and II, she organized the local women, made bandages and kept things going at home. She later worked with Eleanor Roosevelt to get the vote for women in North Carolina. She beat several different kinds of cancer before she died in her mid-70's. Her courage, fortitude, tenacity and perseverance were such beacons of light for me; they showed me how to overcome my traumatic childhood and keep moving towards my dreams.

A Possible Dialogue with an Admired Business Professional

"___(Name)___, I just want you to know that the way you have turned your company around and showed an interest in your employees has really impressed me. You clearly have an excellent leadership style, and I think I could learn a great deal from you. May I spend a few minutes with you and ask you a few questions, at your convenience? I'd very much appreciate your suggestions about the dream I have now."

Another possible way to start might be "___(Name)___, your speech really touched my heart. It is amazing all you overcame to get to the level of success you now have. You have really helped me learn how to better support and encourage my students. Could you spare a few moments and give me some guidance about my dream? I really think you could help me and I would very much appreciate your time."

Approaches like these are powerful and effective. Most everyone who has succeeded has overcome obstacles. *They can relate to your needs when you show them respect, courtesy and sincere admiration.* Always honor their time and stick to the core issues of your dream. You'll be delighted with how helpful they can be.

I feel honored and humbled when someone who has heard me speak calls or writes to tell me how I have touched their lives. I go out of my way to be of service to them. It's always been worth it to me.

"FIRED UP!" PRINCIPLE # 8 – Use Motivational Tapes & Seminars

Another way to stay "FIRED UP!" while you're working on your dream is *listening to motivational audiotapes every day. Going to motivational seminars* can also help you overcome your obstacles and succeed. Both activities will keep you on track and accelerate your success. I've been listening to motivational tapes for years. Jack Canfield's CareerTrack tape set *Self-Esteem and Peak Performance* really influenced me as I built my company. *You Deserve* and *Choosing Your Future* by Les Brown helped me to tell my own story and gave me great success tips. Anthony Robbins' *Personal Power* tape set "FIRED UP!" my husband.

Just one word or sentence heard on tape or at a seminar could ignite a spark inside you and get you "FIRED UP!" The price of the seminar and tape would be worth it. Keep doing what it takes to stay motivated. You never know when your sparks will catch fire.

Throughout this book, you'll find I reference many of the excellent seminars I have attended through the years. Just in the last decade, I have taken over 60 workshops. I always want to be learning and growing, honing my skills and opening to new possibilities. Connecting with others who are on a similar path can inspire and motivate you. Another benefit of seminars is validation – having what we already believe be substantiated by others. And of course, the sheer energy of being in a room where others are "FIRED UP!" lights your fire, too.

"FIRED UP!" PRINCIPLE # 9 – "Act As If"

One of the best ways to get "FIRED UP!" about your dream and ignite your sparks is to "act as if" your dream were already real. When I was building my house, I visited it every week, imagining what it would feel like to live there. Driving your dream car or visiting your dream house can make your flames burn higher and brighter. Even *dressing the part* of the dream you want to live can change the way you feel about yourself. *Start "acting as if" your dream were real.* The more vividly you can see, hear and experience your dream, the more likely you are to make it come true.

Florence Griffith Joyner, super sprinter of the 1988 Olympics, uses clothes as a key tool for "acting as if." Wearing brightly colored, dramatic running outfits and elaborately painted fingernails, Florence won three gold medals. *"My outfits represent the belief, determination, discipline and desire to make my dreams come true...."* [3]

Another great example of "acting as if" is Michael J. Fox in the movie, *The Secret of My Success.* He's a mailboy at a big corporation who starts dressing like a high level executive. He starts doing the executive work competently and others treat him with respect. He begins to live *"as if"* he were already that executive. What happens next is fun and entertaining; you might want to rent the movie.

Congratulations on your progress. You've made a great start by releasing your myths. *You deserve to have whatever your heart desires.* Keep moving!

"Nobody can make you feel inferior without your consent."
Eleanor Roosevelt

Remember These Key Points

◆ Myths or limiting beliefs were often picked up in childhood.
◆ Writing a positive statement to take their place puts new programming into your subconscious.
◆ Burning or tearing up the myths list is a powerful way to tell your subconscious that you no longer believe these thoughts.
◆ People you admire will often be happy to help you when you sincerely share from your heart.

Now Take These "FIRED UP!" Action Steps

◆ If you have not done so already, do the myths activity.
◆ Write a letter to your role models, describing how they inspire you and ask them for guidance with your dream.
◆ Listen to a motivational tape daily.

Chapter 7

Dream, Vision, Mission and Purpose
Laying the Core Logs

"Vision is the link between dream and action."
John Naisbitt and Patricia Aburdene

Where Does Your Dream Begin?

As you begin focusing more on what *you* want, you may wonder "How do I begin to define my dreams?" *An excellent place to start is with your life vision, mission and purpose.*

These all relate to your values and what you consider important. In Dr. Martin Luther King Jr.'s famous 1960's speech entitled *I Have a Dream*, his purpose and mission were very clear. He envisioned a world where his nation would "one day rise up and live out its creed... that all men are created equal.... where my children will not be judged by the color of their skin but rather by the content of their character," and "...where black men and white men, Jews and Gentiles, Protestants and Catholics will be able to join hands and say 'free at last, free at last. Thank God Almighty, we are free at last.'" That got him "FIRED UP!" and led him to inspire millions of people, even decades later. Whenever I watch him delivering that speech, I get emotional. He was a great man who lived and died for his principles.

Your life purpose can be such a driving force. It can help you break through any barriers that may have been in your mind and in your environment. It can move you to rise above previous limitations and do more than you ever believed possible.

Vision, Mission and Purpose

Your *vision* is the deepest expression of what you truly want for your life. It is a conscious statement of hope and optimism, of the ideal.

A *mission statement* reflects who you actually are when you are at your best, and it defines how you live and what you do. It is based more on reality and current action.

Your life purpose relates to what you are meant to do in your life, as you feel it in your heart.

In Peter Block's book, *The Empowered Manager*, he used this example of a large health care company's mission statement: "To market health care products that have a demonstrable health benefit to the customer, to be the leader in each product line, to return a fair profit to our stockholders, and to provide good opportunities to our employees." This statement is more specific and focused than a vision would be.

A vision would relate more to how the business is going to be managed, such as treating customers with integrity, providing superior service and carefully researching health products before offering them to the public. *The vision relates to the quality and tone of the work, whereas the mission is more about the nuts and bolts.*

Purpose is the core of both of the mission and the vision. It is often found in the heart and soul of the business founder. Perhaps he or she lost a parent to an illness that could have been treated with the right products, so the founder wants to offer the products which can save other people's lives. Perhaps the founder has a burning desire to excel and be famous; this will have a large impact on how the business is conducted.

It's All About Values

Fundamental to vision, mission and purpose are your core values. Values are the qualities you consider most significant and they have a tremendous impact on your dreams. They shape your attitudes, beliefs and relationships. Know what you value most when planning your ideal life. Start by including what is most important to you. So what are your values?

Here's a list of values that may apply to you.

1. *Financial security*– having the money to handle your economic responsibilities; using it wisely and keeping yourself free from money-related anxiety.
2. *Safety*– having physical, emotional or mental protection where you feel free from attack and danger.
3. *Freedom*– having the opportunity and independence to live the life you choose.
4. *Success*– progressively realizing a worthwhile dream or goal.
5. *Joy*– feeling effective, successful, happy and fulfilled.
6. *Love*– having healthy relationships with family and friends, including a special long-term, one-on-one committed relationship.
7. *Good Health*– being physically, mentally and emotionally sound.
8. *Personal Integrity*– conducting your life honestly, doing what you believe in.
9. *Service*– helping and contributing to the lives of others.
10. *Peace of Mind*– feeling a sense of serenity and freedom from stress.
11. *Ease*– a sense of relaxation and comfort.
12. *Spirituality*– feeling a sense of connection to God, linking you to all other people.
13. *Creativity*– freely expressing your talents and abilities however you choose.
14. *Personal Growth*– continually refining and developing your inner qualities, learning from your mistakes and moving on.
15. *Fame*– celebrity status – public recognition and awareness of who you are on a large scale.
16. *Humility*– being aware of your unskilled behavior and a lack of pridefulness.
17. *Order*– dealing with your environment so everything is structured and well-organized.
18. *Humor*– being able to laugh with others and not take yourself so seriously.
19. *Talent*– unique ability to do a specific skill or art form.

Values Activity

List in order of priority from 1 to 5 which of the values on the previous page is most important to you. Most important would be #1. Feel free to delete any that don't work for you. Or substitute new ones in place of those that were listed.

1._____   2._____

3._____   4._____

5._____

Now study your list. It will provide a great deal of useful data for you. *The top five values will most shape your life decisions and give you the best clues about what really gets you "FIRED UP!"*

Discovering Your Life Purpose

As John-Roger and Peter McWilliams write in the book *Life 101*, "A purpose... is your bellwether, your inner personal divining rod of truth. It tells you, in any given moment, whether you're living your life 'on purpose' or not." Believe it or not, discovering your life purpose can be easy. It can actually be broken down into a simple, clear statement.

You decide what that information means to you and what feels right for you. Be aware that you may have more than one purpose. You may also express your purpose in a variety of ways. For example, a dancer may express her purpose several different ways: by performing in a ballet, teaching others to dance, choreographing shows, teaching health education through dance, writing and designing musical numbers in a movie, fundraising to bring more dance troupes to a given area, working with dance troupes around the world, doing videos or writing books on dance.

The key is to be open and flexible. It's like you are a private detective and the subject of your investigation is your life. You gather as many clues as possible, put them all down on paper and make sense out of them. You'll discover the answers when you relax and take it one step at a time. You may find this a fascinating and profound experience. For many people, it comes as a tremendous relief to know why they are here on Earth and what is truly meaningful.

Your Life Purpose Worksheet

The worksheet on the next page was adapted from Jack Canfield's life purpose technique in the audiotape set *Self-Esteem and Peak Performance*. It takes you through a series of questions to help you develop your life purpose statement. Take about 15 minutes to play with this form. If it's not convenient now, do it later; but do it. This is a very special process. Do it when you can treat it with respect and allow the information to sink in.

You discover your life purpose by knowing what you love to do, what gets you "FIRED UP!" and what makes you unique. What you love to do is clearly an expression of your values. It's as simple as that.

Step 1) What Are Your Best and Most Unique Qualities?

List your best and most unique qualities, and then pick the two that reflect who you are and for which you would most like to be remembered. In the example of the ballet dancer, her most unique qualities are gracefulness and beauty. As you identify yours, start first with a list of all your best traits. Then go back and underline the two that feel really right inside. If you still aren't sure, ask a loved one or a friend what your most unique traits are. *These are often the qualities that people most frequently comment on. They are the traits without which you would not be uniquely you.*

Step 2) How Do You Enjoy Expressing Those Traits?

List all your favorite ways of expressing those qualities, using verbs ending in "ing." Then pick your top two favorite forms of expression. For the ballet dancer, her two favorites are choreographing and dancing. After you list several forms of expression you enjoy, choose your top two. Go back and review them one by one, and see which words really feel right to you, and which ways you most enjoy expressing those traits. You may want to ask for help from a loved one if you need it. *When you express yourself in these two favorite ways, you feel happy and have a sense of positive well-being.* Inside of you, there's a sense of delight and freedom about these two actions.

Your Life Purpose Worksheet

Step 1 List your best and most unique qualities. Which two qualities truly reflect who you are and for which you'd most like to be remembered? Underline these two.

Step 2 List several ways you enjoy expressing or sharing those two qualities. Use action verbs with "ing" endings. Underline your two favorite forms of expression.

Step 3 Describe your version of an ideal world.

Step 4 Combine the three steps above into one sentence that summarizes your life purpose.

Ex. I am underpowering and inspiring others with my love and joy so that everyone contributes for the greatest benefit of all in a peaceful world.

Ex. I am choreographing and dancing with grace and beauty inspiring others to appreciate their health and the health of the world.

Concept for this form from Jack Canfield's *Self-Esteem and Peak Performance* audiotape set, CareerTrack Publications, 1987.

(If there is any resistance at all to a word, then that probably is not your favorite form of expressing.) Now you're ready for Step 3: describing your ideal world.

Your Life Purpose Worksheet

Step 1 List your best and most unique qualities. Which two qualities truly reflect who you are and for which you'd most like to be remembered? Underline these two.

gracefulness, beauty, coordination, teaching ability, femininity, rhythm

Step 2 List several ways you enjoy expressing or sharing those two qualities. Use action verbs with "ing" endings. Underline your two favorite forms of expression.

dancing, rollerblading, choreographing, teaching, running, performing, acting

Step 3 Describe your version of an ideal world.

peaceful, healthy planet, physically fit, where everyone takes care of themselves and respects the environment

Step 4 Combine the three steps above into one sentence that summarizes your life purpose.

I am choreographing and dancing with grace and beauty inspiring others to appreciate their health and the health of the world.

Step 3) What's Your Ideal World?

Here, you simply describe what an ideal world would be like if you could create it from the beginning. (This is a vision statement, because it has wholeness and optimism in it.) Include what you believe are the most vital elements. What would solve world problems that most disturb you, and what would ensure a positive world for the future? These are all *your* choices and your opinions. That's all that matters here. So it's best to not consult anyone else on this question, or you may be influenced by their view of a "perfect" world.

Now you're almost done. You know what makes you unique and your favorite ways of expressing that uniqueness. You also have defined your ideal world. *All of this information forms the foundation of your life purpose.*

Now look over the ballerina's Life Purpose Worksheet on page 45 and read her answers to each of the questions. For her, an ideal world is healthy, peaceful and one where everyone takes care of themselves and the planet. Her gracefulness and beauty are her most unique traits, and her favorite forms of expressing those traits are by dancing and choreographing. Putting all those together into Step 4, one sentence which combines all the above information, she came up with her life purpose: "I am choreographing and dancing with grace and beauty inspiring others to appreciate their health and the health of the world." See how easily this all fits together? Yours can, too.

Step 4) Summarize Your Life Purpose Statement.

Combine all the elements of the above three questions into one single life purpose statement. There are several ways to start. One is to begin with "I am" and then drop in the two verbs. Example: "I am choreographing and dancing." Another way is to write "Using my" then add your two qualities and follow with "I am... so that others may...." Example: "Using my gracefulness and beauty, I am choreographing and dancing in a way that inspires others to take care of themselves and the world."

Yet a third way might be to show how your life's purpose assists the world as a whole. In the case of the ballet dancer, she believes that her dancing will "inspire others to take care of themselves and the world." Whichever way works best for you is the right way. Try it now.

Here are some other examples of life purpose statements. These are all from ordinary people like most of us. They are not blessed with any special gifts that make them more likely to succeed than others. They are simply "FIRED UP!" about their dreams.

◆ Ed, a national trainer who works with youth, developed this life purpose statement: "As a loving, courageous and compassionate man, I inspire the youth of today through fun and enthusiasm and have tremendous impact on their lives." His vision is a world of children who feel good about themselves and are confident and productive members of society. His mission is to teach youth leadership skills with excellence and enthusiasm.

◆ Will, an American working in Bulgaria, writes his: "Honestly and clearly sharing my life experiences and knowledge, I am creating and promoting world community and peace." His vision is a world which is one large community, respecting and appreciating each other's uniqueness. His mission is to bring business tools and techniques to budding entrepreneurs in undeveloped parts of the world and assist them in becoming financially independent.

As you read over these statements, it's obvious how very distinct each one is. Each person finds a unique way to express their purpose and have a meaningful, fulfilling life. Just like you do. As you achieve various goals and realize certain dreams, your expression may change. However, you can use your life purpose statement as a key reference point throughout your life, especially when you are making major decisions and planning each year. *Your true happiness depends on living your life in alignment with your life purpose.*

You might want to share your purpose statement with someone you love and trust. You could copy it onto a 3"x 5" index card and carry it in your wallet or datebook. You could also tape it to your bathroom mirror to remind you why you're here. Whatever you choose to do, *honor it and yourself. You are a rare individual with treasured gifts that only you can express in exactly your way.*

"Live your beliefs and you can turn the world around."
Henry David Thoreau

Remember These Key Points

◆ To determine your dreams, discover your life purpose.
◆ At the core of your mission, vision and purpose are your key values – those things which are most important to you.
◆ Writing a life purpose statement can be easy, if you take it step by step, and use the form provided in this chapter.
◆ Knowing your best traits and how you enjoy expressing them the most will give you important information about your life purpose.
◆ Your happiness depends on living in alignment with your life purpose.

Now Take These "FIRED UP!" Action Steps

◆ If you have not done so already, identify your values using the list in this chapter.
◆ If you have not done so already, complete the life purpose questions in this chapter.
◆ Copy your life purpose on an index card and carry it with you and also put it somewhere you will see it often. Embrace and honor it and yourself.
◆ This week, be sure to schedule time attending to the things you truly value. For example, if love is really important to you, spend time with those you love. If excellent health is a priority for you, then schedule in time to work out in a way that you enjoy.
◆ If you are inspired by Dr. Martin Luther King Jr., check out the video of his *I Have A Dream* speech at the library and watch it.

Chapter 8

Putting It All Together

Expanding the Fire's Foundation

*"Events, circumstances, etc. have their origin in ourselves.
They spring from seeds which we have sown."*
Henry David Thoreau

Do What You Love and Love What You Do

Magic Johnson had a brilliant career in the National Basketball Association as an incredible ballplayer. All of that changed when he announced, much to the shock and chagrin of the American public, that he was resigning from the NBA because he was HIV positive. Magic and his wife then spent the next several months touring the country speaking about the AIDS virus. What surprised many people was Magic's glorious return to pro ball in late 1995. His explanation was simple: he loved the sport and missed it too much to stay away. That's the power of doing something that gets you "FIRED UP!"

We don't know what Magic's life purpose is, but it clearly relates to his love of basketball. If you looked at his list of favorite activities, playing sports would probably be on top, along with spending time with family, friends and teammates.

49

These activities all relate to each other, just as your life purpose and favorite activities do. It makes sense why you love doing the things that get you "FIRED UP!"; they're usually right on target with your life purpose.

Relating what you love doing with your life purpose can give you some terrific ideas of how to have a more fulfilling and joyful life. What you most enjoy reflects your values, and demonstrates how these values affect your behavior. *Often, activities that are fun for you and give you the most satisfaction are in alignment with your life purpose. Things you avoid may conflict with your life purpose.* That's why so many people are unhappy at work. In many cases, their work is not lined up with their life purpose and values; therefore, it doesn't fulfill them. Once you realize this, you'll become more hopeful that your life could be more meaningful. You may need to change jobs or review your priorities. You may choose to get more education or start a part-time business so you can achieve your dreams and goals. When your job conflicts with your life purpose, you need to take action to lead a happier, richer life.

One young woman realized that her life purpose was in conflict with some parts of her current job description. Armed with new awareness and a heartfelt desire to succeed, she approached her boss and renegotiated her job description. She is no longer required to do certain dreaded tasks, and she completes the rest of her job effectively and efficiently. Her attitude has shifted dramatically, so much so that her co-workers have commented on how upbeat and happy she seems now. This is just one instance where *knowing your life purpose, values and preferred activities can improve the quality of your life, helping you do what gets you "FIRED UP!"*

Getting the Big Picture

Awareness is powerful. For many people, just the act of relating their favorite activities with their life purpose gives them much greater clarity about their life vision. Suddenly, their dream is crystal clear. They are enthusiastic, ready to move on and make their vision a reality. Perhaps that's where you are right now; if so, congratulations. You now have dreams you can work toward; dreams that can inspire you to master the tools for success.

"FIRED UP!" PRINCIPLE # 10 – Take Action and Keep Moving

No dream was ever accomplished without taking action. You need to move and do, experimenting with different ideas along the way, to make things happen. If you're still unsure about your dream, remember to take *action anyway. When you move, one way or another, you'll get feedback.* You might want to adopt the idea of "ready-fire-aim." When things go well, you are on track and in alignment with your purpose. If things don't work and you're unhappy and out of balance, it's likely that you are not living according to your purpose. You need to aim again. This feedback is valuable. Learn from it, *determine what you need to do next* and go forward. Keep moving towards your dream of doing what you love.

Those who don't take action simply stagnate. They sit at home, out of work, on unemployment compensation or welfare, or in a dead-end career and they "die" inside. They may even throw a "pity party," but no one comes! You may know some people like this. You need to be careful to insulate yourself from their negativity. By their refusal to move on, they become their own worst enemy. *As soon as they begin taking positive action, they can start to live happily, fulfilling their purpose.*

Doing something worthwhile requires thought and purpose and usually means the person needs to stop feeling sorry for themselves.
🔥   Andrew Shue, the actor from the popular TV drama Melrose Place, created a non-profit organization for young people called "Do Something." Young people apply for grants from this organization to do local community projects. Shue's organization has positively influenced many youngsters around the country, and serves as a great role model for others. Andrew Shue believes the bottom line is that people need to take action, to *"Do something,"* so things can get better.

Maybe you have written out your life purpose. You may have a concise statement about your dream expressing exactly how you want to live. If so, that's terrific! You probably feel all "FIRED UP!" Focus on your dream statement for a while and see, feel and hear it happening. After reflection, you may want to change it a bit, and that's fine. Your dream is always a work in progress. Share this dream only with your trusted dreambuddy or spouse. This is a deeply personal and private statement and one that may be new and tender to you– like an infant. Protect it and keep it close to your heart. If you tell negative thinking people about your dream, they may douse the flames of your fire.

The immense value of knowing your life purpose is shown clearly in this true story. A highly respected psychotherapist who was enormously successful, found that at a certain point in his life, he felt bored. He had the money, success, family and fame. What he really wanted and loved, though, was sculpting. So one day, he left his practice to begin doing what got him "FIRED UP!" He became a sculptor with a strong following, and today he is successful, fulfilled and stimulated. Life is much more meaningful when you live it in alignment with your purpose.

Jack Anderson, noted Washington columnist and political journalist, said, *"Each person's philosophy is the major factor in how their life works out."* Just as in sailing, he said, *"The set of the sail determines the direction of the boat"*; a person's mindset determines the direction of their life.

If you don't know what your vision is by now, that's OK. *Keep moving anyway.* Pick a "practice" dream to use for taking action. It could be something you really want, even though it may not be your ultimate dream. It might be just one small part of it, or it might be a goal you've had for some time and haven't completed yet. It needs to have meaning and value for you; one that will delight you when you achieve it. Using this practice dream will give you the opportunity to learn about taking action with tools that can be applied to any dream or goal in your life.

Take a moment now to verbalize and write down this practice dream. (Do this only if you don't have a good idea of what your life dream is.) Start with the two words "I am" and then use "ing" verbs to complete the sentence. (It may help you to review the Life Purpose guidelines in Chapter 7.) Play with the sentence until it feels right. Keep it fairly short so you can easily remember it. Once you have it, keep it where you'll see it often.

Whether you are working with your life dream or your practice dream, you now have a statement which you can refer to and manifest. *Great! You persisted and created a result.* That's what realizing your dream is all about.

"In my work I have heard the testimonies of thousands of people who have found the courage to take the next step toward living their dreams. Without exception, the sense of joy and exhilaration in these people is entirely compelling."
Alan Cohen

Remember These Key Points

◆ It's important to keep moving, even when you are not 100% sure of your vision or dream. When you move, you get feedback, and that feedback lets you know whether you are on the right track or not. Think "ready-fire-aim."
◆ Negative thinking people will douse the fire of your dream; don't share your purpose or dream statement with them.
◆ Knowing your life purpose, values and preferred activities can improve the quality of your life, by leading you to do what gets you "FIRED UP!"

Now Take These "FIRED UP!" Action Steps

◆ If you have not done so already, relate your favorite activities to your life purpose statement. Make sure they fit with your life purpose.
◆ Write a dream statement of something you truly want which is in harmony with your life purpose and favorite activities. You can use a smaller dream to practice with.
◆ Spend some time visualizing this dream "as if" it is totally real and you are now living it.

The Power of a Dream

"The dream is made.
Enthusiasm is released.
A challenge is accepted and you're released from apathy.
Excellence is claimed and mediocrity is rejected.
Leadership is asserted.
Faith is put in control of your future.
You're free to become more than what you have done.
Hope is renewed and optimism blossoms.
You need God to help you succeed.
Personhood is affirmed.
Success is honored and assured.
Direction is established.
Fears are overpowered.
Focus is fixed.
Opportunities are given a chance to become achievements.
Growth is renewed.
Your relationships are empowered because
goals attract others interested in those goals.
Positive thoughts create positive changes inspired
by your goals.
Your priorities are set in concrete.
Your vision is crystallized.

SET A GOAL AND GO FOR IT!"
Robert H. Schuller

Chapter 9

Expanding the Vision
Finding the Right Base Logs

"Go confidently in the direction of your dreams. Live the life you've imagined."
Henry David Thoreau

A New Business Vision

In 1983 I opened my advertising and training company with tremendous optimism, three employees, attractive office space and no clients. Out of a sense of fairness and integrity, which is what I based my agency on, I did not take any of my former employer's clients. I started from scratch and even spent the first two weeks working for free to fulfill a grand opening commitment for a new shopping area. After that, the whole staff came together and began drumming up new business, using a variety of sales techniques, including visualization. As a group, we all vividly pictured the agency busy and thriving, doing good work for good people, with effective results for our clients. We even imagined two-to-three years from then, doing work on a large scale for big, well-established national companies. I put all of that energy into action, making sales calls, looking for leads, staying "Fired Up!" and connecting with other businesses. Slowly but surely, I built the company on a foundation of excellent work, advertising with integrity, and long-term marketing strategies.

I made lots of mistakes, which turned out to be major learning opportunities. Hiring the wrong people, paying them too much, spending too much on overhead – these were just a few of the lessons. One of the biggest lessons I learned was that I need to be more open about wanting referrals. In the beginning, I was naive and foolish; whenever anyone asked how business was, I always just said, "Great." That was neither accurate nor authentic, because every company has down times. I learned to say, "Business is OK, but we could use some more. Do you know anyone who needs some advertising?" That made a big difference in terms of referrals and the kind of clients coming our way. It took lots of hard work, but I began achieving my goals, building a solid company.

Within three years, we landed Apple Computer New England as an account. We developed an idea for introducing the new Macintosh computer, and the next thing we knew, *we were designing and producing six million newspaper inserts for Apple Computer nationally.* That meant I was flying to Syracuse, NY, getting snowbound in a blizzard, flying the "red eye" to California and meeting with upper level marketing people in Cupertino. I took my art director to Houston, Texas to be on press for three nights to check the print run. Whew – it was very thrilling. Quite an accomplishment for a small New Hampshire ad agency. In a way though, it was exactly what we expected. Three years earlier, we had all imagined this kind of success in our visualization. We all learned *visualization is amazingly powerful.*

How to Get "Fired Up!" and Take Action

Many people have great dreams that never come true because they don't take action. For whatever reason, from myths and negative self-talk to acts of self-sabotage, they fail to work towards making their dreams real. They give up on what's truly important to them. Sometimes, working on the dream seems overwhelming to them. In other cases, they believe they just can't find the time to add one more thing to an already tight schedule. Usually, they have not taken the time to fully envision their ideal life, i.e., to develop a mental picture of it. Many times, they have focused on the price and not the prize.

Your Creative Imagination is Key to Building Your Dreams

Over and over again, your imagination explores limitless possibilities and infinite outcomes. It can mock up your perfect life or paint a picture of defeat. You may already know how this works. A person who stagnates and never gets a job is a perfect example. Every time they go for an interview, they make excuses why it won't work and actually paint a picture of rejection for themselves. They tell themselves they will fail – and they do – they've become a self-fulfilling prophecy of doom. (This is also called catastrophizing – imagining the worst.) Direct your imagination to visualize only positive pictures of success, and not negative pictures, ever. *You need to be vigilant about your mental pictures – they can make a big difference in the outcome of your actions.*

⬤ One very effective salesperson regularly visualizes success at each sale. They may not know how the presentation will go or who they will be meeting, but they see themselves coming out of the building cheering, with their hand up in the air, feeling terrific about having made a sale. They picture the client's check in their hand all ready to be cashed. This visualization works amazingly well, so they hold that mental picture each time they do a new sales presentation.

In sharp contrast to this style, is that of the depressed door-to-door salesperson who approaches people flatly, expecting the worst. Their pitch is, "You don't want to buy any such and such, do you?" And, of course, the person on the other end doesn't buy. How could they? Even the salesperson doesn't believe in their own product. Because they're picturing negative outcomes, they actively create their own failure.

Visualization is very powerful – *what you look at and continually focus on becomes reality.* Visualization has led hundreds of famous athletes to victory, including many renowned Olympians. They won because they focused on victory and saw themselves giving their personal best. This same technique will work for you. *The more clearly you imagine your success, the more likely it is to manifest exactly that way.*

⬤ There was a impressive story about Earl Nightingale, co-founder of Nightingale Conant tapes. The way I heard it, Earl and his wife each kept a dream book of things they would like to own, places they would like to go and so forth. They never showed these dream books to each other, but they both spent time looking at their own. One day Earl landed a very large account and decided to give his wife a big surprise. He drove up in a light blue Silver Cloud Rolls Royce. When his wife saw it, she got so excited, she ran into the house and came out with her dream book. There, pasted in it, was the exact color, make and model car he had bought for her. He had never seen this and did not know it was in her book. It manifested anyway. *Positive picturing worked!*

Mike Vance, former dean of Disney University, who worked very closely with Walt Disney for years, tells the story of the opening day of DisneyWorld in Florida. Someone commented that it was too bad Walt couldn't see this. Knowing how Walt had completely and totally envisioned the whole concept of DisneyWorld during his initial flight over swampland years before, Mike replied "He did see it – that's why it's here."

What you look at and continually focus on will manifest. This next activity will help do that. You need a quiet place, a notebook and pen or a tape recorder. You'll be imagining your dream one, three and five years from now. Although you may not be sure what it looks like right now, your imagination may have some wonderful surprises for you.

One woman who did this visualization saw herself learning how to train dogs in obedience. One year in the future, she saw that she was also teaching seeing-eye dogs to help lead the blind. Three years in the future, she saw that she had started a dog training center of her own. And five years in the future, her center was highly profitable and respected for its unique, loving and effective approach to animal behavior training. All of this came out of her imagination! She was "FIRED UP!" by what showed up, as each dream unfolded in her life. It delighted her and gave her all sorts of ideas about potential future plans. The same thing can happen for you. *Allow yourself to have a rich and rewarding experience. Believe you deserve it.*

As Napoleon Hill wrote in *Think and Grow Rich,* "Whatever the mind can conceive and believe, it can achieve."

Visualization for Expanding Your Dream

Take ten minutes now in a quiet place where you won't be disturbed. Take the phone off the hook or turn the ringer off and close the door. If it helps, you could read what comes next into a tape recorder and then listen to it as you do this activity.

Now close your eyes and take three deep breaths. Allow yourself to relax, deeply and completely. Let go of all thoughts and distractions – let yourself go. Picture yourself as perfectly protected, and know that you are completely safe. Give yourself full permission to see and experience this dream. *Say to yourself silently or aloud, "subconscious, I'm about to experience a picture of my dream fully realized and I allow only that which is for the greatest benefit of all concerned to come forward. I allow my dream to be clear and expansive and I allow it to come fully present for me now."* Take another deep breath.

Picture yourself in a beautiful place outdoors, someplace where you are walking, feeling energized and refreshed. You are excited and full of anticipation. You sit down at a giant white movie screen and watch the movie of you living your dream, fully and completely, joyfully and easily. Notice what you're doing. Feel the energy and satisfaction of living your dream. What are people saying to you? What are you saying? What actions are you taking? Let it all become crystal clear – *see, hear and feel your dream coming true in every area of your life.*

Notice how whole, satisfied and "FIRED UP!" you feel. What is your professional life like? How are you earning your living? Notice that you have plenty of everything you need: money, success, as well as love and peace of mind. What is your personal life like? See your relationships as valuable and meaningful – filled with happiness, love and mutual support. Feel your sparkling vitality as you enjoy radiant health. Notice that you feel more balanced and connected with an energy that is greater than yourself. You feel a true sense of purpose and meaning.

And now expand your dream to one full year from now. What are you doing? How is your life different? What has happened in the past year? Let yourself be loved and supported in your dream. Let yourself have it all. Experience all the positive shifts and victories, large and small, along the way. What is your life like personally, professionally, physically, spiritually? What has improved in your life and how is it better? Be grateful for all the blessings that present themselves.

And now it's three years from today. You are doing even more. Perhaps the dream has grown in a whole new, unexpected way. What direction has your life taken? Who are the people in your life? What is important to you? Picture yourself living the dream even more fully. Has it changed? Are you doing new things? How do you feel about yourself? What is giving you the greatest pleasure? Experience your life as completely successful in all areas. How are your personal relationships? How are your finances? How do you want them to be? If you need to make adjustments, do so. How is your professional life? What are you doing? Notice how satisfying it is. How do you feel about yourself? See the confident, joyful you living your dream fully.

Now, make the dream even bigger. *Imagine it five years from now.* See, hear and feel yourself as highly successful, living your ideal life. What is happening? What are you telling yourself and what are others saying to you? Notice how terrific it feels to be living your dream, effectively and easily. Notice that you feel abundant in every area of your life, and that you have more success and happiness than you could ever have dreamed of. Observe how "FIRED UP!" you are about your life. If something needs adjusting, do it now. Observe that everything you need is there and that you are continually moving and expanding your horizons. Picture this very clearly and let it sink into your awareness. *Know that you are worthy of wonderful things – of having all your dreams come true.*

Finally, take another deep breath and bring yourself back to today, into your current surroundings. Slowly start to open your eyes and review what you've just experienced. Take a few minutes to jot down or dictate notes. Be sure to record what you were doing one year, three years and five years from now.

As you review what you have just experienced, you may find yourself awed by the growth and dimensions of your dream, and how many directions it took. *When you take action on your intentions, miracles can happen.*

A good example of this is Leigh Moorehouse, who had lost three friends to breast cancer. In 1996 she decided to take action and create greater awareness of the alarming increase in breast cancer and its fatalities. She set out in the summer in her kayak and paddled all the way from Key Largo, Florida to Eastport, Maine – *2100 miles by ocean* – to raise $100,000 for breast cancer research. Her next goal is to do the Pacific Coast from Washington State to Baja, California. In her typically modest fashion, Leigh says of her incredible journey, "I'm just an average person trying to do something."

This is only one example of what being "FIRED UP!" about your dreams can do. There are thousands of other stories like this – including yours in the future. *Let yourself have the life you've always dreamed of – you deserve it.*

> *"The imagination is the preview of what's to come*
> *in your life."*
> Albert Einstein

Remember These Key Points

◆ Many people have dreams that never come true because they don't take action.
◆ Your creative imagination is a key resource to building your dreams.
◆ What you look at and continually focus on will manifest. The more clearly you imagine your success, the more likely it is to manifest exactly that way.
◆ Your imagination can show you how your dream might expand your life.
◆ When you take action on your intentions, miracles can happen.

Now Take These "FIRED UP!" Action Steps

◆ If you have not done so already, visualize your dream as described in this chapter.
◆ Review your notes from this experience and get used to the idea of having all your dreams come true. What would change in your life? How would it be better?

YOU WILL GET IT

"If you want a thing bad enough
to go out and fight for it,
to work day and night for it,
to give up your time, your peace and sleep for it.
If all that you dream and scheme is about it,
and life seems useless and worthless without it...
if you gladly sweat for it and fret for it
and plan for it
and lose all your terror of the opposition for it...
if you simply go after that thing you want
with all of your capacity, strength and sagacity,
faith, hope and confidence and stern pertinacity...
if neither cold, poverty, famine,
nor gout, sickness nor pain,
of body and brain,
can keep you away from the thing
that you want...
if dogged and grim
you beseech and beset it,
with the help of God,
you WILL get it!"

Berton Bradley

Chapter 10

The Dream Creates Action

Laying the Best Kindling

"The great aim of education is not knowledge but action."
Herbert Spencer

You Need an Action Plan to Succeed

In 1987 a non-profit organization called Success for Women Entrepreneurs hosted a daylong conference for female entrepreneurs and women in business. The first major event of its kind, it attracted 250 excited women from New England. With excellent speakers from all over the country presenting a myriad of timely and fascinating topics, participants raved about the value of the day. They had the chance to learn, interview experts and most of all, share their experiences with other female entrepreneurs. The whole event was a huge success, and it laid the foundation for other women's groups to begin their work. As one of the founding board members of the group, and then president, I headed a team of dynamic women who all actively volunteered their time, energy and resources to help create the conference. It could not have happened without tremendous organization and planning. What made it all happen was a *strong action plan*, with clearly spelled-out roles and deadlines and substantial follow-through. That action plan, step by step, took us from the birth of the idea to the thank you notes after the conference was all over. It gave us a framework and structure from which to move and continually take action. It was highly effective.

"FIRED UP!" PRINCIPLE # 11 – Have a Plan

🔥 *The most successful ventures occur because of planning and <u>action</u>.* DisneyWorld® succeeded because after Walt flew over the swamps of Florida, he envisioned the entire concept and went back and made a plan. He got a team together and took action. In his imagination, he knew what DisneyWorld would look like one, three, five, ten and even twenty years later. He had a magnificent plan for the future and it worked.

In this chapter, you will build on your dream and develop a plan for achieving it. Ideas not acted on become incompletes and cause frustrations. Ideas put into practice can result in incredible outcomes, victories and inventions. The telephone, television and mini-computer were all the result of ideas put into action. So were the airplane and automobile. None of these inventions would exist if their creators hadn't had a plan where they continually took action, learned from their mistakes and made adjustments. Now's the time to make your great ideas work for you and your dream.

Your Dream is Your Catalyst for Success

Always remember that while dreams are absolutely essential for you to move ahead and give your life meaning, it's what you become in the process that's most important. If you become a wealthy person by using people, you'll be very lonely and disliked. When you consistently help others realize their dream, you'll automatically achieve yours and most people will love you all the way to the top.

Here's a brief synopsis of how having a dream leads to success. The dream creates action. By taking action we overcome fear. In overcoming fear, we develop faith and strength. With faith and strength, we build belief in ourselves. As our belief increases, we gain confidence. With confidence, we develop self-esteem and expansive thinking. Applying all these, we get *results* which lead to our success.

Using the "Fired Up!" Action Plan for Dreambuilding

This is a valuable tool that you can use over and over again to build a dream and develop a plan for making it come true. You may want to make a copy of it from p. 250- 251 in the Appendix, or use it for reference. It'll help you get moving on your dreams in a concrete, practical way. While the plan itself is two pages long, it is chunked down here and in other chapters into small, easily manageable sections. All too often, people have great ideas but never make any plan for achieving them. Cemeteries are full of them. And the world is deprived of untold great ideas. You don't want that to happen to you. Start *moving* today. A good place to begin is by completing this part of your *action* plan.

"Fired Up!" Action Plan for Dreambuilding

Name   Date

My Dream: (Positively Stated as a Choice, Specific, Powerful, Emotionally Fulfilling)

_____

_____

Where I envision this dream 1 year, 3 years, 5 years from now

1 year: _____

3 years: _____

5 years: _____

Get your notes out from the visualization you did in the last chapter where you expanded your dream. First fill in the top section called "My Dream." This is where you write a brief, vivid description of your dream. *State it positively in the present tense, specifically detailing what you are doing and how you are seeing, hearing and feeling it.* Use descriptive words so you get "Fired Up!" Write it down as clearly as possible. Be sure it's something you really do want. *The test for whether you really want something is this. Just ask yourself the question: "If I could have it right now, would I really take it?" If the answer is yes, you do want it. If the is answer is no or not now, don't put your energy into it.*

Look over your notes from the process you just did and let your mind wander back to what you pictured you were doing and what was happening. Be sure to write it as though it were happening right now. Things we write in future tense almost never happen because they always stay in the future. We only have today; tomorrow is always in the future. Visualize them happening *now*, in the present moment.

Describe the development of your dream one, three and five years from now. Again, use the visualization you just did as a reference point. Pay attention to whatever ideas pop into your head and jot them down in the space provided on the previous page. If you aren't sure how the dream will evolve, just make it up and have fun with it.

What kinds of things would you like to have happening five years from now? Who would you like to be working with? What do you want the quality of your life to be? Look ahead to three years from now. What do you want to happen in that time period? How is the dream developing towards that five year picture? Then look at one year from now. What actions have you taken? How is the dream growing and taking shape? Remember, you are just playing with ideas at this point; you are not making any commitments. So let yourself DREAM BIG and create a wonderfully fulfilling vision of the life you want.

"FIRED UP!" Action Plan for Dreambuilding

Name   Date

My Dream: (Positively Stated as a Choice, Specific, Powerful, Emotionally Fulfilling)
I am creating a new business, working in joy and harmony with others while
expressing my leadership and imagination

Where I envision this dream 1 year, 3 years, 5 years from now
1 year: Myself and 2 other people come together to work toward a business full-time
3 years: 10-500 people work together to develop distribution and market products
5 years: 500-5000 people work together in harmony creating possibilities and
            financial independence

Here's how an entrepreneur completed the top of the "FIRED UP!" Action Plan for Dreambuilding, just to give you an example. In his vision, his new business utilized his leadership and imagination to work with an exciting and cooperative team. As he mapped out his one, three and five year plans, he envisioned the business growing steadily, from 2 to 500 to 5000 people, serving their customer base, developing distributors and gaining financial independence. Since he completed this form, he has started his own business, following-through on his marketing plan.

As you do this, be clear and specific about how you want your dream to feel, look and sound one, three and five years from now. Let your imagination give you some creative hints. *Your life can be even better than your wildest dreams; it just takes planning, action and being "FIRED UP!"*

Here's another example of how someone else completed the "FIRED UP!" Action Plan for Dreambuilding. Barry is a high-level executive who wanted more balance and joy in his life, both at work and at home. His vision (shown below) included specific action steps at home and at work. Rather than drastic change, this represented a gradual improvement of what was already effective in his life. He wanted greater harmony, service and enthusiasm.

"FIRED UP!" Action Plan for Dreambuilding

Name   Date

My Dream: (Positively Stated as a Choice, Specific, Powerful, Emotionally Fulfilling)
I am creating enthusiasm and harmony in my work and home using my loving and imagination

Where I envision this dream 1 year, 3 years, 5 years from now
1 year: Coaching at some level one of my kids activities and supporting my wife in her growth
3 years: Serving at a more senior level of my company while enjoying time off with my family
5 years: Continuing leadership at a senior level of my company with the support of my people so they are enthused by my leadership

---

Your life may already be exactly how you want it in many areas, but you might want to make some minor adjustments so you can do more of what you love. If that's the case, great – just picture your life exactly as you want it to be in all areas and notice where you need to make some changes. It doesn't need to be a whirlwind change – it can be a very gentle, relaxed, methodical process. If you do want to make significant changes and start living your life with more fulfillment, realizing your greatest dreams, *you can do it.* The "FIRED UP!" Action Plan for Dreambuilding is a key tool to making that happen.

> *"The method of enterprising is to plan with audacity, and execute with vigour; to sketch out a map of possibilities; And then to treat them as probabilities."*
> Bovee

Remember These Key Points

◆ The greatest successes occur because of planning and action.
◆ Ideas not acted on become incompletes and frustration. Ideas acted on can result in incredible victories and inventions.
◆ To see if you really want something, ask, "If I could have it right now, would I take it?" If you answer yes, you do want it. If you answer no or not now, don't put your energy into it.
◆ This "FIRED UP!" Action Plan for Dreambuilding is a valuable tool you can use over and over to build a dream and develop a plan for making it come true.
◆ The dream creates action → Action overcomes fear → Fear turns to faith and strength → Faith and strength build belief → Belief leads to confidence → Confidence builds high self-esteem and expansive thinking → All these lead to success.

Now Take These "FIRED UP!" Action Steps

◆ If you have not done so already, complete the top part of the "FIRED UP!" Action Plan For Dreambuilding in this chapter.
◆ Copy your dream description with one, three and five year expansion statements and put it where you will see it every day.
◆ Think about each of your dreams and use the test question in the section above. Keep a record of those dreams you want now, and those you may not want until several years from now. Notice if some things actually leave your dream list altogether.

Chapter 11

Map Out Your Success

Building the Fire

"The action of the child inventing a new game with his playmates; Einstein formulating a theory of relativity; the housewife devising a new sauce for the meat; a young author writing his first novel; all of these are in terms of definition, Creative, and there is no attempt to set them in some order of more or less Creative."
Carl R. Rogers

Ideas Come to You In A Creative Way

Have you ever watched a group of small children spontaneously playacting a scene? They find a pile of leaves, for example, and then all of a sudden, they have transformed the leaves into a fort and created fictional characters for each child to act out. Every child has input, and they frequently blurt out their ideas as they pop into their heads. What generally results is a highly imaginative, satisfying game that is absorbing and fun. Adults are like that too.

People don't think in a linear, organized fashion. Ideas pop in and out, some of which can take us in entirely new directions. This is where some of your best inventive thinking can occur. As you take action on your dreams, capturing these creative thoughts is critical. (Be sure to have paper and pen or tape recorder with you at all times so you can save your ideas – you never know when or how they'll show up.)

"FIRED UP!" PRINCIPLE #12 – Capture Your Creativity on Paper

A unique way to view the action required to achieve your dream is the dreammap. It's literally a map of the things you need to do do make your dreams come true. In a sense, it represents a system or vehicle you can use to drive your way to success. A dreammap captures all your "random" thoughts. It looks like a chart with several branches going in different directions with your core dream in the center. This concept is widely used by many training organizations, originating in the United Kingdom with a man named Tony Buzan. He called it a "mindmap;" I have renamed it here for use when focusing on your dream. *A dreammap allows you to capture both your planned and seemingly random "popcorn" ideas quickly and easily. It provides a great springboard for even more spontaneous imagination.*

Many large corporations throughout the country use this tool for planning and flowchart development. In fact, there is a training company in the Midwest that specializes in what they call "graphic mindmaps," which include pictures and symbols rather than words, since this approach can catch many different ideas.

When you use colored markers and a large piece of construction paper, it helps to make the dreammap even more expansive. Some companies use large brown kraft paper and spread it out, taping it over walls when they're tackling a problem or issue. That way several people can participate and spin off each other's ideas.

Walt Disney used this concept brilliantly with storyboards and continuous input from his employees. This technique still works so well that *The Hunchback of Notre Dame*, one of Disney's animation films, was created in exactly the same manner. Various sketches of scenes would be laid out on a giant board and the animators came together and had story meetings, filling in the gaps, rejecting what didn't work.

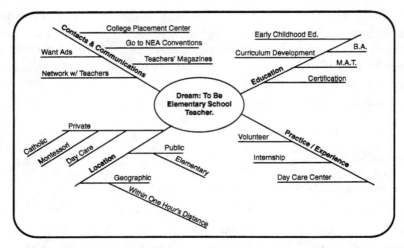

A dreammap is a highly effective way of resolving an issue, planning a strategy for new growth or introducing new products. *It's also an exceptional tool for helping you make your dreams come true.*

Dream of Being an Elementary School Teacher

As an example of what a dreammap looks like, above is one for a woman who wanted to become an elementary school teacher. She brainstormed various possibilities, considering many different options of how she could get her job. One branch off the center is Education, since she needs to develop certain skills and obtain certification to be qualified to teach. Offshoots of that might be a Bachelor's degree or Masters of Arts in Teaching, and early childhood education training.

Another consideration is where she could teach, hence the branch called Location, that spawned thoughts about the geographic territory where she wanted to work. It also brought up the type of school system, public or private, which led to even more detail about which type of private school.

A third direction led to the branch of Practice and Experience, which included offshoots of volunteer internship and day care center work. And the fourth major branch is Contacts and Communications – how to find out about jobs. This branch has a multitude of offshoots, from teachers' magazines to attending National Education Association conventions, to networking with other teachers, to placement offices and more.

There are many more branches that could be placed on this dreammap – it's still in its infancy stage. But it gives you a clear picture of how your dreammap can evolve as more ideas pop into your head. *If you get a new idea that doesn't relate to an existing branch, just create a new one.*

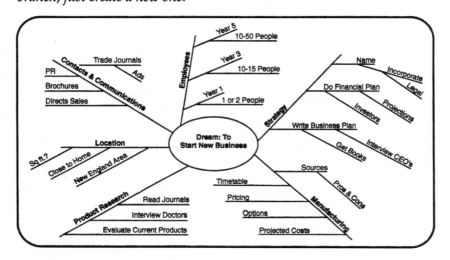

Dream of Starting a New Manufacturing Business

Let's take a look at the dreammap of an entrepreneur starting a new business in medical products manufacturing. His dream is "I am creating a new business working in joy and harmony with others using my leadership and imagination." This dreammap is far more elaborate than the previous one, because it's for the development of a brand new company. Each one of the major directional branches could have an entire dreammap page to itself. Marketing, Manufacturing and Strategy branches need more in-depth detailing. But this overview map is a valuable starting point and it shows him which steps he needs to take first.

The dreammap is such an effective strategic tool that some businesses have dreammaps for every step of a given project. They are consolidated into a notebook and given to every member of the work team, so everyone knows the plan and can more easily add to the maps as the project develops.

A dreammap is also useful when tracking how a project got to a certain point, and it aids in troubleshooting along the way.

Building A Networking Business

This person's dream was to utilize networking as a vehicle to make their dreams come true. They need to plug into a system that's already been developed and proven by successful people. All they need to do is duplicate that system to be effective. They don't have to concern themselves with "reinventing the wheel"; they just duplicate what already works.

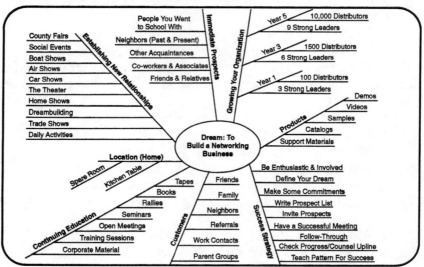

<u>Map Out Your Dream</u>

Now take out your action plan with the descriptions of your dream and the one, three and five year statements. Here's what you need to make your dreammap.

- A large piece of paper – either white or brown Kraft paper or construction paper – some people even like graph paper. (If you hang your map on a wall as you develop it, put up two layers of paper so the markers don't bleed through to your wall.)
- Colorful broad felt-tip <u>non-permanent</u> markers- it helps to make each major branch a different color, and you may want to draw in pictures rather than write words.
- Your Action Plan for Dreambuilding.
- At least half an hour alone in a quiet place.
- A notebook for recording your ideas and thoughts later.
- Artists' white tape or masking tape.

Once you have all your tools assembled, *take a look at your action plan, especially the one, three and five year statements.* As you read these over, you'll get ideas spontaneously about what needs to happen so you can reach your goals. Start jotting down different branches and ideas and let them come to life on your page. It's fine if it's very busy and crowded – this is strictly for you. Brainstorm as many branches as you can, remembering to group them under major branches wherever possible.

Ask Yourself These Questions

These questions may stimulate you to think of new branches and ideas. (There may be a couple of questions that aren't relevant to your dream – depending on what it is. If that's the case, ignore the question.)

- *What resources* or *skills* do you need for your dream?
- *Where* do you want to do your dream?
- *Who* do you need to contact to make your dream happen?
- *How* can you reach your five year goal?
- *What* homework or *research* do you need to do?
- *Which professionals* are needed for your dream (lawyers, CPA's, etc.)?
- *How much money* do you need for your dream?
- Where can you get *experience* in this field?
- Who has already succeeded in this field that you can use as a reference or a *mentor* for counseling and support?
- *What else* do you need to make your dream happen?
- What kind of *help* will you need from co-workers or family?
- How will you *get the word out* about your dream? (Only share your dream with those who can help you or who you believe will support you.)
- Who *benefits* from your dream?
- What *needs to change* in your life for you to have your dream?

Be Open to the Wealth of Infinite Possibilities

Some people play and have fun with dreammaps for hours. Let the little kid inside you be very present, because they're highly creative.

Now that you have a preliminary dreammap, you can develop it even more to gain greater insight. Sit down and share your dreammap with three or four supportive people;

this is an excellent way to gather an abundance of valuable concepts and suggestions. The process is exciting and makes your dream seem more real. It's quite possible these people may very well have exactly the contact you need to make a vital connection in realizing your dream.

The dreammap is a place to collect ideas as a strategic tool. It's not a commitment, so allow yourself to be as spontaneous as possible when creating the map. The time for decisions and commitments is later – *this is the time to play and let your imagination run free.*

"Man alone, of all the creatures of earth, can change his own pattern. Man alone is architect of his destiny...."
William James

Remember These Key Points

◆ People don't think in a linear, organized fashion. Ideas pop in and out, some of which can take us in entirely new directions.
◆ A dreammap is an excellent tool for charting your creative ideas as they show up.
◆ Using colored markers and pictures or graphics on your dreammap helps get your playful kid inside involved.
◆ It is very useful to ask yourself the questions in this chapter to make your dream real. Your answers can tell much of what you need to make your dream happen.
◆ You can use a dreammap with any goal, dream or project.

Now Take These "FIRED UP!" Action Steps

◆ If you have not done so already, create your own dreammap.
◆ Be sure to ask yourself the questions in this chapter.
◆ After you've created your dreammap, invite a few people you trust (who will support you) to contribute ideas. Add their ideas to your dreammap and watch it grow.

IT COULDN'T BE DONE

"Somebody said that it couldn't be done,
But he with a chuckle replied,
That 'maybe it couldn't,' but he would be one
Who wouldn't say so till he tried.
So he buckled right in with the trace of a grin
on his face. If he worried, he hid it.
He started to sing as he tackled the thing
That couldn't be done, and he did it.
Somebody scoffed: 'Oh, you'll never do that,
At least no one has ever done it;'
But he took off his coat and he took off his hat,
And the first thing we knew he'd begun it,
With a lift of his chin and a bit of a grin,
Without any doubting or quiddit,
He started to sing as he tackled the thing
That couldn't be done, and he did it.
There are thousands to tell you it cannot be done,
There are thousands to prophecy failure;
There are thousands to point out to you, one by one,
The dangers that wait to assail you,
But just buckle in with a bit of a grin,
Just take off your coat and get to it;
Just start to sing as you tackle the thing
That 'cannot be done,' and you'll do it."

Edgar A. Guest

Chapter 12

A Dream That Touched over 50,000

The Flame Ignited and Burning Bright

"The most important thing in your life is to live your life for something more than your life."
William James

New Beginnings

Picture yourself as a shy sixth grade boy dealing with the pressures of middle school. Some of the older boys in your neighborhood are ganging up on younger kids like you; some are pressuring you to start smoking, and others are even talking about sex. There's this cute girl, Karen, in your fifth period history class that you have a crush on, but you don't know how to ask her out. There's lots of things you'd like to talk over with your dad – like girls and drugs, but you're not sure where to start. *Then one day you hear about this great new program called Project Safeguard.*

You and your dad get a whole day off from school and work, and you go to fun workshops at this education center. There you learn what the new "cool" drugs are and how to refuse them. You listen to a former addict talk about his experiences and vow inside never to choose that lifestyle. You take a workshop about how girls and boys relate and realize you can ask Karen to the dance, just by being her friend and sharing what you have in common. In the afternoon, new techniques for handling negative peer pressure and feeling good about yourself give you some ideas about how to handle those kids in your neighborhood. Then you get "FIRED UP!" about your future in a seminar called "Reach for the Stars."

On the way home, you and your dad have a different kind of conversation, and you find you can ask him things you've always wanted to. He's open and shares with you honestly, because he has new tools for communicating with his kids. Both of you feel "FIRED UP!" about the day and closer to each other. Before bed that night, your dad tells you what a terrific son you are. *A modern fairy tale? No, it's a genuine reality for thousands of kids in New Hampshire, Massachusetts and Florida.*

Every year, sixth, eighth and eleventh graders, and their parents take a day out and learn how to communicate better. *All of this happens because of the efforts of one remarkable sixth grade science teacher.* A parent himself, Warren Berry took on the challenges of introducing a brand new form of education into the public school system, and succeeded in creating a program that has already impacted over 50,000 people – *Project Safeguard.*

The Dream

Warren Berry was a man with a vision. As a 40 year old sixth grade science teacher in Merrimack, NH, Warren treasured his children and knew how important they were to his life. Their sports and interests were top priority to him and his wife, and they did their best to set a good example and build their children's self-esteem.

Warren knew *there was one adventure he didn't want his children experiencing – the ever-present lure of drugs.* As he prepared the curriculum for his sixth graders, Warren wanted to create a drug education unit that was dramatic and *effective.* He had watched all the fear-based programs fail – you know the ones who say, "This is your brain; this is your brain on drugs," as an egg gets scrambled. He also knew that the government advertising "Just Say No" had been a joke to his students. *Something was missing in all these campaigns – the family.*

Warren believed the most powerful way to make drug education hit home was to include parents. He wanted to take the students and parents off-site to a neutral setting where such a difficult topic could be approached freshly. In the fall of 1987 Warren sat down with his Science Department Coordinator, Marge Chiafery and then Principal, Tom Levesque. The more he talked and added colorful description and intensity, the more they listened. They were "FIRED UP!" by Warren's enthusiasm – it was contagious. (Perhaps you've had this same experience sharing your dream with others. The enthusiasm can catch like wildfire.)

Marge and Tom added clarity, focus and energy to his plans. Six months later, after literally hundreds of hours of work, jumping over seemingly impossible hurdles, they launched a new concept called *Project Safeguard (Student and Family Education Guards Us Against Reliance on Drugs.)* This drug and health awareness program focused on self-esteem and communication, bringing parents and students together. In the spring of 1988 over 100 students and 116 parents walked through the doors of New Hampshire College. They left that afternoon enriched, inspired and informed – with several tools to help them discuss tough issues with each other.

The Challenges

Project Safeguard didn't just happen; there were enormous challenges. Things like busing, parking, registration kits, speakers, topics, fire codes, logistics, emergency plans and the other details all raised a different set of problems. Project Safeguard could never exist without great cooperation and volunteer effort. Working together, *they did whatever it took to make it happen. This is key to making dreams come true.*

1. Overcoming the Negativity – Why is it that when one person has a great idea, there are always others who can give a dozen excuses why it won't work? We all need to be careful of the "naysayers," toxic people who don't have their own dream and try to steal those of others. When Warren first created Project Safeguard, his biggest challenge was convincing others it was *possible.* (This is one of Les Brown's major principles of success for people who are so beaten down they don't know how to continue working on their dream. Consider that it's possible.) Some felt that parents wouldn't attend, that they wouldn't take a day off from work to come, that there were too many organizational nightmares and that it simply could not be done.

That idea of "it can't be done" is one that faces most people with a dream. That's where positivity, faith, action and the sheer determination of being "FIRED UP!" win out. Warren's perseverance and enthusiasm led him to be innovative as he met and overcame each challenge. Warren got others "FIRED UP!" about his dream, creating a dynamic network of "worker bees." As Helen Keller said, *"We can do anything if we stick to it long enough."*

2. Fund-raising – One of the main tasks was raising money to pay speakers and cover expenses. That's where some of these worker bees helped. After endless hours exploring funding options, Warren, Marge and Tom were finally rewarded for all their hard work by earning an $8500 grant from the Federal Drug Free Schools and Communities Act of 1986, through the New Hampshire Department of Education. *What a triumph – both a statewide and federal board got "FIRED UP!" too, and gave life to the dream!* Warren's commitment paid off and proved what Goethe wrote, *"There is one elementary truth, the ignorance of which kills countless ideas and splendid plans: that the moment one definitely commits oneself, then providence moves, too."*

A program of this size needs nearly $10,000 a year (per school system) to keep going, plus a generous amount of volunteer time. While Warren was fortunate to receive the grant, there are always enormous expenses and more money is needed each year. With the state of the economy, funding for education has been increasingly difficult.

How do you raise money when people don't seem to have any? Warren did it with "people people." These are individuals who could get others "FIRED UP!" about Project Safeguard. They believed so strongly in the dream that they called up big companies and asked for help. Some of those people had so much faith and commitment that they donated their time and services and created a video about Project Safeguard – which is an effective sales tool.

Civic groups like Rotary and Lions Clubs often donate money and small local businesses contribute cash and services. Even the

Merrimack School Board now budgets $5000 annually to support Project Safeguard.

Warren knows full well that Project Safeguard wouldn't be alive and well without his volunteers and sponsors. He always acknowledges them for their help. That's something people who live their dreams do regularly – humbly express their gratitude and appreciation and recognize their "cheerleaders" and mentors. *People need to feel valued and know their efforts mean something.*

3. The Power of the Press – Early on, support from the press was crucial, and Project Safeguard was blessed with goodwill in the local community. The town paper, the *Merrimack Village Crier*, wrote several positive articles about the program, followed by other stories in the *Nashua Telegraph* and the *Union Leader*. These same papers continue writing about the program.

4. Time – Wouldn't it be great if there were 28 hours or more in every day? Almost everyone with a dream would love to have more hours in a day. *How do you balance work and home and the dream? How do you find the hours to do everything you need to do to make your dream come true?* There's not enough time in the day to do *everything* that needs to be done. Therefore it's essential to set strong priorities, stay "FIRED UP!" about your dream and keep going for it.

Warren knows this dilemma quite well. He is pleased his children enjoy hanging out at home. He and his wife Lisa have worked hard to create a loving, nurturing environment where their children can use their independence to learn and grow. Warren's family is his first priority. Balancing family with Project Safeguard is challenging. Participation in the Project Safeguard programs held at his children's schools was powerful and positive for the whole family. But running the program generally requires hundreds of hours each year. That could have taken a toll on Warren's family life, so he asked for lots of help and explored options as he strived to balance the two.

One of Warren's goals is to obtain a large grant for the program and take a year-long sabbatical to do Project Safeguard on a national basis. That would give him more time to devote to his dream, while still maintaining a balance with his family.

In the meantime, *he does whatever it takes* to make it all work and appreciates the love and patience of his family and friends.

What really keeps him "FIRED UP!" is his love of children and his faith in teachers. "I have this belief that we, as educators, can do far more than what people give us credit for. We don't need to bring in so-called experts – we have everything we need inside the schools. I am a big supporter of teacher empowerment. I think more schools should give their teachers the power to go out and do these kinds of things. Then the schools would be richer environments for kids and teachers alike."

5. Organization and Structure – Just visualize preparing for a full day of training with over 100 students, 100 parents, 30 speakers, ten exhibitors and countless volunteers! Consider all the materials needed – nametags, information packets, maps, schedules, evaluation forms, pencils, paper. Think about the logistical nightmares of scheduling ten different speaker rooms, a cafeteria, display space and check-in area. Every day, for three days, all these things need to be handled, safely and intelligently.

Here is where Warren's team of volunteers come in. From parent committees and bus drivers to business leaders and cafeteria workers, everyone pulls together to make sure that everything goes smoothly. Miraculously, it works. Not perfectly, but it works. *A positive attitude and teamwork make it all possible.*

The Specifics

What happens at Project Safeguard? Starting early in the morning, everyone arrives and snacks on muffins while they listen to the opening assembly. Usually an inspiring speaker gets everyone "FIRED UP!" for their first session, which is about 55 minutes long. Some sessions are for parents only, some just for kids, but most are for both. There's a ten minute break between them. Lunchtime gives families time to discuss what they have learned, and to use new communication tools.

Picture yourself in a seminar called "The ABC's of Drugs," or "Adventure in Trust and Communication." You could learn about "Fighting Fair: Separating Problems / Personalities," "Finding the Best in Each Other," "How to Communicate with Your Children About Sex/AIDS." Or you could find out about "Abuse and

Misuse... in Our Own Backyard" or "You Know What They Say" (peer pressure). After all that, you could "Reach for the Stars" and start "Winning at Life." Sounds fun and fulfilling, doesn't it?

The Results

From the beginning, the program has been a great success. Of the initial 100 students, 76 had at least 1 parent attend. This participation rate has grown each year. As of 1996 over 50000 people in New Hampshire, Florida and Massachusetts have taken the program. The average participation rate by parents in NH is 79%.

Project Safeguard is perceived as a win-win by parents, teachers and students. In 1991 a formal evaluation was conducted by Community Organization Research Associates of Durham, NH, interviewing both parents and students. The author of the study, Dr. Yvonne M. Vissing, concludes, *"Project Safeguard was 'not just a day out of school,' but an unforgettable life experience for the students."* Because the conference had introduced topics with education and intervention skills before most of them had become involved in those high risk behaviors, they felt they had truly been able to prevent problems. Parents were equally grateful for having had the opportunity to discuss the Project.

Qualities that Support Warren's Success

There are some key personality traits that help people achieve their dreams. Being "FIRED UP!" is just the beginning. For Warren, those qualities include *perseverance, patience, flexibility* and most of all, a *positive attitude.* He also *has tremendous commitment* to the concept of the family as a unit. In addition, Warren is what I call an "educational entrepreneur" – a teacher who goes beyond the existing lesson plan to develop something new, exciting and timely for our youth. His passion for innovation and assisting others led to a brand new, effective way of approaching drug and health education.

The desire to create positive change came from Warren's experience in the Army Reserves. After combat training, he studied Public Affairs all over the world, and learned about the power of the media, public relations and how to develop rapport with people. *He realized that he could make a difference, and that is reflected in his life purpose – "To create positive change."* He does that with his family as a parent, in his classroom as a teacher and with Project Safeguard as a program innovator.

What Next?

Most people who stay "FIRED UP!" make their dreams come true and keep on going. They go on to develop larger dreams and new visions. This is definitely true of Warren, as he envisions Project Safeguard five years from now – "I'd like to see Project Safeguard expand so that any community that wanted to run a program could do so successfully. I'd also like to see us establish a database and a network where all schools could come together and share information. The whole key is the parent and child coming together in a non-threatening environment, where both parties can get something out of it and walk away feeling like they've strengthened the bonds between them with self-esteem and communication. I'd love to see that happening all over the country."

Postscript

Warren Berry is neither rich nor poor, neither famous nor a saint. *He's a man with vision, a man with courage and a man with a commitment to the youth of this country.* He is an ordinary man who has made an extraordinary difference in his community. The fire inside him burns brightly. His dedication, humility and creativity have led to a program that benefits families all over the state of New Hampshire, and in five years – perhaps, all over America.

Remember These Key Points

◆ The idea that "It can't be done" is one that faces most people with a dream, and that's where a positive attitude, faith, action and the sheer determination from being "FIRED UP!" win out.

◆ It's smart to acknowledge people who help you with your dream. Express your appreciation and recognize your cheerleaders, so they feel valued.

◆ One way to balance family life and time spent on your dream is to get lots of help and prioritize your life. Keep looking for solutions.

◆ Patience, flexibility, enthusiasm and commitment are all essential qualities in making your dream come true.

Now Take These "Fired Up!" Action Steps

◆ Review your address book and think about which people you could approach about doing more to help you make your dream come true.
◆ If you have children, spend some time tonight talking with them more intimately about the things that really matter. If you don't have children, talk to a close friend or loved one about your dreams and values.

"There are no extraordinary people. They're all very ordinary but they make extraordinary decisions."
Robert H. Schuller

"Cherish your visions and your dreams as they are the children of your soul; the blueprints of your ultimate achievements."
Napoleon Hill

LIVING THE DREAM

"If you have built castles in the air,
your work need not be lost;
that is where they should be.
Now put foundations under them."
Henry David Thoreau

"...Anything in life can happen
If you give your best in all you do.
Ain't no limits for those who want it
Take a chance and let it all come true.
Shake your fears and hold your head high
You can make it if you really try.
'Cause no one else can live the dream but you."
Joe and Jolyn Skinner
Dreamin' – 1996 Olympics

Chapter 13

Make the Most of Your Resources

Build Your Fire Right Where You Are

*"Tell everyone what you want to do and someone
will want to help you do it."*
W. Clement Stone

"FIRED UP!" PRINCIPLE # 13 – Tap Into Your Resources

*Webster defines resource as "a reserve supply of support; something
to which one has recourse in difficulty; an ability to meet and handle a
situation."* Resources are infinite; they can be tangible, such as a
bank or a book, and they can be intangible, such as a sense of
peace or good health. Project Safeguard's Warren Berry had
significant resources including– the countless volunteers who
helped organize everything, the grant he received, the seminar
speakers, the college which provided the location for the event,
plus his personal commitment, time and energy to follow-through
with his vision. Ranging from legal, financial and professional to
educational, spiritual and motivational, among others, *resources
are absolutely invaluable in helping you achieve your dreams.*

● In July 1996 U.S. Olympic gymnast Kerri Strug made history as she led the women's team to victory. A quiet and barely visible team member until that event, Kerri had worked hard to get to this point. Moving from coach to coach over the years, she finished seventh in the 1995 world championships in Japan. But she was also confused and panicked at that event, and in need of support. She returned to the rugged training of Bela Karolyi, knowing she'd be second in importance to prodigy Dominique Moceanu. Kerry's disposition was what concerned her coach the most. Frequently injured and generally high strung, Kerri often had trouble sleeping.

After rigorous training with Karolyi and an emphasis on "team first," Kerri led the U.S. team through the first two days of the Olympic competition with excellence. Then came the fateful event. Dominique Moceanu failed at both vault attempts. Even though Kerri had injured herself on her first vault, she knew the only way the team could win the gold was to do the second vault. Cheered on by Karolyi, Kerri prayed for help and charged down the runway for an outstanding vault performance. She couldn't stand after she was done; her ankle was sprained so badly. But she had done it – she had won the gold medal for her team and her country, and her life would never be the same again.[4]

None of Kerri's success could have occurred without *substantial resources*. Her coach, team members and family were people resources. Funding for her trips enabled her to go get the training she needed. And in those last few moments, she turned to God for the inner strength to carry on and triumph. No one, no matter how famous or wealthy, can make their dreams come true without utilizing resources.

As you get "FIRED UP!" about your dream, you may find you need several resources to achieve it. You may not even be aware of exactly which resources you currently have and which ones you need to develop. On the following three pages are Resource Lists for people starting a conventional, franchise or networking distribution business. Take a moment to read over the lists. Divided into 11 categories, there are specific resources suggested, and there could be dozens of offshoot resources under each one of those. These lists are just examples and aren't meant to be official or comprehensive; some topics may not be relevant to you and your dream.

RESOURCE LIST FOR STARTING A CONVENTIONAL BUSINESS

1. ACTION PLAN OR BUSINESS PLAN
-MARKETING, ADVERTISING & RELATIONSHIPS
-PRODUCT OR SERVICE DEVELOPMENT
-MANUFACTURING   -INVENTORY
-SHIPPING   -EQUIPMENT
-SUPPLIES   -STAFFING

2. LEGAL
-REGISTRATION   -CONTRACTS
-INCORPORATION   -PRECEDENTS
-ZONING   -TRADEMARKS/PATENTS

3. FINANCIAL
-LOCATION, RENT ETC.   -CASH, LOANS
-INVESTORS   -ACCOUNTANT/BOOKKEEPER
-ACCOUNTING SYSTEM   -SPONSORS
-INSURANCE   -INVESTMENTS

4. FACILITIES/SUPPLIES
-OFFICE SPACE/HOME   -TELEPHONE
-EQUIPMENT/SALES KITS   -TOOLS
-EMPLOYEES/FAMILY   -BUILDING/ REAL ESTATE

5. INDUSTRY SPECIFIC
-MENTORS/ EXPERTS/CONSULTANTS   -ASSOCIATIONS
-RESEARCH   -PUBLICATIONS
-TRADE SHOWS   -CONVENTIONS

6. EDUCATION & TRAINING
-DEGREES   -CERTIFICATION
-SEMINARS   -REQUIRED UPGRADES

7. PERSONAL SUPPORT STRUCTURE
-FAMILY   -FRIENDS
-DREAMBUDDY   -MENTOR

8. MOTIVATION & INSPIRATION
-BOOKS & TAPES   -SEMINARS
-TOOLS LIKE IMAGERY & AFFIRMATIONS -VIDEOS

9. TIME MANAGEMENT
-PLANNER/ CALENDAR   -SCHEDULING
-BALANCING HOME & WORK

10. HEALTH (PHYSICAL & MENTAL)
-NUTRITION   -EXERCISE & REST
-VITAMINS, SUPPLEMENTS   -STRESS MANAGEMENT

11. SPIRITUAL
-PRAYER   -CONTEMPLATION
-MEDITATION   -DAILY READINGS

RESOURCE LIST FOR STARTING A FRANCHISE BUSINESS

1. BUSINESS PLAN
-MARKETING, ADVERTISING & RELATIONSHIPS
-PRODUCT OR SERVICE DEVELOPMENT
-MANUFACTURING   -INVENTORY
-SHIPPING   -EQUIPMENT
-SUPPLIES   -STAFFING

2. LEGAL
-FRANCHISE AGREEMENT   -COMPANY POLICIES
-INCORPORATION   -CORPORATE STANDARDS
-ZONING

3. FINANCIAL
-FRANCHISE FEES/ OPERATING CAPITAL   -LOANS
-INVESTORS   -ACCOUNTANT/BOOKKEEPER
-ACCOUNTING SYSTEM   -LOCATION, RENT ETC.
-INSURANCE   -INVESTMENTS

4. FACILITIES/SUPPLIES
-OFFICE /HOME   -TELEPHONE
-EQUIPMENT/PRODUCTS   -BUILDING/ REAL ESTATE
-EMPLOYEES/FAMILY

5. INDUSTRY SPECIFIC
-MENTORS/ EXPERTS   -ASSOCIATIONS
-FRANCHISE CONTACTS   -PUBLICATIONS
-CONVENTIONS   -FIELD SERVICE

6. EDUCATION & TRAINING
-DEGREES   -CERTIFICATION
-SEMINARS   -REQUIRED UPGRADES
-CORPORATE TRAINING

7. PERSONAL SUPPORT STRUCTURE
-FAMILY   -FRIENDS
-DREAMBUDDY   -MENTOR

8. MOTIVATION & INSPIRATION
-BOOKS & TAPES   -SEMINARS
-TOOLS LIKE IMAGERY & AFFIRMATIONS -VIDEOS

9. TIME MANAGEMENT
-PLANNER/ CALENDAR   -SCHEDULING
-BALANCING HOME & WORK

10. HEALTH (PHYSICAL & MENTAL)
-NUTRITION   -EXERCISE & REST
-VITAMINS, ETC   -STRESS MANAGEMENT

11. SPIRITUAL
-PRAYER   -CONTEMPLATION
-MEDITATION   -DAILY READINGS

RESOURCE LIST FOR STARTING A NETWORKING BUSINESS

1. MARKETING PLAN
-RELATIONSHIPS   -SAMPLE PRODUCTS
-PRESENTATION SUPPLIES   -CATALOG
 BOARD & EASEL OR PEN & PAPER
-PROSPECTING TOOLS

2. LEGAL
-DISTRIBUTOR AGREEMENT   -COMPANY BY-LAWS
                                                  AND RULES OF CONDUCT

3. FINANCIAL
-SALES KIT
-CHECKBOOK

4. FACILITIES/SUPPLIES
-OFFICE SPACE/HOME   -TELEPHONE
-EQUIPMENT/SALES KITS   -PEN/PAPER

5. INDUSTRY SPECIFIC
-SPONSOR & UPLINE LEADER   -CONVENTIONS
-FUNCTIONS   -PUBLICATIONS
-PRODUCT FAIRS

6. EDUCATION & TRAINING
-ONE-ON-ONE COUNSELING   -TRAINING SESSIONS
-SEMINARS & RALLIES   -BOOKS AND TAPES

7. PERSONAL SUPPORT STRUCTURE
-FAMILY & FRIENDS   -BUSINESS ASSOCIATES
-DREAMBUILDING BUDDY   -UPLINE COUNSELOR & ASSOC.

8. MOTIVATION & INSPIRATION
-BOOKS & TAPES   -SEMINARS & RALLIES
-DREAMBUILDING SESSIONS   -VIDEOS

9. TIME MANAGEMENT
-PLANNER/ DATEBOOK   -SCHEDULING
-BALANCING HOME & WORK

10. HEALTH (PHYSICAL & MENTAL)
-NUTRITION   -EXERCISE
-VITAMINS & SUPPLEMENTS   -REST

11. SPIRITUAL
-PRAYER   -CONTEMPLATION
-MEDITATION   -DAILY READING

🔥 For example, a married couple who owned a farm decided they needed to change their lifestyle and began to sell home products and sponsored others to do the same. They needed a minimum of financial resources – to buy a sales kit and support materials; educational – to get the right training and development as people; motivational – to help them stay "FIRED UP!" about their dream; and personal – in terms of people who would be distributors and customers. They didn't need any legal, personnel or manufacturing resources at all. Some businesses are much simpler than others.

"FIRED UP!" PRINCIPLE #14 – Connect with the Right People

Whenever you are beginning a project, starting a new venture or embarking on a new dream, you need to include resources as part of your planning. It would be naive of us to think we could do everything alone. We don't need to reinvent the wheel. We can learn from those who are where we want to be. Their pattern of success can help us succeed by duplicating what they've already achieved. *Taking advantage of the information and tools that are already available to us is intelligent.* You may not know where the answer to one of your challenges will come from; you may not know who has contacts, or who you'll meet next. It has been said that we are all, at most, just seven people away from anyone in the world. In most cases, it would take a maximum of seven contacts to reach Mother Theresa or a U.S. President or a famous CEO.

The key is to make a list of people you can contact and start taking action. You may be better connected than you believe you are. Statistics show that, on average, most people know about 250 other people. People are the greatest resources. From professional contacts and mentors to loved ones and cheerleaders, people can assist us in hundreds of seen and unseen ways. *Sometimes the best way others can help us is to believe in us and in our ability to achieve our dreams.* We can then pass on this belief to others to help them achieve their dreams. Like a spark catching fire, the flames of enthusiasm can spread very quickly. Contrary to popular belief, no one is self-made. It takes the cooperation of other people to realize a big dream. No one can be successful alone.

🔥 Paula Abdul's fiance, Brad, knows this very well. Brad Beckerman, CEO of Groove Track Productions, moved from Connecticut to Los Angeles and was looking for a serious relationship. He told a friend that his ideal partner was someone "normal, athletic and fun – a Paula Abdul type." It just so happened that this friend worked out at the same gym as Paula. He fixed the two of them up on a blind date and they fell in love.

🔥 I also know from personal experience that you can never tell who you'll connect with. When I was handling the Apple Computer New England account, I called my client one day. He was not at his desk, but a man named John answered the phone. Trying to be friendly, I asked John what he did at Apple. It turned out that he was *John Sculley – then CEO of Apple.* Trying to recover gracefully, I brought up sailing, a sport we both happen to love. John asked me what my favorite point of sail was, and we continued talking. Thank God, I had been able to pull my foot out of my mouth in time – it could have been very embarrassing. You never know who's on the other end of the phone.

Using the "Fired Up!" Action Plan with Resources

You're now ready to focus on the action plan for *your* dream. Spend about ten minutes now reviewing which resources you may already have for your dream (office space, motivation, contacts) and which resources you may need to develop (perhaps certifications, equipment, mentors, vision, and courage). What specific results would you like to see from this dream? You may want to retire from your job to work on your business full-time. What strengths do you still need to build to be successful? Maybe you need to learn to ignore negative-thinking people who are trying to steal your dream. Carefully consider each answer. This information will be useful in helping you decide which action steps to take next to make progress on your dream.

Even if you find there are still many resources you need, know you will find them. When you are passionate, committed and "Fired Up!" people will come into your life to help you achieve you dream As prominent business leader Dexter Yager says, *"When the dream's big enough, the facts don't count."* Now, complete the chart on the next page.

Strengths that Need to be Developed for this Dream:
1._____
2._____
3._____

Resources Available	Resources Needed
1.	1.
2	2.
3.	3.
4.	4.

"I believe you can get everything in life you want if
you will just help enough other people get what they want."
Zig Ziglar

Remember These Key Points

◆ To achieve your dream, you need resources, which are tangible or intangible – financial, motivational, spiritual, plus others.

◆ Webster defines resource as "a reserve supply of support; something to which one has recourse in difficulty; an ability to meet and handle a situation."

◆ Taking advantage of the information and tools that are already available to us is intelligent. Benefit from the knowledge and experience of other successful people.

◆ We are, at most, seven people away from anyone in the world.

◆ People can be invaluable to us as resources, especially by believing in us and our dreams. Most people know about 250 other people.

Now Take These "FIRED UP!" Action Steps

◆ If you haven't done so already, read over the resources lists and determine which you already have and those you need to develop. Complete that section of the Action Plan above.

◆ Review your dreammap from earlier in the book to see what other resources you have and which ones you need. Add these to your action plan.

Chapter 14

What About Money? Some New Ideas

Keep a Constant Supply of Kindling

"We believe that getting our finances in order – paying off our debts, learning to share with others, setting financial limits and faithfully living within them – is the beginning of getting our lives free to move forward."
Rich DeVos

Persist and Reap the Rewards

When Jack Canfield and Mark Victor Hansen wrote *Chicken Soup for the Soul*, they took the book to 33 publishers before one said yes! Both were $40,000 in debt, and had to come up with $5000 a month to pay a well-established public relations firm. Every day, they visualized their success. They pasted up a copy of the *New York Times* Bestseller list, with *Chicken Soup* on the top line. They persisted and the one publisher who believed in them was rewarded a thousandfold. *Chicken Soup for the Soul* sold over 3 million copies in the first two years.

Since that time, Jack and Mark have published several other books, including two sequels to *Chicken Soup* and a cookbook. *By the summer of 1996, they had sold 9 million books. They are "FIRED UP!"*

When the president of Random House publishers congratulated them on winning the "Book of the Year" award in 1995, he asked Mark why they didn't come to him to publish the book. Mark replied, "We did, and you turned us down." Imagine how that publisher feels now! And picture how great Jack and Mark feel at having succeeded when so many publishers wouldn't support them.

Jack Canfield and Mark Victor Hansen had a dream and very little money when they started out. They knew they had to invest in themselves to get the book out there, but they had no idea where the money was going to come from. "FIRED UP!" about their dream, they continually took action, asked for help and believed in themselves. They now have huge national bestsellers. They persevered and made millions of dollars.

Many people use their creativity to develop financial resources when working on their dreams. Many people also use their lack of financial resources an an excuse. What about you? Do you have the attitude that nothing is going to get in the way of achieving your dream? That's what champions believe.

We are the wealthiest country in the the world, yet there are homeless, starving people on our streets. While most people are gainfully employed, they still operate from a philosophy of "lack" inside. This "poverty consciousness" is fueled by our national debt and a national obsession with credit card spending. This scarcity consciousness has a built-in negative belief system that says, "There is not enough for everyone, therefore there is not enough for me." This is a limiting belief and it is false. It is very different from an "abundance consciousness," which says there is more than enough for all of us, and that we are all capable of enjoying and sharing that prosperity. *Be sure you are thinking "abundance" rather than "scarcity"; it can make a big difference in how easily you achieve your dreams.*

Fortunately, there are excellent books and techniques to help you change that "poverty" focus into one of wealth and abundance. I highly recommend the following: *Think and Grow Rich* by Napoleon Hill, *Wealth 101* by John-Roger and Peter McWilliams, *Financial Freedom in 8 Minutes a Day* by Ron and Mary Hulnick, *The Richest Man in Babylon* by George Clason and *The Wealthy Barber*, by David Chilton. All of these books have effective suggestions and tools for overcoming debt and cultivating abundance and wealth in all areas of your life.

Wealth 101 is especially good at helping readers understand that abundance is more a state of mind rather than a big bank account or lots of money. In John-Roger's definition, *wealth means "health, happiness, abundance, prosperity, riches, loving, sharing, caring, learning, knowing what you want, opportunity, enjoying and balance."* When you realize that wealth is so much more than money, you get "FIRED UP!" about how truly wealthy you already are. That's important, because *when you are grateful for all the gifts that already exist in your life, you open yourself up to receive more.*

"FIRED UP!" PRINCIPLE #15 – Manage Your Money and Get Out of Debt

Another reason why people sometimes struggle financially is they feel *unworthy* of success or wealth. Again, myths from earlier in life can hold you back today, but only if you let them. It is wise to uncover and release these myths, like we did in Chapter 6. Often these myths are deeply ingrained in your subconscious and they have a powerful hold on you, until you let them go.

I used to think that if I owned my own beautiful home, I wouldn't ever get married. And I very much wanted to be happily married. After I recognized this myth, I released it and built myself a beautiful sunny house on the river. Each week, I watched it grow from a slab of concrete into a lovely contemporary home which became my tranquil refuge. A year and a half after I moved in, I met my husband, who fell in love with the house soon after he fell in love with me!

To uncover any money myths that may be holding you back from fully achieving your dreams and the success you want, spend a few minutes on the following activity.

Money Myths Activity

Get a tape recorder with a blank tape and give yourself 15 minutes alone in a quiet place. Turn the recorder on and just start freely talking about money. Start with statements like "Money is...." or "I think money is...." or "From the viewpoint of my father, money is...," "From the perspective of my mother, money is...," "In the eyes of my religion, money is...," "From the perspective of my profession, money is...," and let yourself ramble on. Pour out any thoughts which come to mind about money. After you are through, take a break.

Half hour later, come back with a pen and paper, and listen to what you said. See if any limiting beliefs about money emerge.

For instance, many people mistakenly believe that money is the "root of all evil." The fact is that *money is just a tool.* It is a fruit of our labor. It does good in the hands of good people.

List all the myths and study them, so you know what may have prevented you from enjoying greater wealth up until now. *Then, draw an X through the page, erase the tape (in the tape recorder and in your mind) and tear up the piece of paper to release those myths. With your new awareness, they won't hold you back any more. Good job. Now you have created an open space inside to receive more abundance, joy and wealth. Nature abhors a vacuum – therefore, give it a vacuum to fill!*

Here are a few of the principles to increase your wealth relative to monthly spending and credit card usage. Let these get you "FIRED UP!" about building your wealth.

TIP #1 Credit Cards

Credit cards aren't recommended unless you pay off the balance each month to avoid paying interest. A helpful technique is to *write down every credit card purchase in your checkbook and subtract it from the balance.* Put a little box or star around it so you know it's a credit card expense and not a check. Then when the bill comes in, you already have the money set aside to pay for these purchases You are not increasing your debt or incurring any finance charges, and you start with a zero balance each month.

TIP #2 Debit Cards

Use a debit card, which automatically withdraws cash directly from your checking account as you spend it. This is a safer method than a credit card because you can only spend what you have in the bank. You can get these debit cards from your bank, and they operate just like a check. It helps to record the amount you spend with your debit card in your time management system. Do it either on the date you spend it or in a separate section, if you don't have your checkbook with you. Remember to record your usage in your checkbook, so you always know how much money is in your account. This kind of card comes in handy when ordering flowers or deliveries over the phone – times when a check may not work.

TIP #3 Lower Interest

There are ways to *cut down on credit card interest expense as you pay off any credit card debt* you may have. Interest rates and annual fees vary a great deal from bank to bank.

⚫ I had an experience with this myself, which may benefit you. One of my credit cards increased my line of credit by $4000 at a low rate. I called to verify that this was not a short-term trick offer and then I asked if I used the increased credit line to pay off other credit cards what my rate would be. Their credit division reviewed my excellent credit history and permanently lowered the interest rate on the entire balance on my card and the new $4000 line. Delighted, I decided to get my other card rates lowered, too. Fifty percent of them did, in fact, lower my rate, which saved me hundreds of dollars in interest.

Do this yourself; ask to speak to someone in customer service and tell them what you want to do. You could also see if you can get a better interest rate by agreeing to shift all your credit card debt and other banking business to the bank with the lowest interest rates. You'll be thrilled to discover that you can often lower your interest rate just by asking!

TIP #4 Freezer Fix

When you go shopping, leave all your credit cards at home, so you are not tempted to spend money you don't have. Also, avoid television shopping. You can spend lots of money on things you really don't need by getting caught up in an infomercial or home shopping show. Another idea is to take all your credit cards and freeze them in an ice block, so that it is more difficult to use them. Consolidating your debt into one or two cards with the lowest interest rates and fees and then paying off more money each month is also a good idea. *Becoming debt-free is one of the best goals you can have*; debt drains your energy and drags you down. Having no debt frees you up and gets you"FIRED UP!"

TIP #5 Seed & Tithe

Seeding and tithing are also powerful tools for creating prosperity. The concept of tithing means to regularly give ten percent of your earnings to an organization which supports you spiritually.

(For more information about that, see chapter 17.) For many people, this organization is their church, but some people give to various non-profit groups in the community which have touched their lives, like the Boys' Club. Tithing is a major premise of the *Richest Man in Babylon.*

Another idea is to tithe ten percent to yourself in a savings account that you do not touch, other than to convert it to wise investments. *The Wealthy Barber* suggests that you have some amount automatically withdrawn from your checking account each month that goes into savings, retirement or a mutual fund. You'll hardly notice it's gone and you get in the habit of building a nest egg.

Seeding is similar to tithing in that you set aside a specific amount to give to whatever organization you choose. The difference is that rather than giving ten percent of your check after you get paid, *you seed in advance for a specific goal or thing.* Let's say you want a new sofa, and you don't have the money now. Sit still quietly and consider what amount you need to seed for that item. Some figure – from $1 to whatever – comes to mind. That's the amount you send off to your church or non-profit organization and you write "seed" on it. Keep a written record of your seed and make notes on when the item shows up. It can be as rapidly as a day, but it usually takes a few weeks or months. Many people, including myself, have had amazing results with seeding.

Mark seeded on a Tuesday for a new apartment. He had a very clear picture in his mind of exactly the kind of place he wanted. He knew it needed to be in a peaceful, quiet area, had to be affordable and close to his job. The very next day he received a tip on a new space which exactly suited his needs, and he moved in shortly afterwards.

The time it takes for the goal to manifest often depends on what you are seeding for, and how attached you are to having it.

"FIRED UP!" PRINCIPLE # 16 – Remain Detached

One of the laws of creating what you want is detachment – not holding on to the desire so tightly that it can't come in. *It's important to remain unattached to the outcome while still maintaining a positive focus.* Some people want their dreams so badly that they push and push and are so attached and contracted that they don't allow any space for the dream to come in. They are focusing from a place of desperation (which is another form of scarcity thinking) and they try to force an outcome which may be premature. That can drive others away. A wiser approach is to take the necessary action, and then let go and give it some time and patience. There has to be room on an energetic as well as physical level for the dream to manifest.

Again, I know exactly how true this is because I have experienced it in my own life. In my early thirties, I really wanted to get married and share my life with a wonderful man. I <u>really</u>, <u>really</u> wanted it. So much so that there was no room for the right man to appear. I probably carried some kind of pushing energy inside and the men I dated would pick up on it subconsciously and be scared. That meant those relationships did not go very far. After taking a personal growth seminar, I came to a place of peace inside of myself where I decided that I would be just fine, even if I spent the rest of my life alone. I no longer <u>had</u> to have a marriage. I was neutral, comfortable and open. Three short months later, my husband came to my office in need of an ad agency. Instead, he ended up with a loving wife, and no one was more surprised than me. I had created space and become detached about getting married. As soon as I did that, the right man appeared!

"FIRED UP!" PRINCIPLE # 17 – Be Patient

Coupled right along with the concept of detachment is patience. I know that it can be difficult to be patient when you are moving on your dream. But, most dreams require a number of things to line up before they come true. That means you want to have patience and faith as you are working through the process. As long as you are taking action and visualizing and moving, things will happen. Remember, there is divine assistance from someone much wiser than any of us. Allow everything to happen in its own perfect time and miracles can occur.

"When one door of happiness closes, another opens; but often we look so long at the closed door that we do not see the one that has been opened for us."
Helen Keller

"There is enough in the world for everyone to have plenty
and to live on happily and to be at peace with his neighbors."
Harry S. Truman

Remember These Key Points

◆ Think "abundance" rather than "scarcity"; it can make a big
difference in how easily you achieve your dreams.
◆ Wealth means "health, happiness, abundance, prosperity,
riches, loving, sharing, caring, learning, knowing what you
want, opportunity, enjoying and balance."
◆ When you are grateful for all the gifts that already exist in your
life, you open the space inside to receive more.
◆ Pay credit cards off each month, or better yet, use a debit card.
◆ Create an open space inside to receive more abundance, joy and
wealth.
◆ Seeding and tithing are powerful tools for creating prosperity.
◆ Remain detached about your dream. Give it room to come in.
Be patient and have faith.

Now Take These "FIRED UP!" Action Steps

◆ If you have not done so already, do the money myths activity in
this chapter.
◆ Review your financial status. Record all your debts, assets and
resources. Make a goal of becoming debt-free, and clean up
your financial status.
◆ Do your best to calculate exactly what you need financially
for your dream. It may well be that you already have all the
money you need to get started.

Chapter 15

Make Each Day Count

Fanning the Flames

"Procrastination is the thief of time."
Edward Young

*"Plan your work for today and every day,
then work your plan."*
Norman Vincent Peale

"FIRED UP!" PRINCIPLE # 18 – Use Your Time Wisely

As you stay "FIRED UP!" about your dream, you'll soon discover that *one of the best ways to support yourself is through effective time management.* You may have taken a time management course before, but I encourage you to approach it from a whole new perspective.

In his book *First Things First*, Stephen Covey recounts an interesting story which goes like this.

In a lecture one time, the instructor said, "We're now going to have a quiz." He pulled out a wide-mouth gallon jar and several large fist-size rocks. He asked the class, "How many of these rocks do you think we can get into the jar?" After many guesses from the class, he began to stuff the rocks in the jar until no more rocks could fit. He then asked "Is the jar full?" The class responded "yes." The instructor said "Aah – wait," and took a bucket of gravel and dumped it into the jar. The gravel filled some of the spaces left by the big rocks. He then asked again "Is the jar full?" This time the class caught on. "Probably not," they replied. "Good," the instructor said, and he brought out a bucket of sand. He dumped the sand into the jar, where it began to fill all the crevices left by the large rocks and the gravel. He asked again, "Is the jar full?" "No," said the class enthusiastically. He then took a quart of water and poured that into the jar, completely saturating all the little areas left by the sand, gravel and rocks. "The point is," he said "that if you had not put the big rocks in first, *you would never have gotten any of them into the jar.*"

Many people try to stuff way too much sand, gravel and water into their lives without taking the time to schedule in the "big rocks." The big rocks represent the most significant things in your life, the ones which give your life joy, meaning and substance. In Chapter 7, you examined what your values are and what is truly most meaningful to you. In the activity below, you have the chance to refine that list even more, by pinpointing your top priorities. This activity is very worthwhile, because *once you know what your big rocks are, you can set up your entire time management program around what is truly most important to you.* It means you are in control – not the outside world. Making your own choices helps you to be "FIRED UP!" about your life. This is key.

Big Rocks Activity

Take a few minutes now and in the left column of the chart on the next page, make a quick list of those things in your life which are most important to you. Don't worry about the order you put them in, just quickly jot them down as they come to mind. Here are some examples – *spiritual life, spouse, children, dream, job, business, volunteer work, health.*

Once you have listed them, go back and in the column on the right, rank them in order of priority in your life. Now you know what items need to go into your calendar or appointment book first. Look over next week's agenda, and schedule in time for each of the big rocks listed above, giving special priority to rocks 1 – 5. When you schedule your big rocks first, you attend to the

Things Most Important to You	Those Things In Order of Priority
_____	1._____
_____	2._____
_____	3._____
_____	4._____
_____	5._____
_____	6._____
_____	7._____
_____	8._____
_____	9._____

most important things in your life, and you feel happier, more fulfilled and "FIRED UP!" This is a significantly different approach than most time planning systems, which have you scheduling according to critical deadlines and other people's agendas. Compromises may be necessary, particularly if you work for someone else. But it's much easier to say "no" to your boss about working late if you have already written a commitment to your children in your book. You can say something like this to your boss as way of explanation: "If I had known sooner, I would have rearranged my schedule; but it's too late to do that now. I'll be happy to come in early or stay late tomorrow. Would that be OK with you?" Most of the time, bosses are fine with that approach, when you are clear and reasonable in your presentation. They're also likely to respect you more.

So in addition to using the big rock approach from above, *how can you use your time better?* Here are some tips from various time management programs that can help you stay "FIRED UP!"and on target with your dream.

(**TIP #1 The Right System**)

Get yourself an excellent time management system, whether it's a Franklin Planner®, TimeDesign®, DayRunner® or something similar that is more elaborate than an appointment book. You'll want a system that has at least one full page for each day, and it's best if it's looseleaf in format so that you can put pages in and around your daily sheets. You will take this everywhere, so that whenever you have a thought about something which needs to be done, you can record it in the appropriate place in your time management system.

You will also need a pencil, (never use pen except for vacations), a marker to highlight in your favorite color and some forms that come with your planner called either "Master Task List," "Things to Do" or "Actions Worksheets." (Most of the systems listed come with these forms built-in.) While your new system may be larger than what you have been using, you'll find that it's an invaluable tool to making your dreams come true.

Several years back, I took a course called *The Sales Athlete* by Kathy Aaronson, who wrote a book of the same name. Kathy gave us a test to measure our sales abilities. I scored very high on the test, except for one area – time management. She emphasized how critical it was to get a good time management system, not just an appointment book, to track everything you are doing and record all your creative ideas. That convinced me to get a system. The one she recommended was the TimeDesign® system. Whatever system you get, make sure you use it regularly and choose the color and size that really appeals to you. Many people find they feel more successful and prosperous when they use one of these new systems. That, alone, is a great benefit!

TIP #2 Using the System

At a course called *Managing Accelerated Productivity*, I learned a great deal about how to use my new system. <u>First of all, set up your system so you have only one month of dated days in it</u>. There usually is a convenient plastic ruler which comes with the system that helps you easily turn to today's date. Next, <u>have a section for months</u>, where you keep miniature calendars of the rest of the months of the year, so you can write down future commitments and agreements. *Remember, broken agreements destroy relationships and damage your self-esteem. Keep your promises to yourself and others by writing them all down and then taking appropriate action.*

Next, have several sections in the back with dividers for your "big rocks." Label each accordingly and put in any pertinent information in those sections. Things like personal wish lists, couple's visions, sizes and birthdates fit in the back section. Also be sure to have a section for your dream. And put in any relevant paperwork there, like your dreammap and action plan. (By the way, most time systems which have sheets that are 6"wide x 8" long use paper which is a 65% reduction from a regular 8.5"x 11" sheet of paper. So if you want to put something in the system, just reduce it to 65% of its size.) In the back, set up all your addresses and phone numbers, both professional and personal, so you can get to them at all times.

Also be sure to *include a miniature "Feel Good Folder" in this book*, which holds pictures of your loved ones, and letters and cards from others which make you feel good when you see them. Then you can turn to these items when you have a tough day and instantly perk up. Use the zipper-type sections to hold your feel-good items.

One thing that might be going through your mind is what happens if you lose this system. The answer is, don't! You will find it to be such a valuable tool that you will want to keep it with you all the time. Be sure to put your name, address and phone number in the front, so the book can be returned to you, just in case you misplace it.

My husband lost his book a few years ago on Christmas Eve. He left it in a shopping cart at the grocery store in the parking lot. By the time he got home, he realized it was missing. He went back to the store, but the book was gone. He wanted to order one that night to replace it. I told him to wait– it was Christmas Eve and I was certain someone would return it to him. Sure enough, later that night the local post office called and said someone had turned it in there. A postman delivered it to us on Christmas morning! Talk about service!

TIP #3 No More To Do Lists

Here's a question for you. How often do you get to the end of the day and discover there are still things to do on your action list? When I ask large groups this question, almost everyone raises their hand. How does that feel? Not very good. It's best to write down only *what needs to be done on your daily page and keep a separate list of weekly action items.* You can put the weekly page next to your daily page, so that if you have extra time after you complete your daily items, you can move on to the weekly page.

Sometimes the weekly page goes on from week to week as you are in the completion process on large projects. That's fine. But at least this way, you have given yourself a chance to complete your entire page each day and you can feel good about all that you have accomplished. *Once you accomplish a task on your daily or weekly page, highlight it with that favorite color marker.* This rewards the little kid inside you with color for a successfully completed action.

The beauty of this system is that it eliminates the daily "things to do list" that may never get completed, which causes some people to feel like failures each day. *When you limit your daily list to only those few items which absolutely need to be done that day, you are more productive and effective.* Having a whole highlighted page feels great and tells you that you've accomplished what you set out to accomplish. Here's an example of what a daily page and a weekly action sheet look like side by side.

WEEKLY ITEMS		7:00	Monday 22nd
		8:00	
CNIB	Vacation	9:00 Meet with CNIB	
reserve ad space	call travel agent	at their office	call Bill
call Corky	check paper/ discounts		re:quotes
get copy direction		10:00	
lay out art	LPN	11:00	
send to separator	direct mailer status		plan week
ship next Tues.	requote w/ printer	12:00 creative meeting	mail bills
	competition's approach	with staff	
UB	meet w/ client	1:00	
meet on new product		2:00	thank you note
call magazines	A.Con.		to Tom
write PR	get quotes	3:00 interview with NT	
write bro. copy	brainstorm concepts		
art dept layout	comps & ideas	4:00	review action
schedule press time			steps with staff
	Book	5:00 groceries	
	research C. 14	6:00	
	make copy edits		
		7:00 dinner with Jon & Sally	

TIP #4 Daily Success Lists

Another tool is the daily success list. Get yourself one of those attractive books with blank pages in it. Every day, at the end of the day, write down at least ten successes you had that day. Some people may judge themselves negatively and say they had no successes. But realize that every positive action you take, no matter how small, is considered a success because you did *something*. Movement is the key. Every phone call you made is a success. Every project you worked on is a success. Whether you receive the desired outcome or not, you have taken positive action, and action is always rewarded. The only real problem is not moving at all; that creates stagnation and frustration.

There is a salesman who believes that for every ten "no's" he receives, he gets one "yes." So he actually thanks the "no" people enthusiastically, because he figures he is one step closer to a "yes." He understands that continually moving and asking for what he wants is the key.

Some of the things you are working on may still be in progress, but you took the necessary action today and that is a win. Let's face it, some days just getting out of bed and going to work is a success, because you may not feel like it. *Tracking your successes consistently gives you an incredible boost to your self-esteem.*

I had a wonderful experience with this in the *Technologies for Creating* course. Part of our weekly assignment was to record our successes. I was stunned at what a difference it made. I did it for about 300 days that year, and when I looked back at the book at the end of the year, I saw how much I had accomplished. It said to me, "You are a person who gets things done. You are successful and effective." I was "FIRED UP!" about my ability to achieve. I know it may seem silly, but it works. Try it for at least two months. When you look back over all that you have done, you learn that you do a great deal and you are a winner.

TIP #5 Live in the Present

Another key to time management is living in the present moment. In *Wealth 101*, John-Roger and Peter McWilliams recount a poignant fable about how the universe was created. This fable indicates the real value of the present moment.

God wanted to give all humans a gift, the gift of their highest level of consciousness, the spark of the divine inside each one. God and all of earth's creatures were trying to decide when and where to hide this gift. After much deliberation, the creatures suggested that the gift and the time when the gift could be accessed be named the same thing – *the present*. Especially since humans are so rarely focused on the here and now – too often, they are living in the past or the future.

Although this story is fiction, it makes a lot of sense. *When you're living in the now, you're making the most of every minute and every day.* The present is your most resourceful state. It's the only time you can take action.

Shaquille O'Neal, championship basketball player, is a great example of this. He has had a tremendous number of opportunities come his way and he is taking advantage of all of them. By the summer of 1996, he had written four books, appeared in two movies, led his National Basketball Association team to victory, promoted a wide range of products and had been phenomenally successful. He is making the most of today, every day.

By living every moment, you take action, get results and triumph. You can be "FIRED UP!"about your life and carry that enthusiasm out into the world. And when you combine the resourceful state of being "FIRED UP!" in the present with your creative imagination, your dream becomes much more alive and attainable.

"Time is an invention. Now is a reality. So much creativity is happening for the simple reason that we have withdrawn ourselves from past and future. Our whole energy remains blocked, either in the past or in the future. When you withdraw all your energy from past and future, a tremendous explosion happens. That explosion is creativity."
B. S. R.[5]

Remember These Key Points

◆ One of the best ways to support yourself is through effective time management (which is really managing yourself).

◆ When you schedule your big rocks first, you attend to the most important things in your life, and you feel happier, more fulfilled and "FIRED UP!" about life.

◆ Get yourself an excellent time management system, whether it's a Franklin Planner®, TimeDesign®, DayRunner® or something else.

◆ Broken agreements destroy relationships and damage your self-esteem. Keep your promises to yourself and others by writing them all down, and taking appropriate action.

◆ To be effective and productive, write down only what needs to be done on your daily page and keep a list of weekly action items next to the daily sheet.

◆ Record your successes every day – you'll experience a huge boost to your self-esteem.

◆ Live in the present moment – it is your most resourceful state, and the only time you can take action.

Now Take These "FIRED UP!" Action Steps

◆ Review the resources section in the back of the book and examine time management systems. Ask successful people what systems they use and find out what they like about them.

◆ When you're ready, invest in a new system which looks great and helps you stay organized and "FIRED UP!"

◆ Then set it up as suggested in Tips 2 & 3. Use it every day and always keep it with you.

ONE MOMENT IN TIME

*"Give me one moment in time
When I'm more than I thought I could be.
When all of my dreams
are a heartbeat away
And the answers are all up to me.
Give me one moment in time,
When I'm racing with destiny
Then in that one moment of time
I will feel,
I will feel
eternity."*

Song by Hammond and Bettis
Sung by Whitney Houston

Chapter 16

Upgrade Your Vitality
Breathe Life into the Fire

*"Inwardly, we know how to participate in our own healing,
physically and emotionally. We can become inspired to shape a
higher, more ideal future, and when we do, miracles happen."*
James Redfield

"FIRED UP!" PRINCIPLE # 19 – Take Care of Your Health

Be aware that your physical and mental health are critical
resources to living your dreams. Feeling good physically and
mentally helps to keep you "FIRED UP!" about life and your
dream. *Physical energy is a resource many people overlook.* Just think
how your life would change if you became seriously ill with a
long-term disease or if you were critically injured in a car accident. It might be more difficult to be "FIRED UP!" all the time. Yet
there are many role models, like Christopher Reeve, of severely
disabled people who do incredible things and inspire the rest of
us. Taking care of your physical and mental health is just good
common sense, but can be forgotten in the pursuit of the "ideal"
job, personal or professional life.

⚫ I witnessed how poor health can destroy your life all too personally through my mother's long-term illness and subsequent death. I saw a brilliant, artistic, beautiful woman disintegrate into a jaundiced, frail shell of a human being, in constant pain. After 15 years in and out of the hospital, she finally died at 45. Her illness and death colored my life and health choices significantly. As I have aged, I have learned to take very good care of myself. That starts first with a healthy and balanced diet, followed by regular, fun exercise and meditation. Perhaps because of all the hospital visits, I developed an aversion to treating illness with medication, and sought alternative treatments.

One of my constant companions in health maintenance is a book by physician James Balch called *Prescription for Nutritional Healing*. Dr. Balch recommends natural treatments like vitamins, minerals, homeopathy and herbs that can be used to heal almost any illness or disease. He doesn't discourage traditional medical treatments when needed; but he does suggest that you can take many easy, inexpensive actions to prevent disease and costly care. My husband and I have been using this reference tool for years with impressive results. We have had far fewer colds, and we are more vital and healthy than ever. After three serious car accidents, I have also found chiropractors have helped me enormously to eliminate back pain and keep me physically on track.

Here are a few key tips for staying "FIRED UP!" physically, which also helps you to feel better mentally. Some may be familiar to you; but the question is, are you doing them? (Note that these are suggestions for you to consider. It's important that you consult your physician to determine what's best for you.)

TIP #1 Take Vitamins, Minerals and Antioxidants

Certainly, a well-balanced diet is the best source of excellent nutrition, but because of the extensive processing of many foods and the fact that most Americans do not eat as well as they could, the next best sources are vitamins, minerals and supplements. Therefore, it's smart to take quality, natural multivitamin and multi-mineral supplements. There also has been a great deal of research done in the past decade about the power of antioxidants and how they are critical to eradicating free radicals, which can hurt your organs and cause disease. Vitamin C is a very powerful healer, and taking 5000+ milligrams of Vitamin C a day, along with Selenium, when you are feeling tired and run-down can make the difference between staying well and getting a cold. Other antioxidants recommended include: Vitamins A & D, Vitamin E for skin and Co-Enzyme Q-10, which has been used for decades in Japan to clear up mouth sores and dental problems. Vitamin B (especially B-6) and Iron are important for women. Also, many sleep disorders have been eliminated by taking proper amounts of Calcium, Magnesium and Choline. Calcium can also prevent osteoporosis. Another item to consider adding to your diet is some form of kelp. All of these are available at a good health food or vitamin store as well as through some marketing organizations who have vitamin lines.

TIP #2 Exercise Four/Five Times a Week

Much as we may not want to admit it, we all know exercise is important. Again, the latest research shows that 30 minutes of exercise which gets your heart rate up and which you enjoy, four times a week can add years to your life. Find some sport or activity that you really love to do, something which gets you "FIRED UP!" even if it's dancing around the living room to your favorite 60's music, and do it regularly.

Develop some kind of reward system for yourself, like buying new clothes for that great new body, or taking a weekend trip. Find a way to include your partner in this activity, if you can.

TIP #3 Eat Four/Five Fruits and Vegetables a Day

Of the hundreds of diet and nutrition books on the market, the one concept that appears over and over again is to *eat lots of fruits and vegetables and cut sugar, fat and salt.* Dean Ornish's book *Eat More, Weigh Less* features some excellent recipes and your local bookstore can offer you other choices. It's easy to work four or five servings of fruits and vegetables into your day, when you plan it. Juice in the morning counts, and have fruit instead of a candy bar for dessert. A hearty salad may cover two or three servings of various vegetables, and carrot sticks and celery make great dippers into a yogurt garden dip. Vegetable juice fills you up, and milkshakes made of skim milk with strawberries and bananas are a great way to start your day. Dried fruit is also delicious.

TIP #4 Drink Lots of Water

This is another tip most of us have heard for a long time, but now more than ever, it's important to drink plenty of water to keep you fit and "FIRED UP!" Drink at least 8 (8-10 oz) glasses of water every day, preferably filtered or bottled. More and more, we are discovering that ground water has been contaminated with pollutants or excess additives. So drink water that's safe. It fills you up, keeps your skin young and elastic and it keeps you energized. It also flushes out toxins more quickly.

TIP #5 Sleep 8+ Hours

Again, here is another truth that has been validated by research. *Sleep for at least 8 hours every night to maintain maximum energy levels, mental clarity, patience and health.* Many Americans and Japanese suffer from severe sleep deprivation, which leads to costly and dangerous mistakes on the job, less patience and flexibility and greater irritability and discord. Although you may think you can get by with less sleep, the research shows that all of us need at least eight hours, so plan your time accordingly.

There may be times when you are doing what it takes to achieve your goal and you sleep less. Then it's important to take a nap during the day to help you maintain your energy and equilibrium.

Also remember that your sleep state is a wonderful resource for your dream. You can program your subconscious by asking it to work on particular aspects of your dream; you are often given answers in your sleep state. All of that keeps you "FIRED UP!" about your dream and moving towards the life you've always wanted.

A Man to Admire

Remember that *even with significant physical shortcomings and health problems, you can make your dream come true.* W. Mitchell is a great example of this. At age 46, he was burned beyond recognition in a horrific motorcycle accident. That would be enough to stop most people. But Mitchell kept going, enduring 16 surgeries and the loss of his fingers. Many people would be totally overwhelmed to suddenly be dependent on others for simple life tasks like eating and going to the bathroom. Mitchell, a former Marine, never quit. He recovered, and co-founded a successful wood-burning stove business with two friends. But at age 50, he faced an even greater challenge; he survived a terrible plane crash and ended up paralyzed from the waist down. A fighter, Mitchell worked constantly to regain his independence and decided to put himself on the line in a big way. Elected as mayor for Crested Butte, Colorado, he later ran for Congress with the slogan "Not just another pretty face." Incredibly, he went on to live the life of his dreams, marrying, flying and public speaking. He has appeared on national TV and his positive attitude and commitment to life keeps him "FIRED UP!" His philosophy is "It's not what happens to you, it's what you do about it."[6]

"FIRED UP!" PRINCIPLE # 20 – Laugh About It

One of the most powerful healing agents in the world is laughter. Norman Cousins, in his book *Anatomy of an Illness*, details how he cured himself of cancer by watching funny movies. Have you ever had the experience of pure joy and laughter when you're among friends? Do you know that very deep belly laugh that frees your whole body? That laughter heals you by releasing endorphins into your body. Laughter opens you up and gets the energy flowing inside you.

My 40th birthday party was just such an occasion. Sixteen of my dearest friends gathered at an elegant restaurant to share dinner with me. My husband had 40 long-stemmed red roses waiting for me and our best man brought a Pocahontas birthday cake. All night long, as we wined and dined, people told stories about me and I laughed and laughed until I cried. My sides actually hurt from all the laughing that night when I went home. It was a night of great joy and it helped me make a smooth transition into my 40's.

"FIRED UP!" PRINCIPLE # 21 – Dreams Keep You Alive

Another factor in recovering from illness or injury is the power of dreams. In the movie *Flashdance*, her boyfriend tells Alex, the main character, "When you give up your dreams, you die." And the converse is true, too. *When you have dreams to live for, you can recover from anything.* That is certainly true of W. Mitchell, and countless athletes who have triumphed over serious injuries. Here are two true stories that illustrate the point.

🔥 My friend, Jon Choate, was working as an industrial filmmaker in the early 1960's. This was his passion and dream, and Robin Eichele, his film writer, shared the dream. While Jon was out pitching new projects to potential clients, Robin became very ill with brain encephalitis. Suddenly, he was in the hospital, barely able to move, dangerously close to death. The prognosis was grim. Jon visited his friend and was deeply saddened by Robin's condition. But Jon kept pursuing their mutual dream, and one day he landed his first big film project. There was only one problem – he needed Robin to write it.

Completely "FIRED UP!" about the project and about his belief in Robin, Jon went to the hospital and said to Robin, "I need you. This is our dream. You've got to write this." Robin replied that he was too sick to do anything and that Jon would just have to find someone else. Jon insisted; he told Robin he was the *one* man for the job. Then, a miracle happened. When Robin realized that he was needed, that his dream of writing films could come true, he sat upright in bed, asked for a typewriter and began writing. In a few days, his hospital room was a sea of paperwork, and he was cheerfully yelling at the nurses to bring him more typewriter ribbons. That film was the first of dozens more that he wrote. In a few months, he recovered completely from the illness which had struck him down. The power of the dream got him "FIRED UP!" and kept him alive.

🔥 In 1983 Joan Benoit, renowned Olympic marathon runner, underwent surgery on both Achilles tendons. Seemingly recovered, she began prepping for the 1984 Olympics. Only two months before the trials, she had severe pain in her right knee, which slowed down her running. For a while, her doctor injected cortisone into her knees. But the pain returned to such an extent that she could barely walk. Courageously, Benoit took a major risk. With only 17 days to go before the Olympic trials, she underwent orthoscopic surgery. Afterwards, she felt no pain. But later, she overcompensated with her left leg, hurting her hamstring. After her initial uncertainty, she decided to start the trials and see how far she could go. Not only did she make the trials, she excelled. On August 5, 1984, she led the pack of runners on a 26 mile Olympic marathon. She made medical and sports history and took the gold medal. Her dream got her "FIRED UP!" and led her to victory.[7]

Take care of your body, and your health will support you as you go for your dreams. We all need energy and vitality to do whatever it takes to make our dreams come true and stay "FIRED UP!" Focusing on good health is a great way to do that.

Remember These Key Points

◆ Your health is a key resource towards staying "FIRED UP!" and living your dream.
◆ Exercise 4/5 times a week, 30 minutes a session, doing something you love.
◆ Drink at least 8 glasses of filtered or bottled water a day.
◆ Eat 4/5 servings of fruit and vegetables every day.
◆ Take vitamins, minerals and antioxidants daily.
◆ Laughter can heal many an illness.
◆ The power of a dream can revive people who are injured or seriously ill.

Now Take These "FIRED UP!" Action Steps

◆ Investigate alternative medicine including homeopathy, Bach flower remedies, chiropractic care, massage therapy, acupuncture and such.
◆ Schedule a regular exercise program into your time management system and stick to it.
◆ Check out Louise Hayes' book *Learning to Love Yourself*. The back of the book features every major illness, its meaning and an affirmation you can use to help overcome it.
◆ Rent or borrow some movies which you find funny from comedians you like, such as Bill Cosby, Robin Williams, Brett Butler, Paula Poundstone or others.

"Feel the flame forever burn
Teaching lessons we must learn
To bring us closer to the power of a dream."
1996 Olympics Song

DREAM BIG

"The poorest of men is not without a cent;
it is the man without a dream."
Anonymous

"Dream no small dreams,
for they have no power
to move
the hearts of men."
Johann Wolfgang Van Guethe

"The only way to discover
the limits of the possible
is to go beyond them
into the impossible."
Arthur C. Clarke

Chapter 17

Attitude and Divine Assistance

Rekindle the Fire at the Source

"Every great and commanding movement in the annals
of the world is the triumph of enthusiasm.
Nothing great was ever achieved without it."
Ralph Waldo Emerson

How's Your Attitude?

In 1914 Thomas Edison, one of the world's great thinkers, faced a very difficult challenge. His laboratory and all the work inside it caught fire and burned to the ground. Instead of being dismayed and quitting, like so many people would have done, he said, "All the mistakes are burned up. Thank God we can start anew." That's the mark of a true optimist, one who faces the world with a positive perspective, no matter what. Your attitude is a critical resource in maintaining enthusiasm for your dream and staying "FIRED UP!"

Are You an Optimist?

Believe it or not, your attitude is completely within your control. It is one of the few things that is. In his audiotape series, *The Power of Optimism*, Alan Loy McGinnis concludes, after studying

121

the lives of thousands of successful people: "The road to a happy and successful life is paved with optimism." That's not to say life won't provide you with challenges nor that you should ignore the problems that present themselves. Inside each problem is a solution and a lesson. *"What happens to you happens for you."* And as Richard Bach writes in *Illusions*, "There is no such thing as a problem without a gift for you in its hands. You seek problems because you need their gifts."

That's where attitude comes in. How we view a particular situation and handle it is our choice; we can become negative and pessimistic or we can look for the solutions and draw on our own resources.

Sally Jesse Raphael is one of media's most visible and successful talk show hosts. She has both a daily TV and nightly radio show. Speaking of her early years in a letter to Andy Andrews in *Storms of Perfection*, she says, *"Eighteen firings later somehow, like the Peter Principle, I always got fired 'up' – and was more determined than ever to be successful."*

Growing in a Foreign Country

I certainly know how important attitude is in my life. When I was 16, I went to live in Jamaica with a Jamaican family I had meet a few years earlier. I taught English voluntarily for a month as part of my senior project in school.

Even though I had tutored throughout high school, I was not expecting the classes in Kingston to be so large. 45 students were in one class, 65 in another. Classrooms were concrete three-sided rooms with an open wall to let the air in.

The rigorous school discipline was also a surprise. Hearing loud noises one day, I rushed to see what was happening. I ran to break up a fight only to find students cheering as a teacher was beating a boy who had been unruly. I was horrified. In the early 1970's, Jamaican schools still maintained the British tradition of corporal punishment, something I have never subscribed to. That day was a turning point in my attitude. In spite of my fear, I made an even deeper conscious choice to make a difference in the lives of my students and to teach without corporal punishment.

Enthusiastic and "FIRED UP!" I spent time with my students on a personal level. I took them on a field trip to the zoo right next door; something that had never been done at the school. I got to know my students as people and learned that many never had money for lunch or even milk. These children were bright and hungry to learn about the world; but many would never get beyond grade nine. They would then go to work to support their families or become farmers. But they still wanted to reach out; they became pen pals to my students in the United States.

My experience as one of only two white teachers in an all-black junior high school was very powerful. Many of the teachers there were optimistic and hopeful; they welcomed me and shared their stories with me. I learned that no matter what the system is or the rules are, *one person can make a difference and have a positive impact.*

My experience in Jamaica got me so "FIRED UP!" that I did my thesis on Jamaican education. I returned there several times while in college and later to do more research. I learned a great deal about myself and about people and grew wiser from my time there. Happily, Jamaican education has improved significantly since that time and there is more hope for the children there today.

As you move forward on your dream, you may find lulls in the process, times when things don't go smoothly and doors which don't get opened. That's the point at which you need to draw on your inner resources, keep having faith and rekindle your sparks inside. It's always an internal choice. You never know what kind of good fortune will come out of adversity. At a minimum, you can learn and grow from it, making you stronger and more capable of handling future challenges.

A New Dream is Born

Julio Iglesias was a professional soccer player in Madrid, living that dream. One day he was severely hurt in a car crash and became paralyzed. He spent a long time in the hospital, and while there, a nurse gave him a guitar. Little did she know she would be launching the career of one of the world's most successful and popular singers. Had that car crash not happened, Julio might still be playing soccer!

Just Keep On Going

Norman Vincent Peale's book *The Power of Positive Thinking* was on the bestseller list for 186 weeks and sold over 20 million copies. Yet it was rejected by dozens and dozens of publishers before it was printed. It was his wife's belief and persistence that got the manuscript into the hands of the man who finally published it. Through this book, Peale taught millions of people how to turn around their negative thinking and start creating positive pictures for themselves. He showed others how to get "FIRED UP!" and stay up.

Starting Small and Making A Big Difference

🔥 W. Clement Stone was the founder and chairman of the Combined Insurance Company of America, which he started with only $100. It became a multi-million dollar organization and he went on to create *Success Magazine*. He teamed up with Napoleon Hill, the author of *Think and Grow Rich* to write *Success through a Positive Mental Attitude*, which is still a popular motivational book for creating success and prosperity.

"FIRED UP!" PRINCIPLE # 22 – It Could Happen

🔥 In the Disney film *Angels in the Outfield* there's a young black child, J.P., who lives in a foster home because his mother had been homeless, raising him in the front seat of their car. In spite of his background, he hopes his mother will come back and get him or that some loving person will adopt him. His entire philosophy of life is summed up in his wistful phrase which he repeats over and over to himself and others, "*It could happen.*"

That line is key to the whole movie and to what happens to J.P. and Roger, the movie's main character. In the end, J.P. gets his wish. A loving man and coach of the Angels baseball team adopts the two boys. The philosophy of "*It could happen*" paid off.

Les Brown, famed speaker, author, television personality and motivator, teaches people to open up their minds and realize "*It's possible.*" Once that door is open, all sorts of miracles can take place. So adopt a philosophy of possibility and realize that your dream *can* happen.

"FIRED UP!" PRINCIPLE # 23 – Learn From Your Mistakes

Mary Lou Retton was the 1984 Olympic gold medalist in gymnastics who earned a perfect 10. She advises, "*Never ever give up on your dreams and don't be afraid to fail, because failure makes you a stronger person.*"

Stay "FIRED UP!" With These Suggestions

So how do you use a positive attitude to stay "FIRED UP!" and keep going? Here are just a few suggestions:

◆ When you have a setback, *look for the lesson* in it. Ask yourself, what can I learn from this experience? Make notes about it.

◆ *Accept the setback.* Then visualize it turning out with a positive outcome. See it with perfect clarity as a victory, with the benefit yet to be realized. Experience this fully inside.

◆ *Be careful how you label* each of your experiences. It's better to consider something a learning opportunity rather than a failure. This attitude will also help you regard yourself in a positive way – knowing you aren't a failure, but rather a student of life, who is learning and growing. Be very careful about the words you use; words create feelings. Support and encourage yourself; be gentle with yourself. When you catch yourself mentally saying something negative to yourself, say "Deflect" or "Cancel that." Keep negativity out of your thinking.

◆ *Ignore failure statistics.* Ignorance can be bliss. In 1983 when I opened my business, four out of five small businesses failed nationally. Today, the success rate is much higher, and 50% of all new businesses are started by women. And according to the U.S. Department of Labor, women-owned businesses now employ more people than all Fortune 500 companies. If I had known the failure statistics in 1983, I might never have tried to open my company. You never know what will happen until you take action.

◆ *Avoid negative people.* They're the ones who are constantly complaining and whining about everyone and everything – blaming everyone else for their problems. They're never happy for you when you succeed, because they're unhappy inside.

◆ *Seek positive mentors.* Associate with people who are more successful than you; people you can emulate and learn from. Duplicate their pattern of success.

◆ If you face a challenge, *keep going.* Make a dreammap, fill out an action plan and start moving.

◆ If you are stuck, the best thing you can do is *get out of your inertia.* Do something constructive which you know you can complete. Create a feeling of accomplishment for yourself. That might mean washing your car, doing the laundry, helping someone or working out. Do *something.*

◆ *Be grateful.* In spite of your challenges, you still have many gifts to be thankful for. Without lessons and mistakes, we don't learn and grow. Be grateful you can learn and keep going.

"The best way out is through."
Helen Keller

Turn to God as a Resource

"God is the silent partner in all great enterprises."
Abraham Lincoln

*"We are headed towards a point in time in history where the
spiritual energy is so powerful. All people need to do is turn
toward the energy and ask. In the Bible it says 'Ask and you
shall receive.' God is waiting and all you need to do is ask even
a little bit for help, and it will be there. A lot of people either
don't ask or turn their backs."*
Tim Piering

God is the greatest resource that is often overlooked. Asking
for God's help as you create your dream is one of the wisest
things you can do.

Trusting in God and receiving His blessings is a wonderful
way to stay "FIRED UP!"about your life. In fact, fire is one of the
scriptures' teaching tools. When Moses encountered the "burning
bush," he was stunned by God's presence in his life. I certainly
felt God's presence as I walked over those burning coals in my
firewalk.

Whatever your personal religious philosophy, turn inside to
your divine heart and you will find incredible answers. The spark
of the divine resides inside each of us, and we are co-creators of
our lives with God. We can use that partnership with God for the
greatest benefit of all, to live our dreams and to stay "FIRED UP!"
about life. Or we can turn away from this incredible resource and
try to do it alone. That is a much more difficult path.

Enthusiasm

Enthusiasm and joy are evidence of God's presence among us.
In fact, the actual root derivation of the word enthusiasm is
"in God." Inspiration means living *in spirit*, connecting with the
divinity present within each of us.

On a personal basis, I find God has been my partner in
many areas of my life, and for that I am supremely grateful. To be
able to go inside through prayer and meditation and connect with
someone much greater than myself is so healing. *When I am quiet
and I really listen, I find I am given astoundingly correct and profound*

answers to major challenges or issues. Even the concept for this book came to me in meditation and dreams.

As a human being, you have an inner link with God's wisdom which can guide and assist you with issues or concerns. Learn to take quiet time on a regular basis to focus inward and listen to the guidance you receive. It is always there for you and enables you to learn and grow. Regularly call upon this resource for help and you'll be amazed at the gifts you are given. Regular daily meditation and prayer can be powerful tools for focusing all your levels of consciousness and quieting the mind and body. If you look deep inside, and are open to receive assistance from God, you'll have all the answers you need.

What Really Matters Anyway?

In James Moody's book, *Life After Life*, he shares his studies of large numbers of patients who had near death experiences. He recounts that, without exception, all these people, whether children or adult, black, white, Hispanic or Asian, atheist or Christian – all had essentially the same experience. All of these people saw their body from above and felt no pain. Next, they walked down a long tunnel and at the end of the tunnel was a brilliant white light. The form that this light took varied. For some people, it was Jesus or an angel; for others, it was a star or a deceased loved one.

In all cases, each person was asked two questions: *"How have you increased your capacity to love?"* and *"What wisdom have you gained to live your life in a more uplifting manner?"* Then they were all shown all the times in their life where they had withheld their love. They were told that it wasn't over– that they could now go back, but these were the two key questions they needed to ask themselves each day.

As you actively pursue your dreams, you'll find these *two questions are excellent as daily reference tools.* When you view each experience as a learning opportunity – a chance to gain wisdom, rather than a mistake or failure, it gives you a different perspective. Your attitude and peace of mind take quantum leaps when you *accept rather than resist your challenges.* Someone once said, "Pain is resistance to truth."

Increasing your capacity to love yourself and others enables you to be more expansive with others, to help them without even trying to help; it increases your patience, acceptance and compassion. Value every individual and their unique gifts and qualities, while doing your best to create win-win situations for the greatest good of all. This makes any dream more meaningful and worthwhile.

Angels Among Us

Recently, there has been a great deal written about the presence of angels in our lives. *Time* Magazine reported that 70% of Americans fully believe in angels. *Touched by an Angel* is a popular television series, rated #12 nationally. Angels appear in every faith, from Judaism to Christianity to Islam. According to Joan Wester Anderson, the author of *Where Angels Walk*, angels have three purposes: to worship God, serve as heralds between God and His people and to act as caretakers for mankind. It is said that angels work best when we ask them for help very specifically. Whether it's for protection, guidance, help with locating a missing item or reassurance of God's love, angel gifts abound. There are hundreds of stories of angel experiences. Ask angels for assistance with your dream and you'll be amazed at their response. As Billy Graham wrote in his book *Angels*, *"If you are a believer, expect powerful angels to accompany you in your life experiences."*

"FIRED UP!" PRINCIPLE # 24 – Cultivate an Attitude of Gratitude

Make it a point to thank people. Go out of your way to appreciate others. Send handwritten thank-you notes to anyone and everyone who assists with your dream or gives to you in some other way. Do something special for a busy person who helps you; send them balloons or flowers. If you have time, make them a pie or another favorite dessert. Every Christmas, I make key lime pies with chocolate graham cracker crusts for my clients in lieu of a store-bought gift. They love it– so much that they start asking in November when the pies are coming.

Once I had gourmet gift baskets sent to two lawyers. They had won a $65,000 lawsuit for me against a former client who had failed to pay me and several other ad agencies. The attorneys had been successful at getting my bills paid and I wanted to thank them in a special way. They both said that in all the years they had practiced law, no one had ever bothered to thank them with a gift or do anything special for them. They were surprised and delighted.

One of the most valuable ways to maintain patience and stay "FIRED UP!" as you pursue your dream is to express gratitude for the blessings in your life. Thanking God and the angels who have assisted you is an important part of continuing to receive their blessings, demonstrating your faith. Thanking other people for their assistance and support is also essential, and encourages others to want to help you again. They're more likely to be "FIRED UP!" about your dream when they feel honored and appreciated.

*"A single grateful thought toward heaven is
the most perfect prayer."*
G.E. Lessing

*"Expect the best,
convert problems into opportunities,
be dissatisfied with the status quo.
Focus on where you want to go,
instead of where you're coming from;
and most importantly,
decide to be happy."*
Denis Waitley

Remember These Key Points

◆ Your attitude is a key resource towards staying "FIRED UP!" and living your dream.
◆ The best way to handle a problem is to look for the lesson and keep moving.
◆ Avoid negative-thinking people and ignore failure statistics.
◆ Adopt an attitude of possibility.
◆ Learn from your mistakes.
◆ Every day, ask yourself "How have I increased my capacity to love?" and "What wisdom have I gained in order to live my life in a more uplifting manner?"
◆ God is a tremendous resource.
◆ All the answers are available to you, when you take the time to be quiet, focus inward and listen.
◆ Ask God and the angels for help with your dream. Be specific.
◆ Adopt an attitude of gratitude.

Now Take These "Fired Up!" Action Steps

◆ Read any of the books recommended in this chapter. *The Power of Positive Thinking* is a great resource for cultivating optimism.
◆ Review your most recent challenge and re-frame it. Look at it differently. Visualize it as successful and see it perfectly.
◆ When you find yourself talking to yourself negatively, say "Deflect" or "Cancel that."
◆ Spend some time in quiet prayer and ask God for assistance with your dreams. Be very specific. Write down the answers you get and act on them.

Chapter 18

Using Affirmations to Build Your Dream
Add More Fuel to the Fire

*"Affirmation means to make firm, solid, more real. Thoughts –
not very solid – when repeated over and over, become more firm.
They become feelings, behaviors, experiences, and things. What
we think about, we can become."*
John-Roger

Let Go of Negative Thinking

You probably have already seen the value of uncovering and
replacing the myths that might have stopped you in the past.
Perhaps there are still some negative beliefs that linger. One of
the best ways to eliminate these is through the use of affirmations.

"FIRED UP!" PRINCIPLE # 25 – Use Affirmations

Made popular over the last 20 years, *affirmations are positive
present tense statements that people say to themselves daily to help bring
about change and high self-esteem.* Remember how the national
research says we have 40,000 to 50,000 thoughts a day and that
75%-85% are negative? We want to change our internal self-talk

to all *positive* in support of our dreams. That's where affirmations help. Although experts' opinions vary about the exact number of days, it's generally believed that *any affirmation said consistently every day for 32 days* will change the programming of the subconscious. For particularly deep-seated myths, it may require a few months' worth of repeating affirmations. When you stick with the affirmation, it will impact you. This may seem surprisingly simple, but affirmations work amazingly well. They can help you stay "FIRED UP!" and on track with your action plan.

Even Better Than I Had Hoped

As the owner of an advertising and training company, I have discovered the value of affirmations when used in business. A few years ago, I learned that my office manager had the chance to go for her dream of living in Montreal, and I encouraged her and began to search for a replacement. In addition to placing ads, I created a statement following all the guidelines given later in this chapter. It read "I am attracting the perfect employee to Brightwork Advertising and Training," and I kept repeating it each day in the shower. Within two weeks, a young man came to apply for the job.

While discussing his abilities, he casually mentioned that he also had experience as a graphic designer and showed me his portfolio, which was impressive. After interviewing several other individuals, I hired the young man. This employee now does two jobs; he serves as office manager as well as a graphic designer. His arrival also meant that I needed freelancer designers less and less, which saved the company money. *Indeed, the perfect employee had shown up–* in ways I had never dreamed of. Hiring him got me "FIRED UP!" about the power of affirmations!

Letting Go of the Old and Affirming the New

In addition to that story, I have had great success with affirmations for several years. As a result of a rather rough childhood, I became expert at dealing with all sorts of life crises and problems. Such situations were a central part of my life, and all that drama and angst was exhausting.

In 1988 I started saying to myself regularly, *"I choose to have my lessons come to me through joy rather than through crisis."* Today, my life is very different. My blessings abound; I have a wonderful husband, a successful business, great friends, a beautiful, comfortable home and frisky, playful cats. I feel much more peaceful now than in the past. Issues still come up, but I find they are usually small and manageable. I am healthy and my stress levels have dropped significantly.

How Do Affirmations Work?

One of the reasons affirmations work so well is that they refocus your consciousness. Many times, people tend to focus on the problem rather than the solution, which just creates more problems. *What you focus your attention on manifests.* To experience how this works, do a little experiment right now. Hold your right hand open and imagine that a warm pat of butter is sitting in the middle of your palm. Now increase the heat in your hand and feel the butter melt in your palm. Got it? Good. That's just a tiny example of how focused attention works.

Focus on What You Want

If you are short on cash, concentrate on abundance and prosperity rather than lack. Most people just look at their unpaid bills and feel frustrated. When you want more money in your life, develop affirmations which fit your style and meet your needs. There are books devoted to financial abundance and wealth-building, some with terrific affirmations, like: "My financial wealth increases daily, as I pursue my dreams." Another might be, "My income is dramatically increasing in a wide variety of ways." Or how about "I easily attract money whenever I need it"?

Earl Nightingale, co-founder of Nightingale-Conant Tapes, started the company with a book called *The Strangest Secret*. In essence, the secret was, "You become what you think about most." Think about your dream, your successes and your abilities. Focus on what you want, not on what you don't want.

Affirmations alone won't bring about significant change; they need to be coupled with action. Sitting at home all day saying affirmations about a new job won't get Bob hired. He needs to review the want ads, network with others in his field and go on interviews. However, his affirmation is a dynamic tool that can assist Bob in the process. It will train his consciousness to expect and accept the ideal job for him when he finds it. *Affirmations are a great way to reeducate your subconscious about your capacity to succeed and stay "FIRED UP!" about your life.*

Guidelines for Creating Effective Affirmations

Programming-in a poorly phrased affirmation can actually do more damage than good. It's the old adage: "Be careful what you ask for, you just might get it." For example, if the affirmation is "I am attracting a new car for very little money," you may be given your family's old clunker, only to find out that the transmission is broken! A better choice would be to say "I am attracting a perfectly working, affordable car that is for my greatest benefit." By being more specific, you eliminate any chance of the car being defective.

Effective affirmations:

◆*Are always phrased in the positive.* When you say, "Don't think about polka dotted giraffes," what immediately comes to mind? Polka dotted giraffes! Focus on what you want – not on what you wish to change. For example, say "I am trim, energetic and healthy," rather than "I am no longer fat." Eliminate any words that cause you to have a negative picture. If you include the negative idea in your affirmation, you are unintentionally reinforcing what you don't want.

◆*Are stated in the present tense* using "I am," and often coupled with action verbs ending in "ing." (e.g. "I am easily attracting the ideal job.") If someone says they will be healthy, that's always in the future – it's not now. You want to start picturing and experiencing the victory today, *right now.* Remember, we can only be in our most resourceful state when we are "living in the present"; we can't change the past and we're not yet living in the future. If there's a quality we want in the future, we need to affirm it in the present – otherwise it will always be out there "someday." Did you know that "someday" generally means "never"? For example, say "I am totally healthy," rather than "I will be healthy tomorrow." Tomorrow will always be in the future. Make it happen now!

◆*Are only about you.* When people create affirmations about others, it doesn't work. A mother may say, for example, "My son is cleaning his room every night." Her affirmation won't help because it's up to her son. What she could do instead is say, "I have a beautiful and orderly house," and she could ask her son for help. The affirmation is only effective for the actions *she* takes, which in this case is requesting her son's cooperation.

◆*Need to have a visual picture associated with them.* If you say, "I am "FIRED UP!" about my dream," make sure you have a picture in your head of what that looks like. You might envision yourself as excited, listening to your favorite inspirational music, dressed for success, living your dream life. Or you may sense a feeling of greatness, knowing you are fulfilling your true purpose and seeing yourself as poised and confident.

Whatever your affirmation means to you, get a clear vision of it mentally, so you can recognize it when it appears in your life. *This is especially important when your affirmation is about a state of mind or something abstract.* If you're affirming being peaceful and relaxed, you may want to imagine yourself by a lake daydreaming quietly, or lying on a beach on a Caribbean island. Maybe you'll picture a clean desk with all the bills paid and plenty of money in the checking account.

Whatever it is, make sure you can see it so that when you achieve it, you'll know it. If you want a big, beautiful house, what's it look like in your mind? Is it a colonial, a cape, a contemporary, a ranch, a log cabin, or another style? Is it brand new, under construction, an antique or something else? Look through architectural magazines or house plan books and get a crystal clear picture of what you want. That way you'll know it instantly when you see it manifest.

◆*Need to have positive emotional components,* such as "I am easily and joyfully attracting an ideal mate." Adding strong, positive emotion makes the affirmation seem more real to your subconscious and enlists the support of the little kid inside you. The best affirmations get you "FIRED UP!" about your goal. A businessman who is speaking at an upcoming conference might say, "I am powerfully presenting my speech with clarity and confidence," to get himself "FIRED UP!" for the event. I personally like to add "ease" into affirmations because I want it to happen gracefully. So many people make life more difficult than it has to be – why not make it as easy as possible?

◆*Need to be short enough to remember,* since you need to say them often. More than about 10-15 words is usually too much for the mind to hold. Try yours out for a day or two; if you find yourself forgetting the affirmation, you may want to reword it so it's catchy and memorable – like a slogan or jingle.

◆*Need to be said every day,* at least once or twice a day until something positive happens. Some affirmations may take several months or even years to achieve, while others may take effect in a few weeks. It often depends on your answers to these three questions. 1) How deeply ingrained was your negative belief which the affirmation is replacing? 2) Have you let go of the negative belief? 3) Are you stretching towards a huge goal? Be aware that your affirmations may take more time to take effect than you now believe they will due to those variables. You need to keep moving towards your dream and be as patient as you can, until you achieve it. *Affirmations only work when you act on them.*

Record Your Affirmations

Mary Ann Somerville, an international trainer, uses a very direct and effective method that can help you ingrain your affirmations on all levels of your consciousness. She recommends recording them into a tape recorder in a very specific manner. Speak to yourself very lovingly in a soothing and supportive voice. It goes like this. Let's say your affirmation is "I am healthy and wealthy." Record that onto your tape with the loving intonation she suggests. Then say your name in third person: "Bonnie is healthy," and then say it in second person: "You, Bonnie, are healthy." Do this with all your affirmations and listen to the tape daily, repeating each phrase. Playing your tape in the car on the way to work can start your day off in a positive way. This can quickly help you start to replace old programming.

If you prefer not to tape record your affirmations, that's fine. Just be sure to say the affirmations every day for 32 days consistently. If you miss a day, start over. You might consider giving your written affirmations some special focus. Creatively decorate the paper on which you wrote them with stickers or color.

Affirmations For Your Dream

Now, to use this new information to achieve your dream, look at the "FIRED UP!"Action Plan on the next page where the Dream Affirmation section appears. There's space for five affirmations. Take a few minutes now and think about the affirmations you could create to support your dream. These need to be statements that will assist you in achieving your goals. You are by no means limited to only five – just use five as a starting point.

For someone who is working towards getting a new job in their chosen field, one affirmation might read, "I am easily conducting informational interviews with field experts," or "I am networking effectively, making contacts with the right people." In the case of the man who wanted to start his own business, his affirmations were:

" I have a clear and powerful vision for my business."
" I am creating numerous financing options for my business."
" I am expanding my personal network."
" I am attracting a strong team."
" I have a joyful and productive relationship with my mentor."

These are all on target for his dream. They relate specifically and directly to the tasks he needs to accomplish before he can open his business. They are short, emotional and present tense, with a visual picture for him. Using this example, you are now ready to invent affirmations for yourself. Dedicate some energy to writing affirmations which will support *your* vision. Remember the guidelines, and have fun with this. Do it now!

Your Dream Affirmations:

1._____

2._____

3._____

4._____

5._____

The act of originating and writing down your affirmations sends a powerful message to your subconscious – this is something you really want and you're starting to invest energy into getting the outcome. *Affirmations help us unlearn negative programming and adopt new thoughts and belief systems about ourselves.* You're in control, rather than the negative programming. You decide how you think and feel about yourself – you're in charge.

Developing affirmations for your dream lets your subconscious know you are in charge of your dream, and that it is meaningful and worth doing. You'll be amazed how the energy in your life unites with your vision once you commit it to writing. The man who wanted to start his own business had already named his company, printed business cards, connected with other professionals and explored financing options within two months of creating his affirmations. Within ten months, he used all of these tools and opened his business. He is actively making his dream come to life and he's "FIRED UP!" *You can be, too.*

> *"The great end of life is not knowledge but action."*
> Thomas Henry Huxley

Remember These Key Points

◆ Affirmations are positive statements that people say to themselves daily to help bring about change and enhance their self-esteem. They help us to unlearn negative programming and adopt new thoughts, opinions and belief systems.
◆ What you focus your attention on manifests.
◆ Affirmations alone won't bring about significant change; they need to be coupled with action. They are powerful tools for keeping you "FIRED UP!"
◆ Affirmations need to be positively framed, short, specific, emotional and in the present tense. You need to say them for 32 consecutive days to create shifts in your subconscious.

Now Take These "FIRED UP!" Action Steps

◆ If you have not done so already, create affirmations for your dream. Say them 32 days in a row and see what manifests.
◆ To get even more value from your affirmations, record them on tape as described in this chapter.

Chapter 19

Affirmations in Action

Showering Sparks on the Tinder

Dream Big

🔥 During the past several years, Paul Martin DuBois and his wife, Frances Moore Lappe, have been busy living their dreams. A former college vice-president, author and a director of a non-profit organization, Paul met Frances when they were both reassessing their lives. Lappe wrote *Diet for a Small Planet* in 1971, which discusses how nutrition relates to socioeconomic causes of hunger.

They both decided that the only way to bring about substantive change was to do something on a larger scale. In 1993 they moved to Vermont and formed the Center for Living Democracy, which is home to the American News Service (ANS), an upbeat and positive organization devoted to sharing a different angle on the news.

They often do stories which focus on problem-solving, winning the war on drugs, community-building and education. "This is news about challenge and hard work, success and the lessons of failure... *news people can use*," says DuBois. These stories are now printed in newspapers all over the country and make a strong contrast to the sensationalist gloom-and-doom journalism so prevalent today.

The stories are already being carried by a national service which makes them available to 350 papers around the country. ANS is doing much better than they ever expected. In describing the success of their dream, Lappe says, *"This is a story of miracles that really happen."* Like DuBois and Lappe, your dream can come true, too. [8]

"FIRED UP!" PRINCIPLE # 26 – Use Action Options to Get "FIRED UP!"

The key to creating and using *effective* affirmations is very simple: *choice.* When you use action options to *choose* how you want to put your affirmations into action, it empowers you and gets you "FIRED UP!"

Several years ago, I created a set of affirmation cards, called Radiance and Power Action Cards®, which feature three different action options for each affirmation. The purpose of these cards is to stimulate your thinking about creative ways to take action on your dream. There could be dozens of action steps you might choose for any given affirmation; I just started with three to help you start thinking in new ways and experiencing the concept of flexibility and movement. *Affirmations only work when you keep moving and doing; action options show you how to do that. Choice is very powerful;* making a choice to move on your dream in a particular way shows you're willing to do whatever it takes to make your dream come true.

Read over the examples shown here. Think about which option you would choose to do if you had the affirmation on your dream affirmation list. Are there other ideas that pop into your head about the affirmation and ways to move on it? *Tap into your creative imagination and let it run wild. It is a fountain of original ideas.*

Theme: Dreams

I believe in myself & I am living my dreams.

Action Options:
◆ Brainstorm all the ways to create your dream with a friend.
◆ Find someone you admire in a similar field & interview that person.
◆ Read about success stories in your dream field.

© 1993, A. Snowden McFall

Theme: Wealth

I easily let go of things I no longer need & make room for new things in my life.

Action Options:
◆ Sell items you are not using at a garage sale.
◆ Give old clothes to a friend or charity.
◆ Donate paint to local theatre group.

© 1993, A. Snowden McFall

Notice the action card on wealth. As ideas on how to make room for more abundance in your life, it gives you three options on eliminating current possessions you no longer use. Which of these three steps would you take to create space

---

Theme: Power

I willingly take risks in order to grow.

Action Options:
◆ Try something you've always dreamed of.
◆ Face a longtime fear in a way that supports you.
◆ Open up to someone trustworthy.

© 1993, A. Snowden McFall

Theme: Radiance

I embrace & cherish my own radiance.

Action Options:
◆ Make a list of your unique special qualities.
◆ Create in any way you like– draw, paint, color, decorate, sing, etc.
◆ Do something very special with someone close & let the real you shine!

© 1993, A. Snowden McFall

Theme: Power

I now step into my full power & actively create my life.

Action Options:
◆ Lovingly but firmly speak up when you disagree.
◆ Say no to an invitation that you don't really want to accept.
◆ Plan a day of self-pampering.

© 1993, A. Snowden McFall

Theme: Gratitude

I am deeply grateful for all the gifts in my life.

Action Options:
◆ Make a list of all the blessings in your life.
◆ Write a note of appreciation to 3 people who have made a significant contribution to your life.
◆ Give something of yourself to someone less fortunate.

© 1993, A. Snowden McFall

---

for more prosperity? Is there anything appealing here that you could do within the next four weeks? If it is something you choose to move on, pull out your time management system and schedule it in within the next 28 days.

These cards are examples of how you can make a specific affirmation more real and applicable to your daily life. *Action options take affirmations and make them practical and workable.* They are hands-on tools for working towards your dream.

Above are four more Radiance and Power Action Cards. Look over them now and consider how these options could apply to your life. Notice that on each card, there are always at least three options shown. You might choose to do one, two or even all three; but there is no *one* set way to do it. That applies to your life and your dream, too. *There is no one set way to make anything happen; part of your gift to the world is your uniqueness.* You can always devise a clever new way to take action on any affirmation in a way that gets you "FIRED UP!"

Options Are Key

Remember that sometimes when a person is trying to help somebody, they may tell them exactly how to fix their problem, giving only one solution. *That is often a form of control or manipulation,* even if it's unintentional. *With at least three different options on how to take action, everyone is free to decide for themselves what works best for them.* This is essential, because so many people have rigidly locked themselves into only one way of doing things.

Certain family structures have systems in place that force children to do things in only one way – the "right way." And while it may have been effective when we were children to follow those standards, it can be severely limiting and frustrating to use them as adults going for our dreams. In order to shift, expand and grow, we all need to develop flexibility and be open to new opportunities. Through options, we give ourselves permission and freedom to take appropriate action while stimulating original thinking and creative problem solving. *Choice liberates; singularity limits.*

Creating Your Own Action Options

Now take out your "FIRED UP!" Action Plan, and refer to the Dream Affirmations list you completed in the last chapter. Take

Affirmations:
1. _____
Action Options
a.
b.
c.
2. _____
Action Options
a.
b.
c.
3._____
Action Options
a.
b.
c.
4. _____
Action Options
a.
b.
c.
5._____
Action Options
a.
b.
c.

each of your affirmations and come up with at least three different action options to support each affirmation. *Hint – Look at your dreammap and you will find many of the action options there.*

You are not committing to these actions at this point. You are simply developing some choices of how you can make your dream happen and stay "FIRED UP!" That means you can be as outrageous as you wish; the sky is the limit, and fires burn best when there's lots of fuel.

Let's look at how other people have developed action options.

🔥 One woman wanted to start playing piano again, but she didn't have a keyboard. She developed these options and within one week of creating them, two different solutions surfaced. Someone's child wasn't using their keyboard, and the parents offered to loan it to her indefinitely.

> **Affirmations:**
> 1. I am easily creating a keyboard for my piano playing.
> **Action Options**
> a. Look in local newspapers for sales.
> b. Ask people if they know of keyboards not in use.
> c. Check yard sales for good deals.

Then a new apartment she saw came fully furnished with a grand piano! In a short period of time, a vital element of her dream manifested.

🔥 This woman wanted to become an elementary school teacher. She knew one of the best ways to learn more about teaching was to talk to others already in the field. She went to school socials, to teachers' union meetings and to her children's teachers. They all had a wealth of ideas for her and enabled her to make the right connections.

> **Affirmations:**
> 1. I am easily networking with other educators about jobs.
> **Action Options**
> a. Go to teachers' union and social meetings.
> b. Call all my children's teachers and ask for their ideas.
> c. Go to college placement people and ask for help.

Within a few months, she had a part-time job teaching in an excellent school system. She had taken action and was "FIRED UP!" about her job.

🔥 This man needed to create significant sums of money for a wildlife project. His friends were generating substantial income by sharing products through networking. He decided to use the business as a means to an end. After assisting enough other people in their success, he became financially independent. His dream came true, faster than he imagined.

> **Affirmations:**
> 1. I am effectively creating financial abundance.
> **Action Options**
> a. Sell quality products through networking.
> b. Sponsor and teach others the business.
> c. Cultivate customers who like the products.

Do You Need More Money to Make Your Dream Come True?

It is often necessary to develop another source of income to live your dream fully. If you want to teach people about peace all over the world, and believe it's truly your mission, you are going to need lots of money to do it. There may be grants available; but you may have to earn the money yourself before fully living your dream. There's absolutely nothing wrong with that; it's a very smart and practical way to make things happen. In college, I worked as a telemarketer for a roofing and siding company to make extra money. When I was a teacher, I waitressed and worked at department stores.

Greg got a job working at a Fixed Base Operator so he could be around aircraft and earn flying time. His ultimate dream is to be a commercial pilot. This interim job is an excellent way for him to gain experience in his chosen field and make money to pay for his flight lessons and schooling.

Carolyn wanted a full-time job teaching music to young children, and she wanted to own her own home. For a year, she worked part-time in a school system teaching music and part-time for an optical store selling eyeglasses. The next September, she got a full-time job teaching music in the school district of her choice and she loves it. She just put money down on a condominium and will be moving there soon.

Remember that the key to staying "FIRED UP!" about your dream is to take action. So let's get you moving right now and stoke up your fire. If you have not done so already, pull out your list of affirmations and develop action options for all of them. Use your dreammap as a resource. *Learning how to develop options increases your flexibility and resourcefulness.* Translating large ideas into small, safe and concrete action steps is a powerful tool towards getting what you want out of life. These small steps keep you moving and "FIRED UP!" about life.

"Begin difficult things while they are easy. Do great things when they are small. The difficult things of the world must have once been easy. The great things must have once been small.... A thousand mile journey begins with one step."
Lao-Tse

Remember These Key Points

◆ When you use action options to choose how to put your affirmation into action, you get empowered and "FIRED UP!"
◆ Affirmations work only when you keep moving and doing; action options show you how to do that.
◆ Choice is powerful. Choice liberates; singularity limits.
◆ Look at your dreammap and you will find many of the action options right there. Write them down.
◆ Sometimes, it may be necessary to develop another source of income in order to live your dream.
◆ Remember that the key to staying "FIRED UP!" about your dream is to take action. Developing action options will increase your flexibility and resourcefulness.

Now Take These "FIRED UP!"Action Steps

◆ If you have not done so already, develop three action options for each affirmation of your dream.
◆ Consider asking your dream buddy or another friend for other ideas, so you have a long list of options.
◆ If you like any of the affirmations or action options on the Radiance and Power Action Cards shown in this chapter, add them to your list. Schedule action items into your time management system.

"Beginning is half done."
Robert H. Schuller

*"Life happens at the level of events,
not words."*
Alfred Adler

POWER

"We grow great by dreams.
All big men are dreamers."
Woodrow Wilson

"The greatest power that a
person possesses is
the power to choose."
J. Martin Kohe

"You can make more friends
in two months
by becoming more interested
in other people
than you can
in two years
by trying to get people
interested in you."
Dale Carnegie

Chapter 20

Persistence and Completion
The Tinder Begins to Glow

"Nothing in the world can take the place of persistence.
Talent will not; nothing is more common than
unsuccessful men with talent. Genius will not;
Unrewarded genius is almost a proverb.
Education alone will not;
the world is full of educated derelicts.
Persistence and determination alone are omnipotent."
Calvin Coolidge

"FIRED UP!" PRINCIPLE # 27 – Persistence Pays Off

Basic training in the Army can be grueling for anyone. For Joseph Almond, it was a horrible nightmare, but not because of the training itself. While there, he got a call saying his mother and younger brother had been brutally attacked by a drug addict. Stabbed 84 times, his young mother died. His 11 year old brother, stabbed 31 times, lived and kept saying, "I want my brother." Joseph's platoon rallied around him and gave him the money to fly home. He reunited with his brother, discovered that he would be OK and left him in the care of an aunt, while he completed basic training.

At this point, Joseph got "FIRED UP"! He had a dream of supporting his younger brother after he completed basic training. It usually takes four years to become a non-commissioned officer; Joseph did it in two. He returned home, got custody of his brother and went to work.

Some years later, he became a transition work specialist, helping place people with disabilities in productive jobs. His success rate was very high, and he began to dream of helping people in a larger way. In 1993 he read Les Brown's book *Live Your Dreams* and got inspired to be a speaker. He began speaking in church basements, and word of his powerful style spread. Soon he was getting paid for his talks, as he portrayed the power of the dream and the dignity of the human spirit.

Joseph knew he wanted more. In December 1995 he called Les Brown's Detroit manager and told her his dream was to work for Les. In March 1995 he flew to Les's office and volunteered for a week, learning the systems and getting to know the staff. His expertise with products was evident, as was his enthusiasm and delightful personality. He never met Les that week, but he did leave his video behind for Les to watch. Every week, he called to see if Les had watched his video. He persisted, remained "FIRED UP!" and never gave up.

Then he learned Les was coming to Alabama. Would he be willing to help sell Les's products? Absolutely! Not only did Joseph go to the airport to pick up the products, he ended up meeting Les and giving him a ride to his hotel. Amazingly, they were registered across the hall from each other. Les spent over three hours with Joseph, analyzing his video and coaching him. Joseph was thrilled. He told Joseph, "You have the gift to inspire and motivate others – continue to let God use you." The next day, Joseph took Les to the airport, hoping to see him again soon.

A few weeks later, he called Les's office to say he had quit his job, sold his house and was on his way to volunteer. They told him to go to Orlando, where Les and his wife, Gladys Knight, were attending the National Speakers' Association annual convention. There, Les sat down with Joseph and asked how he could help him. Joseph asked for a job with Les, and he told him why: "I think I can help take your product sales organization to the next level." Les hired Joseph that night and now Joseph is living his dream. He got married, relocated and started working with Les Brown Enterprises. He's completely "FIRED UP!"

Joseph could have used many excuses to stop himself from moving on his dreams. He could have felt sorry for himself and let the tragedies in his life stop him. But he didn't. He kept moving. He drew on his inner and outer resources, had a clear vision and took action. He committed to his dream and made it happen in a big way. *He asked for what he wanted, continually stayed "FIRED UP!" and persisted. He triumphed. You can too. You have the talent, courage, energy and ability to make it happen. All you need to do is believe, commit and follow through.*

"FIRED UP!" PRINCIPLE #28 – Complete What You Start

In his book *The Path of Least Resistance,* Robert Fritz discusses the circle of completion and demonstrates how each phase in the action process has a unique and distinct quality. As you can see in the chart, there are three phases in this circle: *germination, assimilation and completion. Germination* is the initial start-up phase of the project, the beginning. This is usually where you feel the greatest excitement and enthusiasm and are most "FIRED UP!" about your dream. You'll most likely share that energy with others.

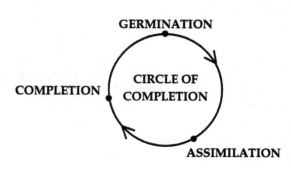

This is also like the beginning part of romantic relationships. It's that first phase of contact when everything the other person does is "perfect," and you're constantly thinking about them. In fact, some people like the aspect of infatuation so much that they don't stay in relationships long enough for them to deepen into mature love and become even more fulfilling. They are stuck in the germination phase and then cheat themselves, believing this phase is the best part.

Assimilation is the phase where people take action. *This is where you're actually doing the things you need to do to make your dream come true.* In Joseph's case, it meant volunteering at Les's office, going to meet Les at the airport, asking for a job and doing whatever it took to make things happen. Those were all part of assimilation or doing. This is where many people get stuck and never completely finish their actions. They get halfway done or they quit just short of realizing their dreams. What is unfortunate about this is that there is a distinct and special energy that you experience every time you complete a project, and that energy gets you "FIRED UP!" to accomplish your next dream. People who stay stuck in assimilation never benefit from that.

Completion is Essential

Incomplete dreams and projects drain large amounts of energy. How does this happen? It can show up in dozens of ways, from half-read books and half-listened to tapes to closets overflowing with clothes you haven't worn in years, to the classic "to do" lists that never get everything crossed off. "What's wrong with that?" you may ask. The problem is that incompletions are a form of self-sabotage which can destroy your self-esteem. Every day, each one of us makes commitments or agreements to do things. Saying you'll be at work on time is an agreement. Setting up lunch with a friend at a certain time and place is an agreement. Saying you'll take out the garbage tonight is an agreement.

Every time you say to yourself or someone else that you will do things, you are making agreements. Some people call them commitments or promises. Most people are pretty good at keeping agreements with others. If they say they will meet someone at two, they do it. People who don't keep agreements don't have many friends, because they aren't trustworthy. You probably know people like this and maybe have let them hurt you. Remember, *broken agreements destroy relationships.*

What about agreements with yourself? This is where most of us need to focus our awareness and make some changes. Here's an example.

Mary goes to bed and realizes she hasn't exercised all week. So she sets her clock for 6:30AM and tells herself that she'll get up and go to the gym for an hour before work. When the alarm rings at 6:30, she rolls over and goes back to sleep. What has just happened? She let herself down. She has broken an agreement with herself and she feels miserable. If she does this enough times, she no longer believes her own word. Her self-esteem slowly diminishes and she may feel tired and anxious. How can she handle this?

Each incompletion is a broken agreement, and as long as something is still hanging out there unfinished, it saps a little bit of energy. *Pile up enough incompletes and you have a frustrated person who feels like a failure.* That's what Mary may be experiencing. *Action is rewarded and inaction leads to stagnancy.*

Incompletion is often linked to procrastination. People who procrastinate may do so for different reasons; from fear of failure to fear of success. Some people are comfortable with chaos and some feel so overwhelmed that they don't know where to begin. Some believe that they work better under pressure, but they let the pressure build until it's super stressful. These are just some of the ways people limit their capacity to achieve.

How Can You Prevent Incompletions?

One way is to use an effective time management system as described in Chapter 15 and *to write every agreement down* on paper, especially agreements with yourself. Always keep your time management system with you and refer to it several times a day. Highlight each agreement as it is successfully accomplished and feel your success.

Another technique is to *say no.* Think very carefully before agreeing to do anything and determine whether you actually want to do it and can do it with your schedule and time constraints. If you are unsure, don't commit to it.

A third technique as discussed earlier is to *renegotiate the agreement.* Rather than breaking agreements, be clear that you are renegotiating agreements. This enables you to maintain your integrity and self-esteem, and it creates trust and respect with your friends and loved ones.

Clean Up Your Home Environment

Another powerful way to eliminate incompletions and "FIRE UP!" your energy is to look at how you live and physically take action. To resolve the incompletion of half-read reading materials, throw out the newspapers and declare the books finished. Recycle empty bottles, jars and cans. Clean out the closets and make room for new clothes. Take the old clothes to the Salvation Army or to a shelter for the homeless. Throw out any old cans or food or half-eaten boxes of stale crackers. Clean up your living environment and eliminate any clutter. Walk around your home and see which areas always catch your eye. Resolve to take action one step at a time and organize them. Find a way to eliminate the things you aren't using and either sell them or give them away to someone who can use them. This is a very powerful and positive exercise. One woman cleaned out all of her closets. The next week, as a surprise, her husband gave her three new dresses. She had created room for the new clothes by getting rid of the old ones. Some call this the "vacuum principle." Nature abhors a vacuum, and something will always come in to fill the void.

Completion Activity

Take some time right now, if you can, and determine one area of your home or work space where you can eliminate things you no longer need and can open up the space for things you want. Perhaps it's cleaning out your desk. Or maybe it's organizing the kitchen cabinets. Maybe you always wanted to sweep the garage floor. Or perhaps your bedroom closet is bulging. Is there laundry or ironing sitting in huge piles? Take action on at least one area where you have a physical incomplete now. Do what needs to be done and allow yourself to feel the powerful and positive burst of satisfaction and energy because you completed that agreement with yourself.

Completion means that you have done what you said you would do, you have finished the task and kept the agreement. With that completion comes a release of confident energy, a sense that you are a successful, powerful person who gets things done. That energy and attitude can help you go a long way towards achieving your dreams and being "FIRED UP!" in life.

Agreements About Your Dream

Now let's return to your dream, the one you have been working with throughout the book. Go to your list of Affirmations and Actions Options from Chapter 19 and your Action Worksheet. You have listed at least 15 different actions you could take to move on your dream. *Now is the commitment phase – where you choose which agreements you want to take action on and you decide when.* On the second page of the Action Plan is a section called *Specific Action Steps* with Target Date and Date Complete. A smaller version is shown here. This is where you write down the specific action option you are choosing to do, a target date and the date when the action was actually completed.

Remember the example of the woman who wanted to become an elementary school teacher? One of her affirmations was about networking. She had three action options on how to do that. So she chose which ones she wanted to do and made a time commitment. She accomplished the first action step on the due date and the second one she completed earlier. Her next step was to list all the other action steps she wanted to take with target dates.

Now it's time for you to take more action on your dream. Make *your action steps small, clear and realistic.* For example, it's

Specific Action Steps:	Target Date	Date Complete
1. Call my children's teachers and discuss ideas with them.	3/1/Yr	3/1/Yr
2. Go to college placement center and ask for help.	3/15/Yr	2/28/Yr

wiser to have an action step like: "Go to the library and look up children's nonprofit organizations in the area," rather than "Research groups serving children." The more specifically and clearly the step is stated, the more likely you will accomplish it easily and efficiently.

Using the Specific Action Steps form that follows, review your action options, get out your time management system, and set some realistic, achievable target dates. It's better to give yourself too much time than to overload a given week and fall short of your goals. I always believe people need to have a reward system built-in for achieving deadlines, and know what that reward is in advance. This enlists the support of your little kid inside and confirms to the adult part of you that a goal has been effectively met. Spend some time thinking about how you would like to reward yourself as you successfully complete your action steps. Perhaps it's a nice dinner out, or a special evening with friends or seeing a new movie. Plan ahead and know exactly how you want to celebrate your accomplishments.

And finally, after you have made your list of action steps with target dates, use the visualization resource you read about earlier. Remember that many professional athletes all over the world in basketball, tennis, golf and other sports use visualization with

Specific Action Steps:	Target Date	Date Complete
1. ——————————————— ——		
2. ——————————————— ——		
3. ——————————————— ——		
4. ——————————————— ——		
5. ——————————————— ——		
6. ——————————————— ——		
7. ——————————————— ——		
8. ——————————————— ——		
9. ——————————————— ——		

tremendous success; they see themselves winning and they often do. They get the part of their brain that knows how to succeed all "FIRED UP!" Every play, every swing, every movement is seen perfectly and clearly. When they are actually playing the sport, they do so with excellence.

Some of them, like Tara Cross Battle, 1996 Olympic member of the U.S. Women's Volleyball team, use music to inspire and motivate themselves. Tara listens to gospel music before games. "It gets me 'FIRED UP!' and ready to go," she explains.

Take a few minutes now and put on some powerful inspiring music. See yourself "FIRED UP!" and successfully taking action on each one of these steps by the target date. *Allow yourself to experience it fully. Feel all the positive emotions and energy; hear the cooperative comments from others you ask for help. Visualize ease and success every step of the way.* When you can see yourself succeeding, you're halfway there. That's great! You can do it!

"Positive 'self-expectancy' is pure and simply optimism, in the face of all odds. 'Self-expectancy' is the key to motivation. It takes the words, pictures, and emotions of the imagination and fuses them into energy and action by commitment. Winners have positive 'self-expectancy' which creates desire."
Denis Waitley

"Small things done consistently over time create big results."
John-Roger

"Action is eloquence."
William Shakespeare

Remember These Key Points

◆ To make your dream come true and stay "FIRED UP!" your next step is *to move, take action and get going.*
◆ The three phases of the Circle of Completion are Germination, Assimilation and Completion. Many people who don't achieve their dreams stay stuck in Assimilation. They cheat themselves of the powerful burst of completion energy which keeps them "FIRED UP!" for the next step.
◆ Incomplete dreams and projects drain large amounts of energy.
◆ Every time you say to yourself or someone else that you'll do something, you are making an agreement.
◆ Another powerful way to eliminate incompletions and get "FIRED UP!" is to physically take action at home. Clean up and clear out the things you're not using and pass them on to some one who can. Dejunk your life.
◆ Make your action steps small, clear and realistic.
◆ You can make your dream come true, with persistence and clarity, coupled with action.

Now Take These "FIRED UP!" Action Steps

◆ If you have not done so already, do the completion activity in this chapter.

◆ If you have not done so, take out your action plan and commit to taking action. Schedule in your action steps into your time management system.

◆ Buy some music which gets you "FIRED UP!" Play it whenever you're visualizing or working on your dream.

"Fall seven times,
stand up eight."
Japanese Proverb

"One can never consent to creep
when one feels
an impulse to soar."
Helen Keller

Chapter 21

The Elf Who Saved Christmas

A Blaze Burning Bright

"Dear Santa Claus:

I am writing this flew line because we all love you and you come to see us in Christmas Eve. Because my mother is sick and they took some money from the check and we wanted some toy for Christmas. If you don't we are going to cry so be sure and come on Christmas to our house and we really do NEED you. So be sure and come. Thanks you

Love yours - Julie

Jeanette - 15, Julie - 14, John - 13, James - 11, Jack - 10, Joy - 7, Janie - 3, Mommy too...

P.S. If you see God, tell him to take care of our daddy, because he died. Thank you so much."

"Dear Santa Claus
    I am writing these few words to
say hello Santa. And I want you to
know the police put my Daddy in jail.
And my mother does not have any
money to buy my little brother any
toys. This year i am only asking for
my 2 little brothers. The old one is
3 year's old and the other one is 1
year old and i would like to tell
you about 3 more sister. One of
them is 14 and 13 and 12. I am
not asking for me but if you have
any money left after you buy my
sister and brothers presents if
you could buy me a little present.
And one more thing thank you for reading
this letter.
                    from Katherine Delgado
P.S. I am 7 years old."

    Just imagine that you were able to grant the wishes of these
two children and help their Christmas dreams come true.
Think of how "FIRED UP!" you would feel to see their joy as they
experienced the wonder of Santa Claus. That's exactly what one
woman and her thousands of volunteers have been doing in
San Antonio, Texas for over 25 years. Louise Locker Elliott, fondly known in the community as "Elf Louise," created her Christmas
project when she was just 19 years old. It has been going strong
ever since. *Her huge heart, loving spirit and unflagging determination
make Santa Claus very real to over 60,000 children every year.*

The Dream

    It all started about ten days before Christmas in 1969.
Like many of us, Louise felt something was missing at the holidays. She watched Johnny Carson read children's "Dear Santa"
letters on TV and was deeply touched by the hope and belief in
them. They reconnected her with the magic of the holidays. To
keep that magic alive, she decided to anonymously answer the
letter of a little girl who would not otherwise receive any gifts.
The next day, she went to the post office and asked to see the

"Dear Santa" letters. There she encountered a formidable stumbling block – the U.S. Postal Service.

Most of us know what it can be like dealing with a government agency; they have strict rules and regulations to follow and rarely bend. Louise encountered the same red tape. The postmaster wouldn't allow her to open the letters; it was against government regulations. She persisted and asked if there was any way she could read just a few of them. They refused. After numerous requests and sincere heartfelt pleading, the post office relented, and allowed her to read the letters after they opened them.

A thrilled Louise sat at the post office for hours, pouring over hundreds of letters, waiting for the right one to jump out at her. It read *"Dear Santa, I know the only reason why you've never given us anything before is because we've never written. Now that we're writing, won't you please bring us...."* and then all the names and ages of the children were listed with a request for just a little something. It continued, *"Please bring us a Christmas tree – we've never had a Christmas tree...."* Imagine how a letter like that would pull at your heart strings. To Louise, it was the most beautiful letter in its purity and trust.

There were several other letters like that, which said things like *"Santa, you must have gotten lost last year, because you didn't bring us anything. My mother's sick and too poor to give us anything. If you have anything left over, please bring us something."* By this time, after she had spent hours in the post office, they finally gave her those 13 letters and wished her well. Unable to disappoint so many needy children, Louise ended up with 65 children to bless with Santa's presence. With only seven days before Christmas, it seemed unlikely these children would receive gifts any other way.

Where There's A Will, There's A Way

Louise now had a strong sense of purpose; she was "FIRED UP!" Perhaps you can remember a time in your life when you were absolutely determined and "FIRED UP!" to do something. You weren't sure how; you just knew you had to find a way. Such was Louise's challenge with getting those presents. She really hadn't thought too much about the actual logistics – her natural spontaneity and desire to give to others had taken over.

Reality hit hard; she had no money and was on a college scholarship. Also, her father had recently died. As Albert Einstein said, *"In the middle of difficulty lies opportunity."* In spite of her challenges, she shared the letters with her generous and supportive mother, who instantly caught the spirit. Together, they immediately took ornaments off their tree, and unearthed games and toys from Louise's childhood, to give to these children.

"FIRED UP!" PRINCIPLE # 29 – Ask for Help

After calling friends and enlisting their help, Louise turned to people she had never met. She visited the local coffee shop, armed with unbridled enthusiasm and 13 "Dear Santa" letters. As she sat at the counter and chatted with people, she shared her wonderful plan. Then she did something that characterizes people who make their dreams come true – *Louise asked for help.*

Think about times in your life when you have reached out in total sincerity and asked for help. Most of the time, you received much more than you asked for, right? Louise had the same experience. People responded generously with toys, other gifts and a little money. On December 22 she approached the gruff, busy gentleman in charge of the Christmas tree lot and shared the letter from the child who had never had a tree. As he read, his whole face transformed; tears streamed down his cheeks and he said, *"This is beautiful. You can have the prettiest tree on my lot."*

The First Christmas Delivery

Picture yourself all ready with the tree and ornaments, out to make a child's dream come true. You'd be filled with excitement, right?

Loaded with the tree, ornaments and lights, Louise and a friend wandered through one of San Antonio's ghettoes late in the night. Unfortunately, they forgot their flashlight, which made it tough to find the right house in the dark. Eventually, they stumbled onto the right street and left the tree with a note saying "Merry Christmas, Santa will be here later," and escaped, undetected. Delighted, the next day, Louise fantasized about how perfect it would be to have Santa actually deliver the other presents. Then these children would truly believe in the miracle of Christmas, rather than just think it was charity.

At the last minute, Louise convinced a rather skinny male friend to dress up as Santa. On Christmas Eve, with adrenaline pumping from sheer anticipation, a "FIRED UP!" Louise and her Santa delivered their gifts from the North Pole throughout the poor sections of San Antonio. Much to their surprise, they discovered that none of the families had anything at all for Christmas; everyone was incredibly grateful for Santa's arrival. None of these people were skeptical, cynical or rude – they all loved the magic and behaved like innocent, trusting little children. Then, inevitably the one child who had written Santa would say, *"I told you Santa would come if we wrote– I told you!"*

By the time Louise and Santa arrived at the last house, it was nearly 2 AM, and everyone was asleep. The blurry-eyed parents stumbled to the door; their eyes lit up like children's, and responded with open joy. They woke their children and giggled with delight. The mother cried softly as she watched her children happily open the gifts and receive what they had asked for. Clearly flabbergasted but thrilled, she welcomed Santa and thanked him: *"I can't believe you're here. My kids wrote you early in the year, and they were so excited. They just knew you would come. I kept trying to explain to them there is no such thing as Santa and here you are. I just can't believe it."*

Throughout all of this, Louise hovered quietly in the background, unnoticed by the families, drinking in their ecstatic reactions. Their gratitude filled her heart with so much love that the Spirit of Christmas truly came alive for her that night. *It also started an adventure that would span over a quarter of a century, touching the lives of millions of people all over Texas and the United States.*

The Challenges She Overcame to Make Her Dream Come True

You've just arrived at this year's Elf Louise headquarters. The smell of hot apple cider wafts through the corridor, along with the sweet melody of Christmas carols. A pleasant woman greets you and asks you to complete a brief questionnaire about your volunteer skills and interests. You wind through the gymnasium-size building and marvel at the hundreds of volunteers sorting through ten foot high metal shelves crammed with toys, wrapping paper, boxes and garbage bags.

To the right, dozens of used bicycles wait for repair. A hundred crimson Santa suits, recently cleaned, hang with shiny black boots and fluffy white beards nearby. Volunteer readers sift through "Dear Santa" letters, many lovingly etched in crayon. As they decipher the innocent requests from little ones, they forward the information to the databank for processing. There, cheerful computer operators process names, family information and gift requests. Amazingly, almost everyone is smiling, in spite of the enormity of the tasks ahead.

A project like Elf Louise requires incredible energy and effort. The challenges have varied throughout the years, but there are definite constants. You may need to overcome similar obstacles as you move on your dream. See if any of these experiences sound familiar and offer solutions you can apply to your dream.

1. Organizational Structure and Changing Locations

Perhaps you have had the experience of trying to start up a new community project. Remember all the phone calls and logistics and organizational snafus? Remember having too few people to do far too much? Louise has faced these same situations.

With over 12,000 families and 60,000 children to support each Christmas, the project requires literally months of planning and volunteer support. Elf Louise also has never had a permanent base of operations. The location for the toys and other gifts has changed each year, depending on which business donates the vacant space. About 80,000 square feet is required to accommodate storage, repair and labor. And it can't be just any 80,000 square feet. It has to be centrally located, near public transportation. It must be well-lit for safety, and have both heat and air conditioning because Texas weather can go to either extreme. And it must be a space with ample storage capacity. Just finding the location is a major job, and that is only the beginning.

With no long-term storage facility, the project organizers scramble every fall. Phones and computers must be installed, tables and lighting must be set up, storage bins and supplies need to be brought in and everything has to start from scratch with very little time to spare. *This happens every single year.*

It is a logistical nightmare which requires careful strategizing to save time and maximize the efforts of volunteer workers. Everything must be highly organized, or the whole thing can fall apart. Think of how challenging that might be. Who could you get to help? Who would support your dream?

In the case of Elf Louise, it's the thousands of volunteers who help. They catch the fire of Louise's enthusiasm and get "FIRED UP!" about the opportunity to give. Starting in October, all the way through Christmas, several thousands of people arrive to do anything and everything. But, as you can well imagine, managing all those people and thousands of toys and gifts can be a monstrous challenge.

So how does Louise do it? She chunks it down into small manageable pieces and delegates the tasks to wonderful supervisory volunteers. These managers make sure every volunteer is interviewed so that each can be appropriately matched to a job. Then they track each task that needs to be handled and who can do them. Shifts are scheduled and timelines are set. Everyone who comes in can help with the project, and all are welcome. Think how terrific it would feel to be immediately included in a project like this and to be unquestionably appreciated for your contribution. That feeling keeps volunteers coming back year after year.

2. Fundraising

You're at the cash register at a toy warehouse. You have 750 Raggedy Ann® dolls, 900 Barbie® dolls, 3000 stuffed animals, 1500 model airplanes, 5000 racing cars, 1000 children's books, 400 Power Rangers®, 500 Barney® dinosaurs, and 10 carts full of baseball and basketball equipment. The total is $42,525, and this is your third trip this week. *Where is next week's cash coming from?*

Elf Louise faces that kind of dilemma every year for eight weeks. Fund-raising, the core of any non-profit project, is an ever-present challenge, in spite of publicity and donations. Over $200,000 is required annually to service the families. How does an all-volunteer organization raise that kind of money? As you may guess, with a great deal of work and the assistance of the local community.

The San Antonio Bar Association donated their services to gain 501C3 non-profit status for the project; something Louise never pursued because of the time and expense required. That status enables the project to receive annual grants from area businesses and private charities, although that is never enough. Creative fund-raisers have provided necessary cash, and a diverse population has staged a myriad of colorful community events.

For several years, the HOW Foundation, a local halfway house for recovering alcoholics, has participated in fund-raising and also volunteers their efforts. *"One man told me later it was the first sober Christmas he had spent in years – because he had a reason to stay sober,"* says Louise. The project gives back as much or more than it receives from volunteers.

Perhaps you know that all forms of media are required to do public service announcements. *In the case of Elf Louise, local media events give the project critical visibility and encourage others to be generous.* Radiothons with special themes have been a tried and true formula. The most lucrative fund-raiser has been the annual golf tournament, which began in 1992. The first year it brought in over $50,000 and the third year it raised over $135,000. Held at the Santero Golf Club, the tournament attracts avid golfers from all over Texas.

3. Toy and Gift Procurement

If you're a parent, you know just how tough it can be to find the right gift when your child has requested the most popular toy of the year, from Game-Boys® to the latest Disney® movie figurines. Remember how frustrated you were when they were all sold out and you didn't know if you could get it before Christmas? Think what that would be like on a scale of 60,000 and then you begin to see the difficulties Louise encounters each year. *Finding the right toys and gifts to match the "Dear Santa" letters requires monumental effort.*

There are seemingly endless shelves full of donated gifts and purchased toys, games and presents. Many people contribute things, although one of the early lessons was to accept only new or "like new" items. A major volunteer job is to sort through all these donations and determine which ones are suitable and which require repair. A whole team of people repair bicycles and assorted broken toys. To date, Elf Louise has never bought any bicycles; all of them have been secondhand and repaired.

In spite of all the contributions, new toys and games must always be purchased. *Louise dreams of connecting up with a national toy distributor for annually donated toys;* right now, she is paying wholesale rates at a local retailer. In the early days, one of the best publicity generators came from her wild shopping sprees. With five or more shopping carts, Louise ran up and down the aisles of a local toy store, grabbing games and toys as quickly as she could. Then she raced back to project headquarters for unloading, sorting and wrapping. The whole thing dazzled the media and frequently ended up on the news. The news coverage also enabled many miracles to take place. Seeing a report that the project desperately needed sports equipment, one retailer drove up and unloaded hundreds of basketballs, just in the nick of time.

4. Identifying the Needy Families

Part of the challenge with a new community program is finding out who to help. Perhaps you have faced the same dilemma. At the beginning, it was nearly impossible to get a few letters from the post office. Today, the post office turns over all the "Dear Santa" letters to her each year. Amazing what a little persistence will do! As Cecile B. De Mille wrote in *Sunshine and Shadow*, *"The person who makes a success of living is the one who sees his goal steadily and aims for it unswervingly."*

Since 1994 the entire community rallies to assist needy children. Fifty different community agencies now provide names and information to the Elf Louise Project. These names are cross-referenced with the existing databank. All letters addressed to "Dear Santa" get answered. The computer records identify the number of children in each family according to their age. This is a vast improvement over the original process of sifting through handwritten letters done in the early days.

5. Keeping the Magic Alive and Maintaining the Enthusiasm

Louise's greatest desire is to keep the magic alive in the project. That's her core value – regardless of how big the project becomes, or how many children are reached. That's also why Louise has resisted the idea of becoming a bureaucratic non-profit infra-structure. Maybe you have encountered the red tape and rigidity of some non-profit groups. That's exactly what Louise wants to avoid. *She fears that if the project becomes more formalized, the joy, spontaneity and wonder would be lost.* That's a compromise she is not willing to make. To Louise, the magic of Christmas is expressed by the exuberance and spontaneous joy that erupts from volunteers as they lovingly wrap, tag and prep packages.

At Elf Louise, buttons and hats help the volunteers stay "FIRED UP!" T-shirts with slogans like *"Ask me if I'm an Elf"* are worn happily by folks from all walks of life, from military generals to tattooed Hell's Angels bikers. *The common denominator is the same–human kindness during the season of giving.* Stepping out beyond the normal confines of day to day life and going the extra mile to make a child smile – that's what the Elf Louise project is all about. Louise describes one volunteer's story.

🔥 "This negative and depressed lady was dragged in by her daughter. Reluctantly, the unhappy soul volunteers. We give her a Santa letter which was a request from two young girls for some new underwear. This sad lady begins to sort through a clothes pile, which was an impossible task because we never had underwear donations. Another woman enters the gym and with 40 volunteers working, this lady walks over to the depressed volunteer. 'You make think this is a weird gift, but I hope you can use it,' she says, and gives the volunteer a box. Inside were two matching girls' sets of underwear. It's things like this that make believers out of people."

6. Balancing Her Life and Time

Probably the single biggest obstacle Louise has faced and overcome has been balancing the rest of her life with the project.

As a psychotherapist with a growing practice, and a wife and mother, Louise has often taken better care of others than herself. *That may sound familiar to you – some dedicated people give so much of themselves to others that they sacrifice their own personal life and health.* Louise has encountered serious health problems along the way. A few years ago, shortly after giving birth, she fell and perilously hurt her back. Restricted to bed and barely able to move, Louise hired a helper and continued to see patients at home. She ran the program through her volunteers, checking in regularly. Eventually she recovered, but she has always struggled with balancing her volunteer efforts with her home and health.

Today she faces medical difficulties with her feet, and she delegates more and more of the project to longtime volunteer Bill Harrison. Regardless of her health concerns, Louise always maintains a positive attitude and a heartfelt conviction that things will get better. Her loving dedication colors everything in her life and enriches the lives of those around her.

The Results of Her Project

In spite of the challenges, the Elf Louise project continues to provide 12,000 families and 60,000 children annually with gifts from Santa Claus that they would never receive otherwise. *Since the project began, over half a million children have received gifts from Elf Louise.* That kind of result is tangible and visible. Sometimes the results are less obvious, but equally meaningful.

One teenage boy explained how the Elf Louise project touched his life. He had written to Santa explaining how his father had lost his job and how everyone in the family was upset and depressed. He didn't ask for presents; he just asked Santa to bring the Spirit of Christmas to his family. Santa did, along with a few gifts. It was such an uplifting experience for his father that it motivated him to go look for work and he soon found another job. The next year, that dad came to volunteer at Elf Louise. He wanted to give back some of the value he had received. Working late one night, he told Louise how the project had restored his faith in himself and the world.

Think how terrific you would feel knowing you had given someone else the hope and strength to keep going. *Chances are good that you have often affected others in a positive way without ever even knowing it.*

For Louise personally, the obvious rewards of the program would have been enough, but she has also received substantial accolades. She was named *Socially Responsible Entrepreneur of the Year for the Southwest* by *Inc.* magazine. The Masonic Grand Lodge of Texas presented her with *The Community Builder Award*, and she received the *Jefferson Award* from none other than Coretta Scott King. Humbled and surprised by this recognition, Louise always hastens to promote her program and compliments all the volunteers who make it possible. She refuses to take the credit alone.

The press has also noticed her good works. *Good Morning America* featured her, and *Southwest Magazine* did a cover story on her. *Reader's Digest* named her one of their "Heroes for Today" and *Woman's World* profiled her. *Parade Magazine* wrote a two page article on the project, and *Good Housekeeping* also did a story on Louise.

She has not let the publicity go to her head, however. What delights her the most is that others around the country have contacted her asking how to set up similar projects in their states. Louise gladly assists them and has even prepared a document called "How to Set Up a Christmas Project." Happily, several cities throughout the country have followed her lead and are running successful programs of their own.

Louise's goal through all the years has been to perpetuate the joyous spirit of Christmas she felt that very first year when she visited those 13 families. Without question, she has achieved and exceeded her goal.

Qualities that Helped Louise Succeed

All of us have key strengths that support our success, such as rare talents or gifts, specific skills or even a fabulous attitude. Think for a minute about the positive feedback you have received in your life. What qualities do you have that people always comment on? What are you most often complimented about? What does your family especially love about you? All of these are clues to the qualities you have to ensure your success in any area of your life. They make you unique.

Louise Locker Elliott has a number of such qualities, not the least of which are *enthusiasm, determination, fearlessness and joy.* Her love for others and her willingness to ask for help have also supported her efforts. Her warmth, accessibility and personal dynamism have captivated many a supporter, from postal workers to wealthy donors. *Her tireless energy, unflagging good nature and heartfelt dedication to children are evident in everything she does.*

Louise also has a rare kind of purity; she absolutely believes in the goodness of all people and the magic that can be present in your life every day, when you choose to look for it. That kind of belief and passion is highly contagious and refreshing in today's world. *Louise is like a spark that lights the flame of hope in the hearts of both adults and children; her own light burns very brightly.*

What's Next?

Like most people who achieve a dream, Louise doesn't rest on her laurels. As she looks to the future, her immediate goals for the program are to increase the number of families reached by the project, improve the quality of the toys, maintain the magic and keep her life balanced. Finding a permanent home and forming a liaison with a national toy manufacturer would also help. Five years from now, she would like to teach seminars to groups about how to make your passion come to life and how to live a life filled with magic. She sees herself expanding her psychotherapy practice to include more group work. One day, she would like to work with a writer and produce a book about the whole

Elf Louise experience. In her typical humble fashion, she says that the biggest lesson to be learned from her experience is that *"One person without money, status or a degree can do something that has a major, positive impact on others." One person, "FIRED UP!" about their dream, can make a difference in the world. Elf Louise, whose dream has touched millions, should know.*

"It's a funny thing about life; if you refuse to accept anything but the best, you very often get it."
Somerset Maugham

"One thing I know: the only ones among you who will be really happy are those who will have sought and found how to serve."
Albert Schweitzer

Remember These Key Points

◆ When you're "FIRED UP!" about a dream, you transcend your normal limitations and find resources, even in strangers.

◆ Most dreams require significant planning, organization and action.

◆ Being willing to ask for help is a key ingredient to succeeding with your dream.

◆ Creative fund-raisers by others who are "FIRED UP!" about your dream can be one of the best ways to help finance it.

◆ Keeping the *magic* alive in your dream is very important to maintaining long-term success. Share the joy, the wins and the accomplishments with others. *You* are the *magic*.

◆ Enthusiasm, determination, fearlessness and joy, along with tireless energy, unflagging good nature and heartfelt dedication are all qualities which helped Louise stay "FIRED UP!" and make her dream come true.

Take These "FIRED UP!" Action Steps Now

◆ If your dream doesn't directly assist other people, consider donating some volunteer time at a local shelter, soup kitchen or non-profit organization. Discover how good you feel when you serve and how "FIRED UP!" you become about your life.
◆ Revisit the holidays this next year from the eyes of a child who might not receive anything. Consider donating to a program like Elf Louise, or doing something on your own.

*"The high destiny of the individual is to serve
rather than to rule."*

Albert Einstein

INSPIRATION

"Nothing has greater,
longer lasting impression
upon another person
than the awareness
that someone has
transcended suffering,
has transcended circumstance,
and is embodying and expressing
a value that inspires
and enobles and lifts life."
Stephen R. Covey

Chapter 22

Paint Your Picture of Success
Stoking the Fire

"Set your sights high, the higher the better.
Expect the most wonderful things to happen, not in the future,
but right now. Realize that nothing is too good.
Allow absolutely nothing to hamper you or hold you up in any way."
Eileen Caddy

A New Way to Picture Your Dreams

You read about how Elf Louise got "FIRED UP!" and overcame many obstacles to achieve her dream. She always knew what she wanted to achieve; the dream burned brightly inside her. She had a clear picture of success in mind, and she stayed focused on her vision. Now you're ready to take your dream one step further, by using your vision to create a powerful tool to help you succeed – a dream collage.

"FIRED UP!" PRINCIPLE # 30 – Create a Dream Collage

A dream collage, or treasure map, as some call it, is a visual repre-
sentation of your completed successful dream. It is a terrific way to stay

"FIRED UP!" about it. It starts with colored poster board or foam-core, perhaps covered with your favorite colored wrapping paper. You paste up pictures and words that represent your fully achieved dream on this board. You can create these images, cut them from magazines and newspapers or use photographs you have taken. A combination of all these things would be great, too. One of the most important elements of your dream collage is that your picture is on it – put yourself in the dream living it to make it seem more real and personal.

In *The Aladdin Factor*, Jack Canfield and Mark Victor Hansen write about a Louisiana millionaire who wanted to help inner city children go on to college. He decided to start with a school in New Orleans that had an 84% dropout rate. He told the students that if they stayed in school, got good grades and had a 95% attendance record, he would pay for their college education. To help them visualize being in college, he took them to several nearby universities, where they spent an entire day following college students around. They went to classes, visited the student union, ate college cafeteria food and got a strong picture of what it would be like to go to school there. Every morning for the next several years, the teachers had the students close their eyes and imagine being a college student. They continually reinforced this positive image for these students. By the time these kids graduated from high school, the dropout rate changed from 84% to less than 20%. The millionaire not only gave the students real incentive, but also an actual way for them to see themselves succeeding; something they could not have imagined before. *Just like visualization, dream collages are powerful motivators.*9

"FIRED UP!" PRINCIPLE # 31 – Let the Little Kid Inside Come Out and Play

Have you ever been to an amusement park and watched the adults? You'll notice many adults are there without children; but they're laughing and playing anyway. One of the reasons DisneyWorld is so successful is that adults get to be kids, too.

Locked inside each of us is a spontaneous, joyful child. Some people are very good at inviting this fun kid to come out and play; while others keep them locked away. It's essential that you invite the little kid inside you to participate in your dream. That kid has incredible imagination and creativity, knows no boundaries and thinks only in terms of possibilities. All of us can benefit by connecting with and accessing the gifts of the kid inside us. This is especially true when creating your dream collage.

🔥 Remember Greg, the man who dreamed of being a commercial pilot? He created a dream collage with pictures of himself flying and several photos of the different airplanes he wanted to fly. In one picture, he cut out the face of the pilot boarding a jet he wanted to fly, and replaced it with a picture of his own face. Within four weeks, he was working for a regional Fixed Base Operator as a linesman. Two weeks later, he was asked to co-pilot the exact jet on his collage! He saw himself flying and he did it. A few months after that, he co-piloted a half-million dollar new Mooney airplane, wearing $1000 headphones. His dream came true in many different ways. He was "FIRED UP!"

Greg's Dream Collage

🔥 Lisa wanted to build her business and create a happy life with a romantic partner. Within a year of creating her dream collage, she was happily married to her new husband, sharing her successful business with him. Lisa has experienced more joy than ever before, and continues to grow and improve her life. She actually has a different collage for every area of her life – finances, health, family, business and such. She has placed the collages strategically around her house, so almost everywhere she looks there's a collage.

Making My Dreams Come True with a Collage

I have personally had astonishing results with dream collages. In 1989 I created the collage shown below, mainly focusing on my personal life. I wasn't married yet, and I wanted to find a healthy life partner. So I picked out key words to get me "FIRED UP!" like "The Best Man Ever." I cut out a picture of a wedding dress I liked, along with pictures of places I wanted to visit with my new husband. In the upper left hand corner, I put a picture of myself with words from a magazine that said "Her Brilliant Career," "High Profile Creativity" and "Women to Watch in the 1990's." These phrases kept the flame alive inside of me and inspired me to achieve. There were also photos of sailboats, since that's my favorite hobby, plus other meaningful words and pictures.

Snowden's Dream Collage

With the exception of the trip to Australia, which we're going to take at a later date, *everything on this collage has come true!* In 1991 I married "The Best Man Ever" in a dress very similar to the one on the collage which I designed and had made in pink. We went to the Caribbean for our honeymoon and have since chartered large sailboats there. I exercise and take care of myself.

The most amazing thing about the collage was something I would never have predicted. That little upper left-hand corner about my career, "High Profile Creativity," came true in incredible ways. In 1991 I received a national award from the Small Business Administration for my work in helping to create a non-profit organization to help women start and stay in business. *That award resulted in my flying to Washington DC., and going to a ceremony in the Rose Garden at the White House with then President Bush. Seven of us were honored at a Congressional luncheon with over 700 people. This led to exposure in national magazines.* Based on my personal experience, dream collages are powerful and effective. My husband, Spencer, and I now have a couple's dream collage of our lives together. It covers every aspect from romance and travel to our spiritual life and finances. It's about five feet long and sits in our bedroom. We look at it regularly for inspiration and to keep on track.

Here's one more example of how collages work.

Carolyn's Dream Collage

Carolyn wanted to teach music to elementary school children in creative and fun ways. Her collage shows her with her musical instruments and children at the age groups she wanted to be working with. She created this collage in the winter. The following fall, she had a part-time job teaching music in several elementary schools. A year later, she was employed full-time teaching music at the same school she had chosen! The pictures got her "FIRED UP!" to believe in her success.

Now It's Your Turn

Schedule an entire morning, afternoon or evening for this activity, because it is fun and engrossing. You'll be amazed at how real your dream becomes and how "FIRED UP!" you get looking at it. Here's what you need to get started:

♦A large piece of poster board or foamcore.
♦Tape or glue.
♦Magazines with the topics and themes that reflect your dream.
♦Construction paper and markers to make words and pictures.
♦A photo of yourself.
♦A pair of scissors.
♦Your imagination.

Where Do You Get Your Ideas?

Review your notes, including any comments you may have recorded after your visualizations. Focus on your dream description and action plan for now, and for one year, three years and five years from now. *Imagine you are painting a picture of your success that fully portrays all you want to create and live as your dream.* Look for pictures and words in magazines and cut out everything that appeals to you. You can also use photographs. Take your time and make sure what you want is completely represented. If you need additional money for your dream, draw a pot of gold or show dollar signs. You might want to consider putting the word "easy" on your collage to help you achieve your dream with ease. *Definitely include a picture of yourself on the collage* – this is essential to your ability to see yourself as successful.

Once you have all the pieces of your collage, including all the words, photos and graphics you want (remember the picture of yourself), review them to be sure each one works for you. *Be specific.*

Here's a great idea. Write a fake check to yourself for a large sum of money, say $1,000,000 and put it on your collage.

Comedian Jim Carrey is living proof that this works. In 1995 he was paid $10,000,000 twice for making movies. In his interview with Barbara Walters, he revealed that he had written a check to himself several years before for $10,000,000 with a description on the bottom– "for services rendered as an actor by 1995." He carried that check with him in his wallet for years, saw himself getting paid that amount and achieved it. You can do the same thing.

As you create your dream collage, if you are building a business, show photos of the crowds of people that would associate with you and buy your products or services. Include a sales report with excellent results and profits on it. Also include photos of the products or services you are selling. If you're starting a non-profit group, include photos of the people you want to help, and show a steady stream of cash flow and positive results.

Make your collage vivid, so your dream comes "alive" when you look at it. Test each picture emotionally – does it get you "FIRED UP!" or not? If not, leave it off your dream collage. A good way to find out is if you get goosebumps or some other positive reaction. This indicates the picture has meaning and value for you.

Once you're happy with all the pieces of the collage, lay them out on the board, which may be in color or covered in your favorite glittery wrapping paper. Play with the layout and move things around until everything looks just right and then tape or glue them down. If you glued it, lay it flat and allow everything to dry thoroughly.

Once your completed collage has dried, put it where you will see it every day. A good location is the refrigerator door. *Look at it daily, notice how you're doing and give yourself credit for your successes. Let it get you "FIRED UP!" and help you move closer and closer towards achieving your dream;* just as it did for Sally.

A Dream Come True

Sally Garrett's lifelong dream was to go to Africa to study wildlife. As a student at Antioch College in New England, she began to find ways to make her dream come true.

First, she created a large dream collage which she hung on her bulletin board. It was covered with pictures of Africa, a *National Geographic* map and a photograph from a camera catalog where the lens focused on a wild heron with a notepad and pencil nearby. That completely expressed what she wanted to be doing – studying wildlife. Sally studied her dream collage daily; she visualized herself living her dream, and took consistent action. In the fall of 1991 she set out to make her dream come true. At Antioch, she networked with a wildlife writer to find out how she could do research in Africa. That led her to connect with Professor Bill Barklow, who had just received a study grant for Tanzania.

Between October 1991 and June of 1992, Sally scrambled to create the resources to go to Africa; she depleted her savings and had to rush through her final classwork so she could make the trip. She booked three different sets of flight reservations for Tanzania, not knowing when the expedition would be leaving or if she would be part of it. Finally, she got word that the departure date was in June and she would be conducting research on hippopotamus communication.

Alone and completely "FIRED UP!" this courageous woman traveled across the ocean and landed in Tanzania, "the most foreign place" she had ever experienced. Nearly missing her connection with the safari, she joined the expedition and headed for the bush. There she spent her days observing two groups of hippos and their interactions with each other. She very fondly remembers sitting there that first night thinking with great joy, "I am living my dream. This is wonderful and it's real." Sally had never felt more empowered in her life.

Many adventures challenged her courage and wit during her time in Africa, such as getting stranded overnight on a local bus and being hassled for traveling alone. But she triumphed over the difficulties and ended up spending four glorious months in Tanzania, Kenya and Zimbabwe.

The reference point of success with her dream proved a powerful reserve when she went home. Shortly after her return, she came face to face with chaos and turmoil, as she dealt with some serious family problems. But the act of having achieved her dream, of having manifested her dream collage so perfectly, served to spur her on and keep her going, no matter what challenges she faced. As she now says, "Once you know you have made your dream come true, you know you can do it again. It's just a question of choosing what dream to work on. I can do anything now." Sally's courage and success are inspirations for her and her friends; they get us "FIRED UP!" too.

Now you have a powerful and exciting dream collage to work from. Show it only to people who will encourage you. Keep it to yourself and only show it those who believe in and appreciate your dream. Congratulations on your work; you have made a terrific tool for realizing your dreams.

Remember These Key Points

◆ A *dream collage,* or treasure map, as some call it, is a visual representation of your successful, completed dream. It's a super way to stay "FIRED UP!" about your dream while doing what it takes to accomplish it.

◆ Imagine you are painting a picture of your success that fully portrays all you want to be, do and have so you can live your dream.

◆ To make a dream collage, you need a large piece of poster board or foamcore, plus tape or glue. Use magazines, photos and words with the topics and themes you want on your collage, Colored markers are useful to make words and pictures. You also need a photo of yourself, a pair of scissors and your imagination. Invite your little kid inside to come out and play.

Now Take These "FIRED UP!" Action Steps

◆ If you have not done so already, create your own dream collage.

◆ Once your completed collage has dried, put it where you'll see it every day, like the refrigerator door. Focus on it every day, notice how you're doing and give yourself credit for your successes. Let it get you "FIRED UP!" and move you closer and closer towards achieving your dream.

"Dream lofty dreams,
and as you dream, so shall you become.
Your vision is the promise
of what you shall at last unveil."
John Ruskin

THE GIFT OF DREAMS

"We grow by dreams.
All great men and women are dreamers.
Some of us let dreams die though;
but others nourish and protect them and
nurse them through bad days and tough times,
'till the sunshine and light
which always comes."
Woodrow Wilson

"If you advance in the direction of your dream
and endeavor to live the life
which you have imagined,
you will meet success unexpected
in common hours.
You will put something behind you,
you will pass invisible boundaries.
New universal and more liberal laws will begin to establish
themselves around and within you.
Or old laws will be expanded and
interpreted in your favor.
In a more liberal sense, you will live
with the license of
a higher order of being."
Henry David Thoreau

Chapter 23

Yes, You Can Do the Impossible!
Friction Produces Fire, Too

*"All who have accomplished great things have had a great aim,
have fixed their gaze on a goal which was high,
one which sometimes seemed impossible."*
Orison Swett Marden

"FIRED UP!" PRINCIPLE # 32 – You Can if You Think You Can

As you get "FIRED UP!" about your dream and focus on your collage and the many exciting directions your dream can take, is there any part of you that believes you may not be able to do it? Is there any part of you that says, "This is impossible"? Is there any part of you that douses the flame of your enthusiasm and causes self-doubt? If so, don't be discouraged. That's a common feeling. Just keep on going, regardless of any doubt, doing whatever it takes to achieve your dream. No matter what that voice says, *you can, like any other human being, do the seemingly impossible and transcend your previous limitations.*

How? Part of the answer is related to your self-definition. All of us tend to have a "box" of self-description which we use to define ourselves. We think of ourselves in a certain way and that "box" is the sum of all we have done so far in our lives. This can be healthy in terms of letting you know where you stand and what kind of person you are. But it can also limit you in subtle ways. It goes something like this.

You hear about a person who climbed Mount Everest or won a gold medal in the Olympics or swam the English channel. They are "FIRED UP!" about their lives. But you may say, "I could never do anything like that." The truth is, *you can do all of those things when you truly want to in your heart more than anything else* ; you will then develop the will and determination to make it happen. When your *intention* and *focus* line up with your dream on every level of your being, you can do amazing things. It just doesn't matter what your limits may have been in the past. Together, they help you keep the flame inside you burning bright and enable you to stay "FIRED UP!" about your dream. Here are some examples.

No Disabilities Hold Winnie Back

Winnie Tunison is a deaf and blind woman with a husband and children. Her mission is to encourage blind-deaf people to seek psychological help and become independent. She wants the deaf community to fully accept the blind and deaf population, and she wants the hearing world to treat them as equals, rather than pity them. Sounds impossible, doesn't it? Yet Winnie has accomplished a great deal of her dream.

Deaf from birth, she fell in love with a deaf man who she married. Raised by parents who helped her develop courage and independence, she had always felt competent and safe. She gave birth to two daughters and later she lost her vision; suddenly she felt helpless and alone.

For Winnie, blindness was very different than deafness. She became depressed and desperate when her husband took over all the household chores. Feeling useless, she took an overdose of sleeping pills. After having her stomach pumped, Winnie reached out to her husband and asked him to respect her for who she was and let her lead her life. Fortunately, he listened to her and gave her the space to grow through her new challenges. Winnie started going to counseling. In group therapy, she met others who had what she felt were even worse problems than hers: bulimia, sexual abuse and schizophrenia. After gaining a new perspective, she entered the Helen Keller Institute and learned to be independent and free.

Today, Winnie travels all over the world alone and feels healthy, positive and "FIRED UP!" She has lectured throughout the country and at national conferences for the blind and deaf. She regularly counsels others with the same health concerns, and keeps her flame inside ablaze. In college, she maintains a 3.8 grade point average. She is continually growing and learning, spreading her flame of enthusiasm to others.10

Winnie had more challenges than most of us, yet she overcame them and went on to accomplish great things. She expanded her box of self-definition, got "FIRED UP!" and ignited the fire of her dream. Since she was already a fully functioning deaf person, she had never felt her deafness was an obstacle. Struck with sudden blindness, she learned to have compassion for others who share her challenges. She got a new dream of helping other blind-deaf people and has assisted hundreds of others along the way. *You can achieve your dream, too. You have everything required to succeed: heart, determination, fire, enthusiasm, vision, intention and the ability to take action.*

Mark's Dream: A 24 Hour Miracle

Mark had a dream of raising significant money for a non-profit organization which he supported. He was deeply committed to this organization because it had touched his heart and helped him personally. That was a big reason for his success. He commented later, "When I spoke from my heart, people heard it and just naturally wanted to participate." He had a specific focus and intention; he wanted to raise the money for a promotional campaign to increase the group's visibility and allow more people to take part in its work.

When Mark originally began his project, he gave himself a very short deadline; *he wanted to raise $25,000 in less than 24 hours and have the promotional pieces in hand to show friends the following evening.* Sounds like a big challenge, doesn't it? But remember, Mark had incredible determination, clarity and intention. He was completely "FIRED UP!" He had the tools of the "FIRED UP!" Action Plan and all the techniques you have learned in this book.

Remember the proverb, "Ask and you shall receive. Knock and the door shall be opened unto you"? *Mark started asking for what he wanted; a critical part of achieving any dream.* Late one Saturday night, he called me and asked for help in creating these pieces literally overnight. At first, I just laughed and said "no," but Mark enrolled me in his dream.

He showed me all the benefits of the project and got me "FIRED UP!" by sharing his enormous enthusiasm. We worked all night creating three beautiful brochures and direct mail pieces. We selected photographs, wrote the copy, designed the brochures and went to an all-night color copier company. By 9 AM, Mark had his three pieces in hand, with five hours to spare!

The next challenge was the fund-raising. Using a business plan he had already created, Mark began to call others who were familiar with the organization's work. He told them about his plan, described the brochures and asked for their specific financial support. The fire spread from one to the other and really caught on. After about five hours of calling and asking for help, *he had raised $8000!* Think about that. How often have you let lack of finances stop you from pursuing your dream? In five hours, he raised $8000. If Mark can do it, you can too.

Happy with the results he had achieved so far, and aware he was running out of time in his narrow deadline, Mark re-evaluated his plan. He realized he would need more time and resources to finish. He renegotiated his agreement with himself and decided to ask more people to help him. That night, he met with friends and showed them the three brochures and business plan, and requested their help. They agreed to support him in reaching his goal within 30 days, and applauded his victories so far.

Over the next month, he elaborated on the business plan. He then mailed it with the color copies of the brochures to a long list of people and asked for what he wanted, always sharing the fire of his enthusiasm. "Sometimes asking for what I wanted was a real stretch," said Mark. "Even though at times, the amount I was asking for seemed outrageous, I got it. When I asked with clarity and focus, I got results. If I didn't get specific about what I wanted, or if I wavered, I didn't get very much." He learned to be extremely focused and clear.

He also found that *believing makes it happen.* "I absolutely believed I could do it, and gave no thought to failure. I became somewhat obsessed with the project, which gave me energy. I also learned to continually take action and keep moving, being open to infinite ways to reach my goal." That faith and action paid off. In a month's time, he achieved his dream. *He raised $25,000 in one month and had everything ready for the promotional campaign. He was totally "FIRED UP!" about his success. He did it and you can too.*

Dolphins Work Miracles

🔥 At Dolphins Plus in Key Largo, Florida, the dolphin researchers have discovered that dolphins are powerful healing agents for disabled or sick people. Many times, parents and social workers turn to this organization when doctors can no longer help. One young boy had survived several heart operations, but was very introverted, lonely and silent. He had no friends and felt isolated and empty. His mother brought him to Dolphins Plus to participate in their treatment program.

After several months of feeding and playing with the dolphins, this young boy started talking, laughing and enjoying life. He happily fed the dolphins and rode on their fins. He spoke of how the dolphins were now his friends, and he no longer felt alone. Because of the healing, joyful energy of the dolphins, this boy's whole life had changed. The dolphins had slowly ignited the sparks of life and joy inside the boy.

Another case involved a 30 year old woman who had never spoken because she was severely withdrawn. She didn't smile, laugh or express herself in any way. She, too, entered the dolphin treatment program. She learned how to feed fish to the dolphins, how to play in the water and interact with these spontaneous, friendly creatures. Miraculously, after several months, she finally began to laugh and converse with both the dolphins and the trainers and social workers who knew her. The dolphins had stirred up the sparks inside her and got her "FIRED UP!" about life.

How Do People Do It?

So what is it that enables people to break through their barriers and achieve their dreams? In the stories just described, all the people had many of the same concerns and challenges you face every day. In fact, many of these people also had severe disabilities and health problems, and yet they remained "FIRED UP!" *What can we learn from their successes?* Some key tips apply to anyone seeking to bring a dream to life.

1. *In every case, the person took action.* They did something different than they had before. They changed their self-definition.

2. *Each asked for help in their own way.* They asked, and asked and asked again, clearly and with conviction.

3. *They were passionate about their dream* and their success. It was important to them and it got them "FIRED UP!" to take action.

4. *They faced their fears head-on and overcame them,* often with a great deal of help from others, as well as their own faith and courage.

5. *Taking the action and overcoming the obstacles resulted in joy.*

"FIRED UP!" PRINCIPLE # 33 – Expand Your Self-Definition

So what about you? I'm certain you have had more than one transcendent moment in your life. Perhaps you took Outward Bound or a similar course and scaled mountain faces. Maybe you flew hang-gliders. Or you may have survived a hurricane, tornado or flood. Or possibly you overcame an illness and beat the odds. You may have run in a marathon or given birth even though you were diagnosed as infertile. Whatever it is, you have already made remarkable progress in your life and you have had moments of triumph. Some would even say the fact that you are here today is a victory, since you survived the race of millions of sperm and ended up here.

Expanding Your Box Activity

Take ten minutes now and do this activity. Get yourself a pen or pencil and a piece of paper.

Step 1) Make two columns. On the left side, label the column "Experiences." *Make a list of any extraordinary experiences you have had in your life, any time when your self-definition changed.* These need not be new record setters, simply experiences which were new and exciting for you. All that matters is that they changed your self-perception. Give yourself credit for all you have accomplished in your life and observe how you have expanded your self-definition.

Review every area of your life: physical, personal, professional, academic, spiritual, arts-related, mental, psychological, romantic, financial. Have you had any notable athletic accomplishments? Have you started a business from scratch? Have you met what seemed like an impossible goal or deadline? How have you overcome your fear and triumphed? Have you ever tried skydiving or parasailing? Write it down. Give yourself credit for what you have already done.

Step 2) Now that you have your list, take a few minutes to read it over. On the right side of the page, head the column with the word "New Self-Definitions." Next to each experience, write the expanded self-perception that you gained from that experience. See the chart below for an example of how to do this.

EXPANDING YOUR SELF-DEFINITION

Experiences	New Self-Definitions
1. Did 10K road race.	Learned I could overcome pain and be strong; that I have stamina!
2. Raised $3,000 for cancer.	Learned to ask others for help for good cause and share about my brother's illness.
3. Started at home business.	Learned I can take risks and be an entrepreneur.
4. Became top distributor for first quarter in my region.	Saw I can share my enthusiasm for my products and get others excited, too.
5. Put on one day seminar for my group.	Learned I am a good organizer and networker. Others like my style and want to work with me.

Nothing listed here is a superhuman feat, and yet they are all important accomplishments. They expanded their self-definition and this enabled them to go on to greater things.

Selling Wheat to India

Corky Newcomb knows all about expanding his self-definition. When he was 23 years old, he had a brainstorm. He said to his friend, "Let's get some wheat and sell it to India." At the time, Corky was working in a hotel in Houston Texas in the sales department. Sooner or later, most everyone passes through a hotel, and eventually a wheat grower came in from Montana. He met at length with Corky and assured him that if Corky could get a contract from the Indian government, he could supply the wheat.

It seemed so simple. All Corky had to do was go sell the wheat. He already had great success selling Civil War bullets to Neiman Marcus and he felt like he was on a roll. As he later said, "Confidence is everything in everything."

He called the Indian Embassy in Washington DC and spoke to the Director of Trade Missions. He told the director that he wanted to help all the Indians dying of starvation. The director asked Corky the price per ton of wheat and Corky said it was negotiable. He flew to Washington the next day for a breakfast meeting. It was a worthwhile trip and he returned home encouraged.

The negotiations went back and forth for several weeks. Corky got totally "FIRED UP!" when the Indian government finally gave him a contract for 200,000 tons of wheat – over $40 million!

The Indian government wanted a $3 million performance bond which meant if the wheat wasn't on the docks when the ships arrived, the $3 million would be forfeited. After calling every banker in Houston, Corky persuaded one to take $3 million in warehouse receipts as collateral. Everything was in place.

Except for one thing. The price of milk suddenly dropped in the United States and people began shooting their cows. The price of wheat fell, and a big grain dealer caught wind of Corky's $40 million deal. The competitor came in the back door with a better price that Corky couldn't match. The whole deal fell through.

Corky never forgot the lessons of that experience, and he has applied them all as he built his multi-million dollar golf and toy business, C.N. Is Believing. He invented the Nitelite® Golfball and sold this novel concept to over 70 countries around the world. With an ever-expanding line of new and creative products for families and golfers, he is more successful than he ever dreamed. His philosophy is based on his favorite sport, baseball and it's very simple: "You win some and you lose some. But always remember that at least you got your turn at bat while most everyone else is sitting in the stands just watching life go by."

You have your turn at bat now. You have everything it takes and you've just realized there are several times in your life when you've already done something special. Great work! Take a break and reward yourself. Mark this page for future reference, so you can easily remind yourself of your earlier successes.

"Be realistic: Plan for a miracle.."
B. S. R.[11]

Remember These Key Points

◆ You can, like anyone else, do the seemingly impossible and transcend your previous limitations.

◆ You can achieve your dream. You have everything it takes to succeed– heart, determination, fire, enthusiasm, vision, intention and the ability to take action.

◆ Asking for what you want is essential to achieving any dream.

◆ Believing is key to making it happen.

◆ People who take action make their dreams come true. They stay "FIRED UP!" face their fears head-on and are rewarded with joy.

Now Take These "FIRED UP!" Action Steps

◆ If you haven't done so already, do the Expanding Your Self-Definition Activity.

◆ Read over your new self-definitions.

◆ Examine what new actions you could take to support your dream which would also expand your self-definition and get you "FIRED UP!"

"All life is a chance. So take it!
The person who goes furthest
is the one
who is willing to do
and dare."
Dale Carnegie

"Only those who dare, truly live."
Ruth P. Freedman

REACH

"Some dreams live on in time forever,
Those dreams, you want with all your heart.
And I'll do whatever it takes,
Follow through with the promise I made,
Put it all on the line,
What I hope for at last would be mine.

If I could reach, higher,
Just for one moment touch the sky,
For that one moment in my life...
I'm gonna be stronger.
Know that I've tried my very best,
I'd put my spirit to the test...
If I could reach, higher,
Some days are meant to be remembered.
Those days we rise above the stars.

So I'll go the distance this time.
Seeing more the higher I climb,
That the more I believe,
All the more that this dream will be mine...."

Gloria Estefan and Dianne Warren

For the 1996 Olympics

Chapter 24

How to Overcome Fear

Tending the Flames

*"I believe... that living on the edge, living in and through your
fear, is the summit of life, and that people who refuse to take the
dare condemn themselves to a life of
living death."*
John H. Johnson

Feel the Fear and Do It Anyway!

As you continue to take action on your dreams, you may
discover that even though you are completely "FIRED UP!" doubts
and apprehension still show up. Just like the people you have
read about, you can overcome those concerns and achieve your
dreams. *All you need to do now is identify your obstacles, be open to
solutions and rely on your own strengths to meet your fears head-on
and triumph over them.* As Susan Jeffers' book is titled, *Feel the Fear
and Do It Anyway.*

Here you'll learn how to conquer your fears once and for all,
realize your dream and become more "FIRED UP!" than ever. Each
person in the last chapter succeeded in part because they asked
for help and got others enthused about their dream. We are not

isolated beings. We need others to love, to be loved and to thrive. Now you, too, can ask for support in ways you may have never considered.

"FIRED UP!" PRINCIPLE # 34 – Take Risks and Be Rewarded

1) Choosing Your Dream Supporters – Make a list of people who know about your dream (preferably) and believe in you. They are positive thinking people who support and encourage you. They will give you honest feedback and support you in winning. Ideally, they are "FIRED UP!" about what *they're* doing and about *your* dream. Your dreambuddy would be an obvious choice, and there are probably several other people you can think of. All you need is three or four people who fit this description. (Be sure to eliminate anyone who might be threatened by or be jealous of your dream.) Only choose those who support you. It's sometimes best to exclude close family members, since there is so much emotional history between you.

Once you have picked your dream supporters, ask them if they would be willing to participate in a process which will help you achieve your dream. Always invite a couple of extra people in case someone can't make it. Invite them over for a two or three hour session at your home in the evening or on the weekend, and plan for privacy. This should be a time when you are alone with them without distractions or interruptions. Give yourself at least a week to get ready.

2) Creating Your "Feel Good Folder" – One of the best tools for staying "FIRED UP!" about your dream is a "Feel Good Folder." This is a folder, box or envelope which contains letters, cards, cartoons and symbols which you feel good about every time you see them. Some of the forms which you may have completed in this book could go in your "Feel Good Folder." Birthday cards, thank you notes, letters from people who have told you how much they value and appreciate you are other likely candidates.

Do a little detective work around your home and office to discover past victories and their symbols like awards, certificates, trophies and other items. Look for anything which inspires you or gets you "FIRED UP!" Photos of loved ones, daily success lists, pictures of vacation spots you'd like to visit and any cards which really touch your heart are other suggestions. It's especially important to include an *inventory of your strengths and positive traits* which will help you make your dream come true.

Take a few minutes now to write down your positive attributes. A good rule of thumb is to list at least 25 qualities that will support you in winning. Number your paper from 1 to 25 and let the ideas pop into your head. Be loving with yourself and acknowledge the great person you are. Once you've finished, read over the list and appreciate yourself.

3) Setting the Stage – Before anyone arrives, set the stage properly. *Imagine you are meeting with four people who have the ability to greatly assist you in achieving your dream.* Get yourself completely "FIRED UP!" to share your enthusiasm. Prepare the setting for just that opportunity. Get ready to excite them and get them "FIRED UP!" about how you can make your dream come true. Approach it as though you were making a major sales presentation on your dream to key potential contributors.

Bring out all your data and evidence for why this is important and why you can succeed. Display your dreammap and dream collage. Bring out any other visual symbols of your dream to contribute to the impact you want them to have. Review your expansion list of self-defining experiences from Chapter 23. Have some food and beverages available for everyone's enjoyment. Also provide pens, paper and a stopwatch. Put the answering machine on, get someone to babysit the kids elsewhere, put your pets in another room and plan to have an evening devoted to your dream. Just before everyone arrives, read over your list of unique strengths from number 2.

4) Sharing Your Dream – Your dream supporters have arrived; they've eaten and are comfortable. *Now it's time to get them all "FIRED UP!" Express your joy and enthusiasm about your dream.* Use your props, your dream collage and action plan and describe why this dream is so meaningful to you. Get them excited! Take your time and let your own energy build. Once you have shared fully and feel complete, request their help with the next three steps of the process. *Read the following statement to them out loud before you go on.* (Note – if you don't feel comfortable reading this to them, have them read the Dream Supporters' Instructions found in the Appendix on page 254.)

"Thank you for being here to support me in achieving my dream. Please offer information and feedback in as neutral and honest a manner as possible. Please raise any possible objections or obstacles to my dream in a neutral, calm voice. Thanks for your help."

5) Voicing the Objections – 2 minutes. Ask one of the guests to play the role of recorder and another to serve as timekeeper. Have the recorder write down all the objections that everyone offers. Be sure the recorder participates, too. *Now, face your fears and look at the possible obstacles to your dream.* Have the timekeeper start timing two minutes, and you begin first; list the obstacles that you might encounter. Be sure the recorder writes them down. Next, each Dream Supporter states potential objections.

After two minutes, the timekeeper says "stop," and everyone becomes quiet. No more listing of objections occurs, because you don't want to wallow in negativity or give energy to your fears. *The recorder reads back all the objections out loud, and you pick the top three; these are your greatest potential dreamstealers.* They are easy to identify; often you will experience a drop in the pit of your stomach, or a sense of despair when this objection is brought up. Have the recorder star those three.

6) Overcoming the Objections – 10 minutes. Read the following statement out loud to the Dream Supporters.

"Now it's time to be your most creative and encourage me to over-come my greatest obstacles. Offer as many different ideas and solutions to overcoming those top three obstacles, staying completely positive. Do not allow any negativity into the conversation; just keep brainstorming ideas. Avoid discussions of any one solution; suggest several. Be open and optimistic."

Once you are clear about the three main objections, your Dream Supporters can be a rich resource for you. Have the recorder write down all the solutions to the obstacles as people say them. Take one objection at a time, allowing three minutes for each one. Timekeeper begins. You start with the first one. Give some solutions to that obstacle; how could you overcome it? What could you do? Brainstorm and be creative. Don't censor yourself; mention any ideas that pop into your head. Again, your Dream Supporters contribute. One by one, they all tackle each objection as a group, brainstorming as many different ways to overcome it as possible. The recorder writes down all the solutions and elaborates when appropriate. You offer suggestions to meet each challenge first, and then the group jumps in. At the end of this step, you have three sheets of paper with a variety of ways to overcome each obstacle. These will help keep you "FIRED UP!" and on track.

7) Positive Feedback – 6 minutes. Read to the Dream Supporters:

"You have done a great job. Now is the time to bolster me and give me as much encouragement as possible. Please give me positive feedback, telling me all the reasons why you know I will succeed, and all the good qualities you admire about me. Share from your heart honestly and enthusiastically. Only say positive things and speak generously. Recorder, please continue to write down all the positive comments and share your ideas, too.

Now sit in front of your Dream Supporters. The timekeeper starts, and one by one, each person tells you how much they believe in you and how they admire you. They describe your positive qualities, especially the ones which will help you make your dream come true. Gracefully receive all their feedback. Let their words touch your heart, so you feel renewed and revitalized in your purpose.

When they have finished appreciating you, the recorder gives you the written feedback sheets. You thank your Dream Supporters and describe how much this whole experience has meant to you. Tell them you will keep them informed of your progress as you move forward on your dream.

Express your gratitude again and change the subject to something completely different; just share time together as friends. Do not go back to the objections or discuss your dream anymore during this gathering. Just allow all the valuable information and feedback to smolder inside you. If your flames haven't ignited already, they will ignite later on. Hold the dream close to your heart and let it take shape. Congratulations!

After Your Dream Supporters Leave

Risk and Reward Waterfall Visualization

Go to a room where you will have some private uninterrupted time. You can either dictate this into a tape recorder and play it back for yourself or picture it as you read. Choose whatever works best for you.

Take three deep breaths and relax. Close your eyes. In your imagination, find yourself walking in a very beautiful place outside. It may be the same place you have visited before or a brand new one. You feel totally safe, relaxed and perfectly protected. As you walk, the sun warms your skin, the fresh scents fill your nose and peace envelopes you.

As you continue on the path, you feel a sense of anticipation and eagerness. You find a new area in this beautiful outdoor setting. You hear the rush of water, and as you get closer, you spy a breathtakingly magnificent waterfall. It glistens in the sunlight as it cascades down gently. It's a glorious sight with the water sparkling magnificently in the sunlight. *You realize there is something very special about this waterfall.* You decide to take a swim. Magically, as you step into the water, your clothes come off and you are wearing whatever you wish. As you submerge below the surface, you discover the water and air temperature are perfect. Even if you couldn't swim before, you find that now you can, with ease and grace. You glide through the water, frolicking in the bubbles.

Amazingly, the more time you spend in the waterfall pool, the better you feel. Any aches and pains that may have been in your muscles are gone; you feel vibrantly alive and healthier than ever. You glimpse an area of the waterfall that is particularly brilliant; it has little stars sparkling all around it. You go over to it and notice a little ledge to perch on where the water cascades over you.

Incredibly, the waterfall washes away any doubts, fears, feelings of unworthiness and all old limiting programming. *Any negativity or fear is completely cleansed. Forgiveness and happiness flood your heart; clarity and wisdom fill your mind.* Your body feels energized and powerful; better than you've ever felt before. You allow that sensation to encompass you. You tell yourself you're worthy of wonderful things, like success and peace. You believe you are powerful and creative, making your dream come true. You become more and more energized and refreshed. It's as though you have a brand new perspective– a fresh start on life. You feel "FIRED UP!" and deeply in touch with the dream that lights up your heart.

Slowly, you swim out from that ledge towards land. As you step out of the water, you find you are instantly dry, with your original clothes back on. You feel great, as though you've had a fabulous therapeutic massage, eaten one of the best meals of your life and are ready to tackle any task. *You know in the deepest part of yourself that you can stay "FIRED UP!" achieve your dream and make a positive difference in the world.* You know you have unique gifts to share with others and are eager to do so. Take three deep breaths and completely experience that terrific feeling. When you're ready, mentally come back to the room, open your eyes and savor the sensations.

Congratulations. Well done. Take some time now to reward yourself by watching uplifting movies. Some good ones to consider are *Angels in the Outfield, Flashdance, Mrs. Doubtfire, Field* of *Dreams* and *The Boy Who Could Fly.* All these have positive, inspirational themes, and most of them will make you laugh and celebrate the hero's victory.

Doing the Risk and Reward Process Alone

The process you went through with your Dream Supporters is a powerful tool to use whenever you're pursuing a dream or goal. If you later want to approach another dream by yourself and are unable to get your Dream Supporters together, you can do the process alone and still find it worthwhile. However, first have the experience with your Dream Supporters before doing this alone.

Here are the steps for a "Do It Yourself Risk and Reward Process."

1) Review Your "Feel Good" Folder – Take some time to look over the contents and bask in your own good feelings. Allow yourself to get "FIRED UP!"

2) Set the Stage for Yourself – Get out your dream collage, your dreammap, a timer, some blank action plans, some blank risk and reward sheets from the Appendix and lined paper and pens. Make sure you won't be disturbed for at least two hours.

Step 3) State Your Dream in Writing – Using a blank action plan, write the description of your dream in the top section. If you have a strong image of your dream – write out the one, three and five year descriptions. Let your imagination ignite the fire inside.

Step 4) Listing Objections – Set the timer for one and a half minutes. Now, write down many of the obstacles you think may exist between you and your dream. Just jot them down quickly on paper and don't mull them over. Stop at one minute and thirty seconds. Don't give any energy to these; just be aware of them.

Step 5) Overcome the Objections – Start by selecting the top three that really affect you. These are the most important ones to overcome. Now, one by one, taking about three minutes per objection, create a dreammap with as many solutions as possible as you brainstorm how to overcome them. Do this for all three objections. If you get stuck, take a few minutes to sit quietly and go back to your beautiful spot in nature. Invite three people you consider quite successful and for whom you have great respect. They can be living or dead. Dreamers often envision individuals like Einstein, Edison, Lincoln, Martin Luther King or Amelia Earhart – depending on the dream. Ask each of them for their advice on how to overcome your obstacles. Listen carefully to what each has to say and write down their ideas. Their suggestions can be quite accurate and helpful; so use this resource.

Step 6) Positive Feedback – This is the time to pull out your "Feel Good Folder" and review your positive traits list. It's also helpful to return to your beautiful scene in nature and ask those three individuals to appear again, the ones you admire so much. One by one each of them comes forward. They tell you what qualities you have in common with them, and that you will be successful with your dream. They give you wonderful insights into yourself, and they believe in you fully. Take the time to completely receive their feedback; make notes on what they had to say and appreciate your own talents and abilities in a whole new light.[12]

Excellent work. You now have the tools to overcome any challenge and stay "FIRED UP!" about your dream. Remember, you are a gifted individual with much to share. *Your dream can light up the hearts of others. Share it and make it come true.*

Remember These Key Points

◆ A "Feel Good Folder" is a great way to bolster you self-esteem and get you "FIRED UP!" about your dream and your life.
◆ Like the people in the last chapter, you can overcome any fears as well as obstacles to your dream.
◆ Asking Dream Supporters is an excellent way to develop creative solutions for any challenges to your dream.
◆ Positive feedback from your Dream Supporters can be a useful reference for you as you take action and triumph over challenges.

Now Take These "FIRED UP!" Action Steps

◆ If you have not done so already, review your list of friends and associates and gather your Dream Supporters to help you with your dream.
◆ Prepare yourself for a Risk and Reward session and arrange a time with your Dream Supporters to do the process in this chapter.
◆ After you have done the process, be sure to complete it by doing the Waterfall Visualization.
◆ Reflect back on all the positive work you have done and all the support you have for your dream.

COURAGE

*"Go after your dream
with a sense of entitlement.
Know that you have the power to
achieve it
and that you deserve it.
Be willing to get up into life's face,
grab it by the collar and say,
'Give it up! It's my dream.'"*
Les Brown

*"Come to the edge, he said.
They said, we are afraid.
Come to the edge, he said.
They came.
He pushed them... and they flew."*
Guillaume Apollinaire

Chapter 25

Avoid Dream-Delaying Hooks

Keep Smoldering Embers Alive

*"Giving means extending one's love with no conditions,
no expectations and no boundaries. Peace of mind occurs,
therefore, when we put all our attention into giving and have
no desire to get anything from, or to change, another person.
The giving motivation leads to a sense of inner peace and joy
that is unrelated to time."*
Gerald Jampolsky

"FIRED UP!" PRINCIPLE # 35 – Avoid the Hooks

Do you remember the old vaudeville acts where a performer would be all "FIRED UP!" singing or dancing, and a giant hook would come out and grab the person in mid-act? Or perhaps you've seen the comedy "The Gong Show," where judges would gong the entertainer if they didn't like him. That entertainer's dream of performing would be over, at least for that show. That's what is meant by the term "hooks" to avoid. They're the real life hooks you can get snagged by. They can only douse the flames of your enthusiasm and discourage you from going further on your dream, if you let them. *With your advance awareness of these hooks, you can prevent them from stopping you.*

While people's dreams vary, many want to directly touch others' lives in a positive way. They want to have personal contact with those who benefit from their products or work and experience the results. They can't afford to let dream-delaying hooks get in the way. Here are some examples.

Empowering Inner City Youth

Geoffrey Canada grew up in South Bronx, New York, a poor young man without warm clothes for winter. His father had left home when he was three, but his mother steadfastly tutored her sons and slowly earned a master's degree from Harvard herself. Geoffrey excelled in school, moved to Maine when he was 15 and earned a scholarship to Bowdoin College, where he did his undergraduate work. Later he attended Harvard's Graduate School of Education, and then taught inner-city children in Boston.

Geoffrey decided he wanted to make a direct impact on the city where he was raised. He returned to Harlem to head the Rheedlen Center for Children and Families, which is devoted to salvaging the lives of needy youngsters. Based mostly in public schools, the Rheedlen program provides tutoring assistance, help with homework and recreational programs for qualified children five years old and older. Social workers handle drug and parent counseling. Emergency food and clothing are given to families in crisis. Every year, over 2000 students benefit from the program, and from Geoffrey's own involvement. He teaches martial arts to the children as a form of non-violent self-defense and self-discipline. He cares deeply about the children he works with and feels tremendous satisfaction when he helps others. [13]

Children Preventing Crime

When she was ten years old, Linda Warsaw-Champin saw first-hand how crime can destroy lives. Burglars ransacked her home, leaving her feeling helpless. To do something about her anger, she and her mother started volunteering at a Victim-Witness Assistance Program, where she met dozens of victims of child abuse. She felt outraged, and decided, that even as a youngster, she could take action.

She collected a folder full of crime prevention ideas, information on child safety and addresses and phone numbers of law enforcement and child abuse assistance agencies. She then talked to her junior high school classmates about creating a crime-busters group, and they responded enthusiastically. They designed T-shirts and posters with their own "Kids Against Crime" logo. The group became active in crime prevention by attending trials and inviting guest speakers to their meetings. They acted out plays about gangs, smoking, drugs and molestation. Today, the "Kids Against Crime" group offers a national teen hot line, child fingerprinting, a drop-in center, graffiti clean-ups and crime prevention education. In seven and a half years, memberships have gone from 19 to 4700 worldwide. [14]

Both of these dreams have people as a key component, on the giving and receiving ends. Other people must be involved for the dream to be fully realized. For those whose dream is to help others, it is especially vital to avoid dream-delaying hooks.

Hook # 1 – Anticipated Outcomes

As Richard Bach wrote in *Illusions,* "*If your happiness depends on what somebody else does, ... you do have a problem.*" The outcome of service can never be fully guaranteed or anticipated. If people who are helping others let their self-esteem be affected by how the helpee responds, there can be disappointments.

If Geoffrey Canada, the man who heads the Rheedlen Center, would have his self-esteem tied to whether or not the children in his program succeed, he could easily be let down. As much as he gives his best effort, he won't be able to protect every child in the program, or ensure they all get a good education. If he measured his self-worth by his children's actions, that would be a serious mistake.

In the case of Linda Warsaw-Champin, founder of "Kids Against Crime," she knows that crime all against children is not going to end as a result of her program. It will help, and it will make a difference, but it won't wipe out the problem. She would be foolish to have her feeling of satisfaction about her program and her self-esteem tied into the goal of completely eliminating crimes against children.

The approach to take when you are working on a dream which involves others is always to maintain the philosophy of "for the greatest benefit of all concerned." That way, there are no hooks, and you can give your best without attachment to the outcome. This is sometimes referred to as "high commitment, low investment." You work on your dream; you give it your full effort, but you are not devastated if things don't turn out the way you hoped.

You are "FIRED UP!" and share your vision, but are open to what is best for everyone in the situation. This is a bit tricky. But you need to maintain determination and persist in seeing the dream through. And at the same time, remain uninvested in the final outcome. How do you do this?

Part of the key is to have targeted results which are measurable and enable you to see that the work you do is helping others. Another part is *to realize that if you have touched even one person with your efforts, your work has been worthwhile.* Make your daily success lists, acknowledge baby steps and microscopic changes, along with your bigger accomplishments. Realize that even small achievements add up to significant improvements over time, because it's a process.

Hook #2 - Expecting a Specific Response

Another hook is waiting for a particular response from those being helped. At a Dunn and Bradstreet seminar called "Managing Multiple Priorities," which I took many years ago, the trainer said something very profound: *"Other people's behavior is always about them."* This struck me right between the eyes. Up until that time, I had naively and egotistically thought that my actions were what caused other people to behave the way they did. Once I perceived how true this statement was, that other people behave a certain way because of what is going on in *their* lives, it gave me a great deal of freedom to just be myself and not be upset by the behavior of others.

The boss may not be yelling because he's unhappy with your job performance; he may have just had a fight with his wife and is venting his anger. The child in the cancer wing who won't smile at a volunteer's funny stories may be too sick from chemotherapy to notice anything else. The homeless person who received the coat someone donated may not say thank you because of their shame about being homeless. The prospective buyer of your product or service may decline simply because they might not have the money in their budget. *Other people's behavior is always about them.* It's important to remember that when you are serving and reaching out to others. *Don't take on their emotional reactions as a personal affront. Stay focused on where you're going and feel good about what you are doing, regardless of how others react.*

Hook # 3 – Martyrdom

Webster defines a martyr as *"one who sacrifices his life or something of great value for the sake of principle."* No matter how much your dream means to you, it's not worth you sacrificing your life or health. Behave differently than Joan of Arc, who did everything for others without taking care of herself. It is self-destructive to spend your mortgage money on a good cause. It is not constructive to spend every waking moment at the local battered women's shelter if you are neglecting your own family. It isn't effective to spend so much time doing community service that you don't get your job done at work, causing you to be fired.

The interesting thing about martyrdom is that it's really very selfish, because it keeps one or more people dependent on the martyr and forces a connection that may otherwise not be there. There have been stories about invalids who truly despise their nurses, because they detect the attitude of righteousness and pity which the nurses carry. Righteousness is offensive; it means that someone thinks they're right and someone else is definitely wrong. It's more constructive to focus on the positive aspects of your dream and not condemn anyone else. That will keep you "FIRED UP!" and moving.

In general, an intelligent approach is *to take care of yourself first so that then you can take care of others.* It's not wise for someone to risk their health by working at all hours to help those less fortunate. People are most resourceful and useful when they are healthy and secure. Sacrificing your own livelihood and well-being just to aid others is martyrdom and is unwise. This is a common syndrome among teachers and doctors who work several shifts because they care so much about assisting others.

Managers and leaders sometimes have the same problem; they spend so much time helping their people that they neglect themselves. The problem here is they could burn out and then wouldn't be able to help anyone, including themselves. Balance is the key, as well as taking care of yourself. You may wonder how to resist constant requests for more and more of your time. It may sound trite, but *learn to say "no."* Tell the truth. You are much more effective when you've had rest, and that you are of little to no good to anyone when you're sick. Tell them that you'll return after you have taken care of yourself; then keep your agreement.

Hook # 4 – Quitting Too Soon

When you have a large or complex dream, it may take time and considerable effort to achieve it. Building a big business, writing a book, creating a brand new program for children are all examples of long-term dreams. What happens sometimes is that the dreamer quits too soon, maybe just short of achieving their dream. Remember when we talked about the circle of completion, and how some people never complete? *They rob themselves of the significant satisfaction and burst of energy which results from completion.* Sometimes they quit because they are impatient, or because they are not seeing the results they want fast enough. Another reason they may quit is they allow their finite box of self-definition to limit them. As Winston Churchill once said *"Never, never, never, never give in...."*

Les Brown, nationally recognized author, speaker and television personality recounts a compelling story about his childhood. At a young age, he was misdiagnosed "educable mentally retarded." He was put into classrooms with slower children and told of his limitation. As many children do, he bought into their definition of him.

The turning point in his life came in high school, when he went to meet a buddy in another classroom. The teacher, who didn't know Les, asked him to write something on the board. Les said he couldn't because he was "educable mentally retarded." The teacher said he never wanted to hear Les use those words again, and told him, "Someone's opinion of you does not have to become your reality." The teacher believed in Les and worked with him, showing Les that he was, in fact, intelligent and capable.

Les later went on to work at an area radio station, as an errand boy. With persistence, his dream of being a radio disc jockey paid off. His vision at that time was to be a great on-air talent. By watching, learning and practicing, he knew exactly what he would do when he got the chance. He held on to his dream, and then one day, it paid off. The disc jockey on the air was drunk; the station manager heard him and asked Les to replace him and simply play records without saying a word. Les was ready; he was hungry. He was truly "FIRED UP!" He knew what he wanted and he went for it.

When he got in the studio, he turned up the mic and said, "Look out, this is BLB, Triple P, Les Brown, your platter-playing pappa, there were none before me, and there will be none after me, therefore that makes me the one and only. Young and single, and love to mingle, certified, bona fide, indubitably qualified to bring you satisfaction, a whole lot of action. Look out baby, I'm your love man."

His on-air demonstration of talent launched his professional career. He's now nationally renowned as an uplifting, motivational speaker and celebrity. If he had quit, in high school, at that radio station, or even at any of the dozens of other goal points in his career, he would not have the success he enjoys today. [15]

Hook #5 – Overlooking Small Victories along the Way

We all need to know we are making progress on our goals. We may be impatient with the process and want to see immediate results. Our culture is into instant gratification – buy now, pay later. Television teaches you that weight loss can be instant and permanent with this or that product. Commercials show that the right breath mint can attract a new love. Most dreams take time to come true; most require multiple steps to take full shape. Success is a process.

Charting daily successes will keep you "FIRED UP!" and motivated, so that you know you're on your way. If, for example, a physical therapist felt like a failure because his patient with a broken leg wasn't able to walk normally in one day, he would be missing the big picture. Most dreams take time to come true; most require long-term consistent action to be realized. *Recognizing the progress along the way is imperative – it's a key piece of completion.*

Take stock of your dreams and goals each day, and give yourself credit for all the action steps you took. This will help you to stay "FIRED UP!" and keep the flame inside you alive. It will also let you know how far you've come, and that makes the flames burn bright and tall.

"Your dream is God's gift to you."
Robert H. Schuller

Remember These Key Points

◆ Advance awareness of hooks that can douse your flames prevents you from buying into them.
◆ Make sure your happiness and self-esteem does not depend on the actions of others; create your own happiness and self-esteem inside yourself.
◆ Approach any dream or goal from the standpoint of "the greatest benefit of all concerned."
◆ Remember, "Other people's behavior is always about them."
◆ Don't be a martyr and sacrifice yourself; take care of yourself first so you can take care of others.
◆ Never quit! Keep going and give yourself credit for every step along the way.

Now Take These "FIRED UP!" Action Steps

◆ Look over your dream descriptions. Notice if any of the hooks in this chapter apply to you, and take action to avoid them.
◆ Take two actions today toward your dream.
◆ Acknowledge the successes you've had this week. Write them down and give yourself credit.

Chapter 26

Stay Expansive

Building the Fire Bigger

"When we do something new, something different, we push against the parameters of our comfort zone. If we do the new thing often enough, we overcome the fear, guilt, unworthiness, hurt feelings and anger – and our comfort zone expands."
John-Roger

Expand Rather than Contract

Remaining "FIRED UP!" while pursuing your dream is an ongoing challenge that requires conscious awareness. Monitoring your progress is useful, but knowing what keeps your fire burning and energizes you is even more valuable. Contraction is a word that makes most women think of labor pains, and in fact, *contraction is painful.* It generally means reduction or shortening, pulling in and shutting down. Relative to your dream, it means an emotional state which is less than positive.

All of us have had times in our lives which cause contraction. Losing a sale, getting hurt physically or emotionally, being criticized; we generally respond to these with contraction. The natural human reaction is to turn inward and lick our wounds.

However, there is a much more effective way of dealing with contraction. *Shift into expansion – look for the lesson in the contractive experience and grow from it.*

This story demonstrates the point. To most people, witnessing war-torn Bosnia would be contractive. Seeing all the people suffering and children who were orphaned would melt almost anyone's heart, like it did Gerry McClure's. She and her mother visited Bosnia in 1993 for two weeks, supplying badly needed medical supplies to a refugee center. Gerry was deeply affected by the children's pain. When she returned, her father's diagnosis of terminal cancer further shook her; she knew she needed to do something to make a difference.

Inspiration came to her in a dream and led to the birth of a new business specifically *designed to benefit children.* She started Heaven on Earth, Inc., a company which manufactures several different multiracial and non-denominational dolls meant to represent guardian angels. A minimum 10% of pretax profits are donated to worldwide charities. Each "Angel Gram" doll's tag reads, *"This angel comes to you from above with the message of joy and God's love."* The dolls are available in black, white and Hispanic, with Asian dolls soon to be released, each one also has a cassette of the song, "Your Angel's Always There," an angel pendant for the child to wear, a *Little Book of Angels* and a map showing where donations from Heaven on Earth have gone around the world. With six employees and revenues of over $1 million, the business has been able to donate monies and supplies to the Croatian Emergency Relief Fund, the Children's Welfare Institute in China and International God-Parenthood to Bosnian Children, among others. Gerry's contractive experience led to her realizing that *she wanted to share love and give a sense of hope to others.* 16

What's Contractive and Expansive for You?

As you work on your dream, identify which activities are contractive and which are expansive for you. This will help you be more aware and stay "FIRED UP!" in the direction you want to go. Spending more time in an expansive state will enable you to think bigger, do more and create better results. It keeps your fire blazing.

Expansive actions are those which help you feel larger, more powerful, more successful and more competent. For some people, an expansive action might be viewing an uplifting movie, getting a hug or going dancing. For others, it might mean doing something you have never done before, just for the thrill of it.

These are in sharp contrast to *contractive activities – those actions which make you shut down, feel small, tight, depressed or incompetent.* Watching violent TV shows, spending time complaining about things, criticizing others; all these tend to contract people.

Choose Expansive Activities

Knowing what is expansive and contractive for you assists you in making conscious shifts in behavior and attitude by purposely seeking expansive activities, especially when you're a little tired or depressed. In general, *people who are the most effective in achieving their dreams and staying "FIRED UP!" regularly participate in expansive activities and avoid or transform contractive behavior.*

Consciously choosing which movie to see on the weekend is an example of how this awareness works. If you choose a particularly gruesome horror film, you may have nightmares and feel a sense of free-floating anxiety. On the other hand, when you select a funny movie where you laugh and relax, your body and mind will be freer and more comfortable. You will also be healthier; there is clinical evidence to show that laughter is healing to the body. Doing exercise you enjoy is much more valuable than doing exercise that you loathe. Spending time with upbeat, supportive friends is of more benefit than visiting the office whiners. All of these are the kinds of choices we make daily.

Here is a way to help you determine what is expansive or contractive for you. A series of activities is listed with a blank next to each one. It's important to note that there are no wrong or right answers; there is only information. The same action may be expansive to some, yet contractive to others.

Expansive or Contractive Activities Exercise

Put E in the blank for Expansive if it expands you when you do it, and a C in the blank if this activity is Contractive for you.

_____Exercising	_____Going to a seminar
_____Being under pressure	_____Dancing
_____Rushing to get somewhere	_____Jogging
_____Making a sale	_____Paying bills
_____Going sailing	_____Hugging

_____Paperwork	_____Budgeting
_____Meditating	_____Staying indoors
_____Being in nature	_____Playing with children
_____Visiting parents	_____Doing errands
_____Watching funny movies	_____Writing letters
_____Being judged	_____Making love
_____Taking a hot bath	_____Singing
_____Swimming	_____Listening to music
_____Traveling	_____Arguing
_____Smiling	_____Reading
_____Reading the paper	_____Watching the news
_____Grocery shopping	_____Cooking
_____Doing the laundry	_____Painting or drawing
_____Starting a new project	_____Completing a project
_____Eating	_____Playing basketball
_____Serving others	_____Crying
_____Therapy	_____Sharing successes
_____Daydreaming	_____Cleaning out the closet
_____Seeing friends	_____Playing with pets

Now that you've completed the list, you can learn more about yourself. Some people love to do the laundry because it's a completion, with clean clothes as the result. Others view it as a chore. Some dread making sales calls and others look forward to it with eager anticipation because they are excited about their products or services and where they're going. You may have also found that the answer might have depended on specifics. Seeing certain friends might be expansive; while seeing other friends might be contractive. Meditating and contemplating are usually relaxing for most people, but if you are just learning and don't feel like you're doing them correctly, they may be contractive for a while.

There are moments when paperwork can be really satisfying, and other times when it simply stacks up and you may feel overwhelmed. *All that matters here is that you learn what works for you.* I recommend you highlight all the "E" Expansive activities in your favorite color and keep the list for future reference. Be sure to add other activities that are expansive for you that are not on the list. These are reference points for when you need to get "FIRED UP!"

Any time you find yourself contracting, learn from the experience and deliberately do an expansive activity. Better than that, plan your day around the kinds of experiences you would like to have; those that stir your sparks and set you on fire.

🔥 For me, some of my most expansive experiences have involved travel and exploration. I studied a little art and sculpture in prep school. (My mother had been an artist when she was healthy.) I was looking forward to seeing the work of Michelangelo when I visited Italy. But no one could have prepared me for my reaction to Michelangelo's David. This mammoth sculpture is in Florence, and I wasn't even sure where in the museum it was located. Flipping through my guidebook, I wandered from room to room until I entered the hall where the David is showcased. I took one look and burst into tears. It was spectacular. I didn't expect to react like that – but I felt the incredible power and beauty of the statue. I remembered Michelangelo had said that he had simply cut the rock away to reveal the David.

Years later, I had a similar experience in Paris. The impressionist paintings of Renoir and Monet used to be housed in a quaint museum called Le Jeu du Pomme. When I climbed the stairs and came face to face with Monet's sailing paintings, again, I started crying. I don't know what came over me; I don't usually burst into tears. I was just deeply moved by the beauty and magnificence of what I was witnessing. These were expansive activities for me and are treasured memories.

You may have had moments like these. When we choose our activities wisely with the intention of staying open and expansive, we are much more likely to be moving forward gracefully. Our dreams can be attained much more easily. The fire can be stoked at every level, and the blaze can burn brighter and brighter.

"Thoughts are things; they have tremendous power.
Thoughts of doubt and fear are pathways to failure.
When you conquer negative attitudes of doubt and fear, you
conquer failure. Thoughts crystallize into habit and habit
solidifies into circumstances."
Brian Adams

Remember These Key Points

◆ The most effective way to deal with contraction is to shift into expansion and look for the lesson from the contraction.
◆ Contractive activities are those actions which make you shut down, feel small, tight, depressed or incompetent.
◆ Expansive actions get you "FIRED UP!" and help you feel more powerful, successful and victorious.
◆ The most successful people regularly schedule in expansive activities and transform contractive ones.
◆ Learning what works for you helps you stay "FIRED UP!"

Now Take These "FIRED UP!" Action Steps

◆ If you have not done so already, complete the expansive and contractive activity in this chapter.
◆ Schedule expansive activities into your time management system.
◆ Ask a friend or partner to help you transform a contractive experience into an expansive one by looking for the lessons and changing the outcome.

Chapter 27

28 Tips for Staying "FIRED UP!"

Keep the Fire Burning

"We are built to conquer environment, solve problems,
achieve goals;
and we find no real satisfaction or happiness in life
without obstacles to conquer and goals to achieve."
Maxwell Maltz

"FIRED UP!" PRINCIPLE # 36 – Use Tools to Stay "FIRED UP!"

You've read stories about famous athletes and heroes who kept going no matter what, stayed "FIRED UP!" and achieved their dreams. Even those skilled in personal development have times when it's more difficult to stay motivated, and that's what this chapter is all about. It's chock full of tips which will help you get "FIRED UP!" and stay "FIRED UP!" Use them regularly, especially if you are stuck. If one doesn't do it for you, try another until you get going again. The important thing is to keep moving and keep igniting the sparks of your fire.

Count Your Blessings

Before you review these keys, *consider your many blessings, write them down and be grateful for them.* No matter what your circumstances are, there are positive aspects to your life, as the following story illustrates.

🔥 Becky Ferry is a teenage girl who knows all about what it takes to be a champion. She cares for Jersey cows on the family farm, many of which are blue ribbon winners. What is extraordinary is not that the cows are winners or even that Becky takes great pleasure in their victories. What is noteworthy is Becky's winning attitude after all the tragedy she has faced in her young life.

When she was nine years old, Becky's coat caught on the spinning shaft of a machine that unloads corn from a wagon. Before anyone could stop the machine, she suffered multiple fractures of both her knees and legs. The only safe medical solution was amputation.

Incredibly, the first thing Becky asked when she came out of surgery was, "Will I be able to show cows again?" Her enthusiasm and "FIRED UP!" attitude have carried her a long way, through the grueling months of rehabilitation and physical therapy. She has been fitted with prosthetics, but finds them unwieldy for farm work. When working with her beloved cows, she prefers to wear her "stubbies"– short wide rubber platforms which give her stability and balance but not height.

In spite of her physical disability, she maintains a B average at school and works with the cows ten hours a day. She recently learned to swim again, and looks forward to a future filled with promise, including raising heifers. Her favorite cow, Sunny, a honey colored Jersey, earned the coveted "Farmer's Museum Dairy Cup." *Becky accepted the award with joy; she was truly grateful and "FIRED UP!" That's her fundamental outlook on life and it keeps her going every day.* We could all learn a great deal from Becky's attitude.[17]

Remember This

🔥 Wilma Rudolph, the first woman runner to win three gold medals at a single Olympic event, overcame severe physical disabilities to become an athlete. At four, she was struck with double pneumonia and scarlet fever, losing the use of her left leg. Her family had a "FIRED UP!" attitude, though and began massaging her leg four times a day. By age eleven, she was able to run normally and by high school, she was an outstanding athlete. As a black Southern woman, her challenges were many. But she beat them all to triumph at the Olympics and be named to the Women's Sports Hall of Fame.

Ski instructor Pete Seibert was called crazy when he told others about his dream. From age 12 on, he had the dream of building a top level ski resort in Colorado. Without money, but with lots of vision and focus, he enrolled others in his dream, got them "FIRED UP!"and went on to create and develop one of the most famous resorts in the United States – Vail, Colorado.

Quick Tips For Staying "FIRED UP!"

1. Identify what **you truly want** in your life.
2. **Dreambuild** regularly.
3. **Keep agreements** with yourself and others.
4. Update your **dream collage** and regularly **visualize your dream as completed.**
5. Maintain a **daily success list.**
6. Review and update your **"Feel Good Folder."**
7. Keep a **reward/pamper yourself jar** and use it whenever you take action on your dream.
8. Update your **"FIRED UP!" Action Plan** or make a new one.
9. Update your **"Expanding Your Self -Definition"** list.
10. **Be of service** to someone else.
11. **Ask, ask, ask** for what you want.
12. **Schedule action steps for your dream** in your time management system.
13. Attend **seminars or take courses** about the subject matter of your dream.
14. **Interview experts** in the field of your dream and select a mentor.
15. Say your **affirmations** daily. Make new ones as they come true.
16. Watch **motivational movies**, listen to **audiotapes & read uplifting books.**
17. **Live in the present moment.**
18. **Use music** to inspire, relax or energize yourself.
19. Use all your **resources.**
20. **Play regularly** – honor the little kid inside.
21. **Exercise** in a way that supports you.
22. **Laugh often** and watch funny movies or shows.
23. Spend time with **winners.**
24. Create a **"FIRED UP!" Inspiration Circle.** Meet once a month.
25. Do **random acts of kindness.**
26. Do some sort of **spiritual practice daily.**
27. **Celebrate success and spread joy.**
28. **Tell your story and ask others about theirs.**

Detailed explanations of each tip follow on the next several pages. These are tried and true ways to stay "FIRED UP!" Look for those which most appeal to you, and perhaps they will lead you to new ones. *What matters is that you use everything for your continued growth and advancement, to keep moving and growing towards your dream. Get "FIRED UP!" Stay "FIRED UP!" and live your dream.*

1. Identify What You Truly Want in Your Life

Periodically, update your wish list for life. Often, we change faster than we realize, and what was once important to us no longer is. College majors are good examples. Many students pick a major as a freshman, and choose another by their junior year. It's not unusual for someone to go all the way through school and find that their major is not what they want to do after all. The same may well be true in your life. You may be ready for a change now. Your career may be something totally new a decade from now, and your life's work may shift substantially.

Consider the story of Larry Koning, an obstetrician/gynecologist who is also a Diamond Direct Distributor. As Larry's wife said, "Doctors are ripped away from family life by that crazy beeper." Larry was putting in 60-80 hours a week as a physician and rarely saw Julie or his children. Larry, too, became chagrined at the changes in the medical profession and reordered his life. "You set your priorities and figure out that there are more important things than just being a big-shot physician. Thank heaven [this] came along at the right time for us to focus on where we really want to go in life."

He and Julie successfully run their business together and he spends only half a week at his medical profession. It's the best of both worlds for him, since he can now meet his sons for baseball practice and spend quality time playing with them. Larry believes his products and optimistic attitude provide as many healing benefits as medicine. Clearly, Larry's entire orientation shifted as he became disenchanted with medicine and more excited about the flexibility his business offered him as it helped him balance his life.[18]

Remember the technique from Robert Fritz about listing the things you have in your life which you don't want? (You can review it in Chapter 3.) Every once in a while, make a new list to see where you are. It will help keep you clear about what you truly value and get you "FIRED UP!" about life.

2. Dreambuild Regularly

It's important to dreambuild as often as you can. Whenever the urge strikes you, go drive your dream car. Go tour houses you'd like to live in. Go to car shows, boat shows, air shows, hobby shows and the like, to stay in touch with your dream and meet other dreamers. Do this regularly to keep yourself "FIRED UP!" for where you're going. These activities are inexpensive, don't take much time and can be critical for you to keep going.

3. Keep Agreements with Yourself and Others

Agreements are described throughout this book. *Remember every commitment you make to yourself and others is an agreement, even if you don't say it aloud.* Every time you break an agreement, you are sabotaging yourself and hurting your self-esteem. *If you find your life just isn't working, take a look at your agreements.* Complete them or renegotiate them. Write them down in your time management system. Don't commit to agreements you aren't sure you'll be able to keep.

4. Update Your Dream Collage and Regularly Visualize Your Dream as Completed

Your dream collage or treasure map is a dynamic tool for actually seeing your dream come to life. To many people, seeing is believing. Look at your collage daily to help you believe through seeing. Update it regularly with current pictures, words and symbols as you find your dream manifesting. Either enhance your dream collage or replace it.

Throughout this book, there are a series of visualizations. *Use these often to clearly imagine your dream fully realized.* Each time you do this, it's likely you will experience something special and some new aspect of your dream will appear. *The more clearly you envision your dream, the sooner you'll likely be living it.*

5. Maintain a Daily Success List

I've suggested this several times throughout the book because it works so well in teaching yourself that you are successful; *through these lists, you'll learn to recognize how much you really do accomplish.* Every time I feel like I'm not getting anywhere on my dream, I remember to do my daily success list. In a short period of time, my whole attitude shifts and I am "FIRED UP!" again about what I have done. You can get "FIRED UP!" too.

6. Review and Update Your "Feel Good Folder"

This "Feel Good Folder" was described in detail in Chapter 24. One woman created an artfully decorated hatbox with all her "Feel Good" paraphernalia inside. Another man keeps his in his time management system, so that it is with him all the time. *The purpose of a "Feel Good Folder" is to make you feel good, especially when life doles out a little disappointment.* Keep one at work and one at home. Remember, "Feel Good Folders" usually contain cartoons, cards and thank you notes, postcards of places you might want to visit, pictures of loved ones, newspaper clippings which inspire you and such. Everyone's "Feel Good Folder" is unique and memorable. Make sure yours contains what most motivates and soothes you.

7. Keep a Reward/Pamper Yourself Jar and Use it Whenever You Take Action on Your Dream

Throughout the book, after you've done great work on your dream, I have suggested you reward yourself. That's so the little kid inside you gets involved in the process and so you don't burn out. Some people enjoy the reward process so much that they use a "reward/ pamper yourself jar." This is a jar or bottle which you fill with various pieces of colored paper with rewards written on them. They might say "Get a therapeutic massage," "Go out to dinner with your best friend," "Take a bubble bath," "Play with friends," or "Go dancing." Whatever you consider to be a reward, that's what you write down. Fill the jar with all these goodies and pull one every time you take action on your dream. It will get you "FIRED UP!" to do more.

8. Update Your Action Plan or Make a New One

The "FIRED UP!"Action Plan appears throughout the book, and in the Appendix. It's one of the best vehicles for succeeding at any goal or dream. Use it any time you have a new project that you want to set ablaze. It will ignite you into action.

9. Update Your "Expanding Your Self-Definition" List

As you move on your dream, you will probably transcend previous limitations and break through old fears. Be sure to record these experiences on your list of expansive self-defining activities from Chapter 23. Pay attention to these experiences. They are important landmarks as you grow and change. They will forever change your self-perception. As Oliver Wendell Holmes once said, *"The mind, once expanded to the dimensions of a larger idea, never returns to its original size."*

10. Be of Service to Someone Else

One of the most powerful ways to shift your state from contractive to expansive, or from depressed to positive, is to serve someone else. It can take any form you wish, from volunteering at the local soup kitchen to taking food and blankets to the animal shelter to babysitting a friend's toddlers or something else. *The key to service is that it comes from your heart and that you are giving with no attachment to the outcome.* Invariably, helping someone who is less fortunate than you will give you a wake-up call about how good your life is. It teaches you to appreciate your blessings. You care about others and want to contribute in a positive way. Just remember it doesn't need to be a big, substantial contribution. Little gestures mean a lot, too. The fact that you are focusing outside yourself to serve others will get you "FIRED UP!"

11. Ask, Ask, Ask for What You Want

You'll find other people who are more than willing to help you achieve your dreams; but they are not mind readers! Learn to ask specifically for what you want, like Markita Andrews did.

🔥 Markita Andrews was an eight year old girl whose father had abandoned her and her waitress mother. Both had a dream of traveling around the world. But with their meager income, it seemed unlikely to come true. That all changed at age 13, when Markita read in her Girl Scout magazine that the Scout who sold the most cookies in the country would win an all-expense paid trip around the world. Now Markita had a vehicle to realize her dream and she got "FIRED UP!" Her burning desire to win this trip led her to create a winning action plan.

Dressed in her uniform every day after school, she would visit people and ask them to invest in her dream by buying one or two dozen boxes of cookies. Pretty soon, with her drive and determination, Markita had sold 3256 boxes of Girl Scout Cookies. She won the trip around the world and since then has sold more than 42,000 boxes of cookies!

At age 14, she spoke at the international roundtable of the world's top salespeople. Her advice was to ask for the order, ask, ask, ask. True to her motto, she then asked these salespeople to buy her Girl Scout cookies. At that one session, she sold 10,000 boxes of cookies. She's a perfect example of how asking for what you want is a key to making your dreams come true.[19]

Ask for whatever you need to make your dream come true. Be clear and specific. Visualize success, picture the person saying yes and giving you what you want. See yourself as "FIRED UP!" and victorious. *Let others take part in your dream; they may want to help you. It gets them* "FIRED UP!" *too.*

12. Schedule Action Steps for Your Dream in Your Time Management System

You may currently be doing something else besides living your dream. That's fairly typical and is no problem so long as you take time to focus and work your dream. Lots of people work a second job to get the money to start a new business or change careers. You may want to build a home-based business on the side to earn money for your dream. That's fine, as long as you give regular attention each week to accomplishing your dream. Remember to use your time management system and schedule in action steps and complete them. That's how you live your dream, one step at a time.

13. Attend Seminars or Take Courses about the Subject Matter of Your Dream

If you are pursuing a dream in a different field than the one you're in or the one you prepared for in school, you may find great value in attending seminars or taking college courses in the area of your dream. There are a wealth of advantages to this. First of all, you will gain valuable information about your dream and what it takes to make it happen. Second, you will meet others who may already be in your chosen field and who may know people that would love to help you with your dream. Contacts can be of tremendous assistance in accomplishing your dream. Third, associating with others who are "FIRED UP!" and taking action helps you to stay motivated. Fourth, the instructor or seminar leader may become a valuable resource for you as you move forward. In fact, they may even become a mentor.

14. Interview Experts in the Field of Your Dream and Select a Mentor

The people presenting your seminars or teaching your courses are likely to be experts in the field. If not, they probably know who the experts are, and can help you connect with them. *In general, experts are more than willing to help others.* Think about it. When someone asks you for help or advice, aren't you honored? These experts are people too, and will usually respond generously. Some may even be so supportive that they become a mentor to you. A mentor is a trusted counselor who guides you, and who can save you countless hours and mistakes by sharing their experiences with you.

Ed Gerety has benefitted significantly from the counsel of his mentor. Ed was a fledgling speaker wanting to work with youth. He had the enthusiasm and the drive, but he needed help in terms of positioning himself and launching his career properly. His mentor, another highly successful counselor and youth speaker, gave him excellent guidance and helped Ed launch what is now a dynamic and prosperous career as a motivational youth speaker. His mentor has been invaluable to him. Now both he and Ed are "FIRED UP!" about Ed's career.

15. Say Your Affirmations Daily and Make New Ones as They Come True

Chapter 18 is all about affirmations. You know they are powerful; they work and are really easy to do. Use them every day, and when you have achieved the goal of a specific affirmation, make up a new one to take its place. The more you ingrain your success into your subconscious, the further along you will be with your dream. Create your own set of action options for your dream affirmations and move on them. Stoke your fire.

16. Watch Motivational Movies, Listen to Audiotapes and Read Uplifting Books

There are entire stores and catalogues devoted to inspirational books, tapes and movies. CareerTrack, Nightingale Conant and InterNET Services Corporation all offer excellent audio and video-tapes. The Resources Section of this book suggests dozens of outstanding books, tapes and movies. I especially recommend the following books: *Chicken Soup for the Soul* by Jack Canfield, *Life 101* by John Roger, *Live Your Dreams* by Les Brown and *Random Acts of Kindness.*

Some of my favorite inspirational movies include: *Sister Act, Field of Dreams, The Boy Who Could Fly, Flashdance, Working Girl, Angels in the Outfield, The Secret of My Success, Vision Quest, Hook, Mrs. Doubtfire* and *Mr. Holland's Opus.* These are just a few that work for me. Choose those that appeal to you. I also find that *Parade Magazine* in the Sunday newspaper does a particularly good job of showcasing uplifting stories, and I check it frequently.

17. Live in the Present Moment

It's easy to focus on the future when you're working on a large dream, but you will experience greater joy and success when you live in the present moment. *The present is your most resourceful state. It allows you to be open to new and magical experiences as they present themselves.* Keep agreements for the future and visualize your dream as fully realized and still enjoy today. Remember, the present is a gift you give yourself.

18. Use Music to Inspire, Relax or Energize Yourself

Music is an amazing healing agent, since it can inspire, motivate and soothe you. Taste in music is an individual matter; so choose music which supports you best. Some people like soft jazz or classical music for relaxation; while others like country or folk music. Fast music and rock and roll can energize you and get you "FIRED UP!" Many songwriters feature positive messages which remind you to stay on track. Kenny Loggins, James Taylor, Luther Vandross, Celine Dion, Tuck and Patti, Desiree and Michael Franks, among others, all write songs with meaningful messages which can inspire you to stay focused on your dream.

19. Use All Your Resources

Chapter 13 outlines your resources in detail. Look over that list periodically and determine whether there are some resources available to you which may yet be untapped. *Stay on track by using everything for your advancement and taking advantage of every opportunity.*

20. Play Regularly – Honor the Little Kid Inside You

I personally am a big fan of play, perhaps because I had a painful childhood. My husband is one of the best sources for play ideas, and we schedule in play time every week and weekend. Again, how you like to play is up to you. But some good ideas to consider are: coloring, drawing or painting; sculpting or molding with modeling clay; building something with blocks, cards or paper. Go to an amusement park, try rollerskating or visit a children's museum. Remember that the little kid inside you is a super creative resource for you. You deserve fun and pleasure. They stir up the embers inside of you. Schedule them in. Remember the old adage, "All work and no play makes Jack a dull boy."

21. Exercise in a Way That Supports You

You're probably tired of hearing people talk about the value of exercise, so I won't belabor the point. The truth is, I'm not an exercise fiend myself. But I do exercise fairly often and I find it gives me much more energy for my dreams. It helps my head to be clear, my body to be sound and my blood to flow. *Exercise can sometimes be the perfect way to resolve a problem, because you can put all your effort into working out and forget about your worries.* Afterwards, you're more relaxed and invigorated and able to tackle the challenges. Being healthy, eating right and exercising in ways that support you will all give you greater strength, both physically and mentally. It will help get you "FIRED UP!" with the flames of energy and life.

22. Laugh Often and Watch Funny Movies or Shows

When is the last time you went to a comedy club? Or watched a comedian on television? Or listened to a comedian on audiotape? All of these are interesting ways to stay fresh, open and relaxed about your dream. Having a good sense of humor is healthy on all levels, and will enable you to have more joy along the way.

My husband and I experienced this as we were driving on a trip to New York City listening to an old Robin Williams tape. The trip was over four hours long and somewhat tedious. It was incredible how the tape lightened our moods. Robin is in many respects a creative genius, and hearing his routine brought tears to our eyes. Within half an hour, our attitudes were more positive. We were revitalized and recommitted to the purpose of our journey, which was to participate in a valuable weekend training. So pick up a tape of your favorite humorist and listen to it soon. It can give you a whole new perspective on life.

23. Spend Time With Winners

Winner is a subjective term. In sports, it means someone who has competed and triumphed. A winner in life is someone with an optimistic outlook who has a great attitude about life and gets things done. A winner is joyful and open to opportunity. A winner looks for the best in others, rather than criticizing or complaining. A winner has occasional setbacks, but keeps going, with their goal in mind. If you had the choice, wouldn't you rather spend the day with a winner than a loser? Which one do you think would encourage and inspire you to move forward? Which would show appreciation for you and your victories and give you honest feedback? Think about these questions when you decide who to share your dream with, or even who to spend your free time with. Negative people bring others down; so stay away from them. Hang around with winners as much as possible. You want to keep going up and up.

24. Create a "FIRED UP!" Inspiration Circle– Meet Once a Month

A *"Fired Up!" Inspiration Circle is another marvelous tool for maintaining enthusiasm.* An Inspiration Circle is a group of people who voluntarily come together on a regular basis with the main intent of supporting and encouraging each other on their dreams.

Common activities at these gatherings are success and dream-building discussions, self-disclosure, updates on dream progress, asking for help, saying key affirmations out loud and giving each other positive feedback. Sometimes professional speakers come and speak to the group. Food is often included. Circle members may bring a poem, book, video, song or artwork to share, as people build their inventory of motivational tools. They frequently describe all the things they are grateful for, appreciating their blessings.

When you are establishing or joining a "FIRED UP!" Inspiration Circle, choose the members carefully. Your Dream Supporters from the Chapter 24 Risk and Reward Process would be a great place to start. You might also include other people you know who are working on their dreams, even if their dreams are much different from yours. Make sure they have a winning, caring attitude and will uplift rather than depress others. Use the guidelines for establishing an Inspiration Circle as described in the Appendix on page 254. Get each other "FIRED UP!"

25. Do Random Acts of Kindness

In 1983 a California artist decided she would do unexpected favors for strangers, in an effort to make the world a kinder place. Her actions caught on and the concept of *Random Acts of Kindness* resulted in a bestselling book of the same name, published by the editors of Conari Press. Most of the gestures described in the book are small, simple acts of kindness, and yet they make a large difference in the lives of those they touch. Why? As the book says, "At the foundation of every act of kindness is a simple and compassionate connection between strangers, who, for a moment, aren't strangers anymore.... Kindness, it seems, has the capacity to return us to the very core of our humanity."

Practicing acts of kindness is a wonderful way to quickly get "FIRED UP!" about who you are as a person. Something as seemingly inconsequential as paying a stranger's toll at the tollbooth, or putting money in someone else's parking meter or even smiling at the checkout person at the grocery store can mean a great deal to those other people.

I had a sweet experience with this when a group of us were focusing on kindness as a theme one week. I was grocery shopping and at the checkout counter, I started chatting with the woman in front of me. She was obviously from another country and was getting accustomed to our prices. I commented on how I loved chocolate, as there was a cookbook for sale at the checkout counter with a chocolate cake on the the cover. She said she loved making desserts and trying new recipes but that cookbook was not in this week's budget. As her groceries were being bagged, I bought her the cookbook. To avoid any embarrassment that she might have felt, I quickly added, "It's Kindness Week" and told her that I would like her to have the cookbook. She rewarded me with a great big smile and a simple thank you. Little things can mean a lot. Giving, especially when it's unexpected, is such fun and so heartwarming. Try it and find out for yourself.

26. Do Some Sort of Spiritual Practice Daily

One of the keys to staying "FIRED UP!" is to establish a daily spiritual routine and stick to it. Make it as simple and meaningful for yourself as possible. Like your body, you need to feed your spirit as well.

Your mind, body and spirit are all closely connected and affect each other in many different ways. It's important to keep all of them as healthy, relaxed and clear as possible.

There are several spiritual practices you can adopt to create a greater sense of peace and well-being. Here are just a few.

A. *Read from a Daily Devotional.* You can reap enormous benefits from these readings. It only takes a few minutes to read a page or two. Reading it out loud to yourself or someone else and then discussing it briefly can be powerful and effective. Even if you don't understand everything you read, it's OK; it's a growing process. One of the popular classics which can be read year after year is *My Utmost for His Highest* by Oswald Chambers. Bookstores carry other daily reading books for specific types of people, such as stressed-out women, salespeople, people in recovery and such. Check around to see what works for you.

B. *Pray Daily.* Talk to God and share your heart's concerns, fears and dreams. This is also the time to pray for others you care about. Express your gratitude first; thank God for all your blessings and for His ongoing assistance with your life and dreams. Be open to receive His guidance and to do whatever is for the greatest good of all concerned. Be specific about your concerns, but realize that God's answers will always come to you in a form that is best for you. Know that you don't have all the answers and that God provides a tremendous source of inspiration and support. Sometimes just praying for clarity is a good way to start if you are confused about something in your life. It's worth it to take time to be with God. Even just ten minutes a day can make a world of difference in your life.

C. *Meditate Daily.* The calming affects of meditation can be miraculous. It's surprisingly simple. Many of you practice it now without even realizing it, when you're out walking quietly in nature or sitting silently by a stream. Meditation means quieting the mind and body and focusing inward. Some do this by concentrating on their breathing. It doesn't take long to have good results. You can start out with as little as five minutes a day and work your way up to half an hour or even a full hour, if you wish.

Here's a paraphrased version of Dr. Schuller's approach to meditation from his book *My Soul's Adventure with God:*

◆*Relax* – Let go of the body and all of its distractions.
◆*Retreat* – Leave behind your tensions, stress and passions. Go into neutral.
◆*Receive* – Open to receive God's Spirit within you. Let your self experience the peace available to you.
◆*Resign* – Let go of your ambitions and thoughts.
◆*Recharge* – Let His spirit fill you and revitalize you.
◆*Renew* – Find your soul newly strengthened by God's love.

There are a myriad of tapes on the market which provide guided relaxations and suggestions for focusing inward. There are also all sorts of meditation classes offered through hospitals and community centers. It really doesn't matter *how* you go inside– just that you do something to connect with your own divinity. You can use one of the visualizations from this book. *All that is important is that you pay attention to your inner guidance and give yourself the chance to slow down and just be in the stillness.* You'll be astonished and delighted by the results after you've practiced.

Regular daily devotional reading, meditation and prayer are powerful tools for focusing all the levels of your consciousness and aligning your mind with your purpose. Answers you need for your dream can show up during any of these spiritual routines, or while you're sleeping. Be open to Divine Assistance. Allow yourself to draw on this valuable resource.

27. Celebrate Success and Spread Joy

In the Walt Disney movie, *Pollyanna*, the main character is a wonderful little girl who was orphaned and sent to live with her "crusty" old aunt. In spite of her harsh surroundings and the strict treatment she receives, Pollyanna faithfully maintains a sweet, upbeat disposition and brings joy to people all over her community.

One particularly poignant example of Pollyanna's engaging nature occurred when she visited an elderly woman and her daughter. The older woman was a hypochondriac, and a rather loud, complaining one at that. She stayed in bed all day, whining and moaning and trying to make everyone else's life miserable, too. Pollyanna visited her, and magically transformed the woman's outlook. She took the crystal prisms that were attached to the lamps, and hung them in her sunlit window so that tiny rainbows sparkled throughout the room.

The effect was enchanting, and the old woman was delighted with the results. She settled down, stopped whining and really enjoyed the effect. To Pollyanna, the whole thing was minor and fun; to the woman, it was a very big deal.

That's what I mean when I say spread joy to others. Your actions may be very small and simple, but they can uplift and heal; they get you and others "FIRED UP!" *One way to give joy is to celebrate success. Every time you have a win, share it with someone else who cares about you and who will be happy for you.* Also celebrate with your loved ones when they have a victory. Go out to dinner or have a cupcake together. Do something fun and spontaneous. *Celebrate all of life's little and big special moments along the way; that will make every day more worthwhile for you and others.*

Spreading happiness is a form of service. Joy is contagious. The more you share with others, the more joyful you feel yourself. That's a terrific win-win experience that keeps your fire burning.

28. Tell Your Story and Ask Others About Theirs

Believe it or not, very few people are actively going for their dreams. Many people think about it and want to, but few actually do the work to make their dreams come true. That's where you come in. Your story can inspire and get others "FIRED UP!" to start moving toward their dreams. Tell other people what you are doing and how much it means to you. Discuss your successes and the lessons you've learned. Let them vicariously experience your thrill of making your dream come true.

While you're conversing, *ask others about their dreams*. Even if they haven't done anything about them, they still have dreams. Listen to them and encourage them to describe their vision of how they would like their lives to be. Believe in them and their ability to live their dreams; tell them they can do it. Cheer them on. *Help them get "FIRED UP!" about what could happen for them, and let them feed off your enthusiasm.*

You may find a valuable resource that may have been otherwise been hidden. You may discover that you touch others' lives significantly with your energy and attitude. Your enthusiasm may build and light up others just by sharing about your dream.

You may also have learned a great deal about the process that you can share. *Remember, the name of this book is* FIRED UP!– HOW TO SUCCEED BY MAKING YOUR DREAMS COME TRUE. *Talking with others and discussing what you most love to do benefits others as well as yourself.* Many people really do love to hear about others' dreams. Take the time to share with people you feel will be interested and supportive and you will reap the rewards.

"We are here to live and know life in its multi-dimensions,
to know life in its richness, in all its variety.
And when a man lives multidimensionally,
explores all possibilities available,
never shrinks back from any challenge,
goes, rushes to it, welcomes it, rises to the occasion,
then life becomes a flame, life blooms."
B.S.R.20

FIRE IN MY SOUL

"Wanting a world that's healed and whole,
Looking for ways to reach that goal.
Sending a message out to those who care.
Believing I'll find a way to peace.
Hoping for days when there will be
Loving and freedom ringing everywhere.

There's a fire in, fire in, fire in my soul.
There's a fire in, fire in, fire in my soul.
Maybe the answer's plain to see,
Maybe it's here inside of me.
Would someone please tell me where to start?
Maybe it's up to you and me.
It's our responsibility to let peace prevail in our hearts.

Searching for ways to reach on out.
Moving right through the fear and doubt.
Balancing inner strength and harmony.
Learning to look outside myself.
Finding the ways that I can help.
Promising only those that I will keep.

There's a fire in, fire in, fire in my soul.
There's a fire in, fire in, fire in my soul.
Maybe the answer's plain to see,
Maybe it's here inside of me.
Would someone please tell me where to start?
Maybe it's up to you and me.
It's our responsibility to let peace prevail in our hearts."
Song by Stawn Barber

Chapter 28

You Can Make a Difference in the World

Sharing Your Fire's Warmth with Others

"It seems that you are happy and successful in life if you are doing your thing, you know specifically what your thing is, and that which you are doing earns you the respect of other people, because what you are doing benefits other people as well as yourself."
Denis Waitley

You're "FIRED UP!"

You're using the tools in this book and moving forward in a positive way. You're motivated, excited and starting to live your dreams. Now what?

"FIRED UP!" PRINCIPLE # 37 – Make a Difference!

How about sharing some of your newfound joy and success with others? How about lifting others into a more expansive space, putting smiles on their faces and sharing your blessings?

It's simple. When you feel good, it shows. When you are "FIRED UP!" about your life, your enthusiasm bubbles over and can make a difference in the lives of those around you. In many cases, your excitement helps to uplift others and shake them out of their negativity.

Making a difference doesn't have to be a big deal, either. It can be simple and easy. Perhaps you just bought a new puppy and while on a walk, little children pet it and giggle. Your favorite baseball team just won and you are whistling as you walk down the street; others smile. You feel happy about your experiences that day and smile at the grocery clerk; she feels encouraged. You greet a weary telephone caller with a cheerful "hello"; they feel valued. You extend a little kindness to an elderly neighbor by carrying their bags to the door or sweeping their sidewalk; they feel like somebody cares. You feed the birds and they reward you by chirping and visiting daily. You help others take action on their dreams; they are "FIRED UP!" Or perhaps you just take two minutes to speak to a stranger when no one else has; they appreciate your attention. All of these are examples of being "FIRED UP!" and touching the lives of others. *In your own uncommon way, you can ignite the flames of other people and make a difference in their lives.*

Other People Making a Difference

Growing up in a communist country was not easy for Maria. Both her Bulgarian parents worked hard, and her father's strict disciplinary approach taught her to be strong. At age 14, Maria decided to leave home and go to an English speaking school. It was there that her dream of being a doctor was born. Throughout the next several years, she studied and worked with dedication and fervor. She eventually became a respected physician with a specialty in neurology, and was chosen to work in the University Hospital. But in 1993 she fell in love with an American and moved to the United States to share his vision.

Happily married, she never gave up her longing for practicing medicine. After passing the American medical exams, she expected to resume life as a doctor. Months of interviewing taught her how difficult it was for foreign doctors to work in the U.S. She knew the only way for her to succeed was to get a residency at one of the hospitals in the Boston area. She interviewed with hospitals, made phone calls, observed medical procedures and made professional contacts wherever possible. Maria got "FIRED UP!" She took consistent action on her dream and did everything she could to make it come true.

Just two months later, she heard that she had not been chosen for any of the residencies for which she had applied. Undaunted, she continued to take action. That very same day, while observing at a Boston hospital, she asked an American co-worker to put in a good word for her with the hiring physician there. He did, and later that day, after she had spoken extensively with that physician, she was hired! She triumphed over dozens of other physicians, American and foreign, for the one available residency. She had made her dream come true!

Now she lights up the lives of those she works with and shares her delight at being able to live her dream fully. She is still "FIRED UP!" and not only makes a big difference in the lives of the patients she helps heal, but also in the lives of her medical colleagues. They feel the warmth of her fire, enthusiasm and dedication. It also reminds them why they originally decided to become doctors. Maria has helped them learn to appreciate why they do what they do. This has reignited their internal flames.

Making a Difference in Mississippi

Osceola McCarty worked most all of her life as an uneducated black washer-woman in Hattiesburg, MS. Even when washing machines came into vogue, she preferred to wash clothing by hand in a boiling pot to give the highest quality wash. Amazingly, she charged only 50 cents a bundle, which rose to $10 a bundle in later years.

With no children of her own, Osceola had the dream of helping out other African Americans in the area. In 1995 she donated her whole life savings *of $150,000 to the University of Southern Mississippi for scholarships for black college students.* "I want them to have an education," she says, "I had to work hard all my life. They can have the chance that I didn't have."

Osceola's generosity has astonished her community; so much so that matching funds have been raised by area businesses. Equally common is the question she receives so often: "Why didn't you spend the money on yourself?" She answers with a big, loving smile, "I *am* spending it on myself." Osceola is "FIRED UP!" and making a difference in the lives of others. Every graduating student sets her fire inside ablaze. [21]

At a National Speaker's Association Convention, someone told a story about the Special Olympics in Seattle a few years ago. Nine youngsters, all disabled either physically or mentally, gathered at the start of the 100 yard dash. When the gun sounded, they took off, with enthusiasm for winning the race; all except for one boy, who tripped on the asphalt, tumbled a few times and burst into tears. The other contestants heard him cry. One by one, they all halted, paused and went back to the distraught boy. One Down's syndrome girl bent over him, gave him a kiss on his cheek and said, "This will make it better." *All nine contestants linked arms and walked together over the finish line. They got a standing ovation and the cheering lasted for ten minutes.* The crowd was "FIRED UP!" and touched by the loving support these youngsters had demonstrated for each other.

What Are the Keys To Making a Difference in the World?

In each of these cases, people got "FIRED UP!" about their dream, and in some way reached out and made a difference in the lives of others. Making a difference in the world is not difficult at all. You do it far more often than you realize.

In most examples of making a difference in the world:
◆ Some action is taken, either inwardly or outwardly.
◆ This action contributes in a positive way to someone or something (often by inspiring, healing, helping or creating).
◆ Enthusiasm is present. People are "FIRED UP!"

The interesting thing about touching others while you're "FIRED UP!" is that you often do it without even being consciously aware of it. This next story illustrates this point.

A Little Boy Lights Up Others

My husband and I were sitting in a pancake restaurant on a rainy Saturday. Many people were allowing the weather to dampen their moods; the atmosphere was quiet and glum. All of a sudden, a very young boy sauntered into the restaurant with his parents. After they were seated, the little boy excitedly ran up and down the aisles, giggling all the way. He was simply "FIRED UP!" about life, about eating pancakes and about being out with his parents. His father chased him, laughing and having fun with his exuberant son. Pretty soon almost everyone in the restaurant began smiling. Several people chuckled, lightened by the child's joy. He lit up the whole restaurant, just by being himself, living in the present and enjoying his experience. He made a positive difference that day and each laugh stirred the sparks inside the other people.

The same thing is true of you when you radiate your joy and natural well-being from being "FIRED UP!"about your life, doing what you love.

A Few Tips to Remember

When you are "FIRED UP!" about your dream, your enthusiasm and energy can be enormous. When you value other people and truly want to make a difference in their lives while you live your dream, here are a few tips to remember.

(**TIP #1 Share From Your Heart**)

When you are "FIRED UP!" and the flame inside you burns brightly, *share with others authentically from your heart.* When you are talking about your dream, be sure to mention the challenges along the way and how you overcame them. Let them know what kind of effort and energy you put into your dream, so they can see that it's possible for them, too. Don't let your ego run away with you; understand that everything you have achieved has been through the grace of God, with lots of help along the way from other people. Be humble while sharing your joy; let them know how grateful you are for all the wonderful gifts in your life.

(**TIP #2 Ask Questions and Listen**)

When you're connecting and sharing with others, be sure to ask them what dreams they have and how they feel about them. Ask them to describe what they love to do, and what they have always hoped they could accomplish. Encourage them to keep talking while, most of all, listening carefully to what they have to say. (Remember how, in the beginning of the book, you did the listening exercise with another person? *The most important guideline of that activity was to be quiet and not interrupt the other person.*) Let them have all the time they need to share about their dreams. They will be so appreciative; you'll watch the sparks ignite inside of them and their faces will become animated. They will get "FIRED UP!" right in front of you. Listening is one of the most loving things you can do for someone. Make it a regular part of your interactions with others.

TIP #3 Stay Detached

Remember the law of detachment – be unattached to the outcome of your sharing or making a difference. Service, by its very nature, means contributing to the welfare of others, assisting them in some way, without expecting anything in return. The best kind of service is done lovingly from the heart with the intention of doing work for the greatest benefit of all concerned. You cannot measure your self-worth based on the outcome of the work you do with others. Remember, other people's behavior is always about them. Let them pursue their dreams or not, the way they choose, without fear or concern that they did it your way.

Every year, there's a TV show called *Party for the Planet*, which honors young people from around the country who do special projects to improve the environment. Schools, clubs and organizations with young people of all ages from all walks of life enter and participate, in the competition. The best ones are showcased in a national celebration on television. Each of these groups does their best and works hard to make a difference in the earth itself. Sometimes their results don't turn out the way they expected. Some projects span over years. And there are people who have worked very hard who don't get the national media attention that the winners get. That doesn't mean their work is any less valuable; it just means someone else's project was chosen. If these youngsters were to stop doing their projects because of that, it would show that their hearts were not in it. *When you do service work, let go of any attachment to a specific outcome. Do your personal best; that's the best you can do! Remember, the journey is the success; the outcome is a reward.*

TIP #4 Give Them Freedom

You're "FIRED UP!" living your dream and taking advantage of all that is available to you. Your life is going great, you have tremendous abundance and love, happiness and success. So who would be better than you to help other people with their dreams? Be careful. Fires can be extinguished, too. Definitely share your joy and excitement; by all means listen and engage them in positive, upbeat activities. But give others *their* freedom; don't try to change or "fix" them or have them live their lives your way. That's control and has a negative impact.

Respect that each person is different, learns through different modalities and does things in their own time. Let them. Give them the space they need. Support and encourage them; offer suggestions and help if they want it, but let them do it. Did you ever try something new with your parents when you were a kid – like riding a bike or building a model? They could not do it for you and have it be satisfying to you. You had to do it yourself, your way. That's how you learned and achieved. And that's how others learn, too. As Dale Carnegie said, *"A man convinced against his will is of the same opinion still."* Let people make their own decisions and do what they believe they need to do.

In my many years as a trainer, it has been enormously gratifying to watch people get "FIRED UP!" step into their power and take off in pursuit of their dreams. Most have been successful, and some are still working on it. But out of all the successes, not one has ever done it exactly the same way as the others. Each individual's personal history and unique approach to life has colored and impacted everything about their dream. These factors made their dream real and personal for them. I have loved watching and learning, listening and experiencing the rich diversity of the human heart; it can teach us all so much.

TIP #5 Share Your Love

The best way to make a difference in the lives of others is to sincerely share your love. Authentically share from your heart any caring or empathy you have for others. It means exhibiting kindness, going the extra mile and giving others the benefit of the doubt. It means having more patience and forgiveness for yourself and others. It means letting the past go and living in the present. It means stepping forward and doing what needs to be done to help another human being. Loving means laughing and experiencing joy and sharing the interaction. It means reaching out and touching others genuinely in friendship and goodwill. Celebrate their successes, no matter how small. Encourage them when they face disappointments. Remind them of their talents and greatness. Thank them for being in your life. Continually help them keep their flame alive. Help them stoke the embers if they go out. Help them ignite their dreams and stay "FIRED UP!"

The "Give Kids the World" Foundation

One of the many programs designed to help terminally ill children enjoy their last few months of life is "Give Kids the World." Henri Landwirth founded this international non-profit foundation in 1986 to bring sick children and their families to DisneyWorld, Florida. This program pays expenses for the sick children and their families, including airfare from over forty foreign countries.

In 1989 Henri opened "Kids Village" near DisneyWorld in Kissimmee, which provides housing for 4000 families on 35 acres of land. The village includes a castle and carousel, a lake with live fish, a welcome center, the Gingerbread House dining area and 56 villas. A doctor is always on call to tend to the terminally ill children while they are visiting. The whole purpose of the foundation is to help bring joy into the lives of these children and their families. Happily, they regularly achieve this goal. "The happiest six days of my child's life," was how one parent described their visit. Henri Landwirth was recently honored as one of the twelve most caring people in America. As his life so clearly demonstrates, one person can indeed make a difference.

"We make a living by what we get.
We make a life by what we give."
Winston Churchill

Light Up the World with Your Fire

Some seminars use a wonderful "FIRED UP!" concept to show how powerful it is to share your love to make a difference in the world. With a candle lit as a symbol of the light of love that burns inside each person, they tell this story. If just one person shared their light with two other people and if they in turn shared their light with two more people, if it took the first person one day to share, it would take only 33 days to spread the light of loving around the world. And if it took that first person a little longer, say perhaps one month to share their loving in such a way that two others received it, it would take 33 months to spread the light of loving around the world. And if they were much slower, and it took them a year to share their loving with two others, *it would take only 33 years to spread the light of loving around the world. What a difference that would make.* We'd have a "FIRED UP!" planet! [22]

Always Remember

Inside you is the fire of life. That fire is your passion, your life purpose, your mission, your fulfillment. It burns brightly inside you and ignites when you do what you love and live your dreams. It reignites every time you share your dream with others and make a positive difference in their lives. When you're "FIRED UP!" your fire warms others, igniting their flames and creating enthusiasm and joy.

You can overcome any obstacle, meet any challenge and win. You have greatness inside you. The time to start living the life of your dreams and sharing it with others is now. Ignite the flame inside, stay "FIRED UP!"and keep moving on your dreams. Live your life with joy and success. "FIRED UP!" – *it's not just a state of temporary excitement – it's a way of life that can change the world.*

"I am the master of my fate;
I am the captain of my soul."
William Ernest Henley

"What would you attempt to do
if you knew you could not fail?"
Robert H. Schuller

Remember These Key Points

◆ It's easy to make a difference in the lives of others. Share your "FIRED UP!" energy and ask them about their dreams.

◆ Share your dream with others and ignite the fire inside them.

◆ In most examples of making a difference in the world, some action is taken inwardly or outwardly; this action contributes in some way to someone or something (usually by inspiring, helping, healing or creating); enthusiasm is present. People are "FIRED UP!"

◆ Share authentically from your heart, and really listen to others.

◆ Stay detached; don't be invested in a certain outcome.

◆ Give others their freedom to live their dreams their way.

◆ The best way you can make a difference is to stay "FIRED UP!" and share your love.

Now Take These "FIRED UP!" Action Steps

◆ Actively think about who you'd like to serve and share your dream with. Begin making a difference in the world with the people in your life.

◆ Consider what charities or non-profit groups you admire and whose work you would like to support. Ask yourself, "What could I do to help?"

◆ If you have achieved your dream, it's time for your next dream. Use the tools of this book to start on a new dream and get "FIRED UP!" all over again. Live your life in joy and success. Keep the fire alive inside you and share your love and enthusiasm with others.

Postscript

Share Your "FIRED UP!" Stories

As you continue to move on your dreams and stay "FIRED UP!" about life, *please share your success stories with me.* This is just the first of several "FIRED UP!" books, and I would love to hear how you have used these tools and techniques to ignite your flame and get "FIRED UP!" *Learning about your stories keeps the flame inside of me burning bright and gets me "FIRED UP!" every day.*

Write to me at: "FIRED UP!"- Snowden McFall
                       c/o Brightwork Advertising and Training
                       74 Northeastern Blvd. Unit 20
                       Nashua, NH 03062

You can also get more information about "FIRED UP!" seminars and presentations around the country.

Make a Difference Day

October 28 is International Make a Difference Day. The designation of this day encourages people to volunteer to help others on an otherwise normal day. The fifth annual "Make a Difference Day"in

1995 involved 865,000 people from all 50 states and 24 countries. These people gave of their hearts, wallets and busy schedules to help others. Each year, ten people are named the day's most outstanding participants. They receive national awards and $2000 each in charitable donations from the creator of "Make a Difference Day," *USA WEEKEND*. Fifty Honorable Mentions and special Encore Awards are also presented. These awards are given out during National Volunteers Week in April. This event is held in partnership with The Points of Light Foundation and its network of 501 Volunteer Centers.

IMAGINE THE WORLD AS "FIRED UP!"

"Love alone can unite living beings
so as to complete and fulfill them...
for it alone joins them
by what is deepest in themselves.

All we need is to imagine
our ability to love developing
until it embraces
the totality of men
and of the earth."
Teilhard De Chardin

About the Author

Snowden McFall is a powerful and dynamic speaker, trainer and author. Founder and president of Brightwork Advertising and Training, Inc., Snowden's trademark qualities are her genuine enthusiasm and her ability to get people "FIRED UP!"

Snowden began her professional career as an educator, and is still actively involved with youth through organizations like Project Safeguard and the YMCA. She opened her advertising and training company in 1983, serves as creative director and handles accounts nationally and internationally.

Snowden is featured in the *World's Who's Who of Women*, and *Who's Who in Emerging Leaders in America*. She has also been featured in *Inc.*, *Adweek* and *Entrepreneurial Woman*.

Business NH Magazine chose Snowden as one of eight leaders to make an impact on business in New Hampshire. She was named the "National Women in Business Advocate of the Year" by the Small Business Administration for her nonprofit work helping women entrepreneurs start their own companies. As a result of this, Snowden was honored at a Rose Garden Ceremony at the White House and a Congressional luncheon. A finalist for *Inc.* Magazine's "New England Entrepreneur of the Year," Snowden was also chosen as "New Hampshire Woman of the Year" by the Merrimack Valley Business and Professional Association. She was selected as a finalist for *New Hampshire's Most Powerful Women*, a list awarded by Network Publications.

Snowden is married and loves to sail, travel, write, dance and entertain. *FIRED UP!* is the first of six books.

MEMBER

NATIONAL
SPEAKERS
ASSOCIATION

Other Products and Services

◆ "FIRED UP!" Affirmations Brochure
◆ "FIRED UP!" Creed in 4 Color (see page 263)
◆ "FIRED UP!" Buttons, 2 1/4 inches round
   which read "Ask Me Why I'm "FIRED UP!""™
◆ "FIRED UP!" Post-it® Notes
◆ "FIRED UP!" Acronym (see page vii)
◆ Radiance and Power Action Cards® – affirmation cards
   with action options for each affirmation

Seminars, Trainings and Consulting

◆ "FIRED UP!" One Day Program
◆ "FIRED UP!" One Hour Keynote
◆ "Making a Difference in the World" Weekend Seminar

Consulting Available on a Group or Individual Basis:

◆ Any of the topics listed below
◆ Specific one-on-one **dream consulting** with you to help you
   achieve your dream

Keynotes, Corporate Trainings and Custom Programs:

◆ "FIRED UP!"– Enthusiasm, the Key to Success
◆ Get "FIRED UP!" About Your Business
◆ "FIRE UP!" Your Team
◆ "FIRE UP!" Your Sales Force
◆ Get "FIRED UP!" and Overcome Stress
◆ Women Entrepreneurs: Get "FIRED UP!" for Success
◆ "FIRE UP!" Your Marketing & Advertising
◆ Get "FIRED UP!" About Your Dreams
◆ "FIRE UP!" Your Family-Finding the Best in Each Other

For information on these or other products or services, call
Brightwork Advertising and Training at 603-882-0600.

Your Life Purpose Worksheet

Step 1 List your best and most unique qualities. Which two qualities truly reflect who you are and for which you'd most like to be remembered? Underline these two.

Step 2 List several ways you enjoy expressing or sharing those two qualities. Use action verbs with "ing" endings. Underline your two favorite forms of expression.

Step 3 Describe your version of an ideal world.

Step 4 Combine the three steps above into one sentence that summarizes your life purpose.
Ex. I am <u>empowering</u> and <u>inspiring</u> others with my <u>love</u> and <u>joy</u> so that everyone <u>contributes for the greatest benefit of all in a peaceful world</u>.
Ex. I am <u>choreographing</u> and <u>dancing</u> with <u>grace</u> and <u>beauty</u> inspiring others to <u>appreciate their health and the health of the world</u>.

Concept for this form from Jack Canfield's *Self-Esteem and Peak Performance* audiotape set, CareerTrack Publications, 1987.

"FIRED UP!" Action Plan for Dreambuilding

Name   **Date**

My Dream: (Positively Stated as a Choice, Specific, Powerful, Emotionally Fulfilling)

_____

_____

_____

Where I envision this dream 1 year, 3 years, 5 years from now

1 year:

3 years:

5 years:

Affirmations:

1. _____
   Action Options
   a.
   b.
   c.
2. _____
   Action Options
   a.
   b.
   c.
3. _____
   Action Options
   a.
   b.
   c.
4. _____
   Action Options
   a.
   b.
   c.
5. _____
   Action Options
   a.
   b.
   c.

© 1993 , A. Snowden McFall

Action Steps: Specific Action	Target Date	Date Complete
1. ————————————————		
2. ————————————————		
3. ————————————————		
4. ————————————————		
5. ————————————————		
6. ————————————————		
7. ————————————————		
8. ————————————————		
9. ————————————————		

Results I'd Like to See from this Dream: (Ways I know I'm Succeeding)
1.
2.
3.
4.
5.

Strengths that Need to be Developed for this Dream:
1.
2.
3.

Resources Available
1.
2
3.
4.

Resources Needed
1.
2.
3.
4.

Do it Yourself Risk and Reward Process
(from Chapter 24)

Step 1) Review Your "Feel Good Folder" – Take some time to look over the contents and bask in your own good feelings. Allow yourself to get "FIRED UP!"

Step 2) Set the Stage for Yourself – Get out your dream collage, your dreammap, a timer, some blank action plans, some blank risk and reward sheets from the Appendix and lined paper and pens. Make sure you won't be disturbed for at least two hours.

Step 3) State Your Dream in Writing – Using a blank action plan, write the description of your dream in the top section. When you have a strong image of your dream, write out the one, three and five year descriptions. Let your imagination ignite the fire inside.

Step 4) Listing Objections – Set the timer for one and a half minutes. Now, write down many of the obstacles you think may exist between you and your dream. Just jot them down quickly on paper and don't mull them over. Stop at one minute and thirty seconds. Don't give any energy to these; just be aware of them.

Step 5) Overcome the Objections – Start by selecting the top three that really affect you. These are the most important ones to overcome. Now, one by one, taking about three minutes per objection, create a dreammap with as many solutions as possible as you brainstorm how to overcome them. Do this for all three objections. If you get stuck, take a few minutes to sit quietly and go back to your beautiful spot in nature. Invite three people you label as quite successful and for whom you have great respect. They can be living or dead. Dreamers often envision individuals like Einstein, Edison, Lincoln, Martin Luther King, or Amelia Earhart – depending on the dream. Ask each of them for their advice on how to overcome your obstacles. Listen carefully to what each has to say and write down their ideas. Their suggestions can be quite accurate and helpful, so use this resource.

Step 6) Positive Feedback – This is the time to pull out your "Feel Good Folder" and review your positive traits list. It's also good to return to your beautiful scene in nature and ask those three individuals to appear again; the ones you admired so much. One by one each of them comes forward. They tell you what qualities you have in common with them, and that you will be successful with your dream. They give you wonderful insights into yourself, and they believe in you fully. Take the time to completely receive their feedback; make notes on what they had to say, and appreciate your own talents and abilities in a whole new light.

Dream Supporters' Instructions for Doing the Risk and Reward Process

Read this aloud to your dream supporters or have them read it as you begin these steps from Chapter 24. Do Steps 1, 2 and 3. See pages 194-199.

4) Sharing Your Dream

"Thank you for being here to support me in achieving my dream. Please offer information and feedback in as neutral and honest a manner as possible. Please raise any possible objections or obstacles to my dream in a neutral, calm voice. Thanks for your help."

6) Overcoming the Objection

"Now it's time to be your most creative and encourage me to over-come my greatest obstacles. Offer as many different ideas and solutions to overcoming those top three obstacles, staying completely positive. Do not allow any negativity into the conversation; just keep brainstorming ideas. Avoid discussions of any one solution – suggest several. Be open and optimistic."

7) Positive Feedback

"You have done a great job. Now is the time to bolster me and give me as much encouragement as possible. Please give me positive feedback, telling me all the reasons why you know I will succeed, and all the good qualities you admire about me. Share from your heart honestly and enthusiastically. Only say positive things and speak generously. Recorder, please continue to write down all the positive comments and share your ideas, too.

Instructions for Creating a
FIRED UP! Inspiration Circle
(from pages 228-229)

Guidelines for Organization

1. Select members who are positive doers, with dreams of their own that they're working on. Your Dream Supporters or dreambuddy are likely candidates.
2. It's best to leave your family or loved ones out of the group, as they are frequently too close to be objective.

Once you have decided who will be a part of this circle, then

3. Establish a regular location for meetings and a regular schedule
4. Determine a group mission or focus
5. Determine the length of time the group will continue to meet: three months, six months, a year or other
6. Arrange to have refreshments and a private setting to help everyone feel comfortable

Recommended Activities for FIRED UP! Inspiration Circles

- ◆ laugh and let your little kid inside come out and play
- ◆ share dreambuilding activities
- ◆ share dreammaps and dream collages
- ◆ give updates about your progress and concerns relative to your FIRED UP! Action Plan
- ◆ ask for help with any questions or concerns
- ◆ bring and share an item that inspires you about your dream
- ◆ do guided visualizations
- ◆ share any new motivational books, videos or audiotapes
- ◆ spend time in nature looking for answers to questions about your dream
- ◆ make a list of the things you are grateful for and share it
- ◆ give each other positive feedback and stay FIRED UP!

Notes

1. Lois R. Shea, "Making a Real Difference," *The Boston Globe* (May 14, 1996), pp. 1 & 8.

2. Barbara Sher with Annie Gottlieb, "How to Get What You Really Want," *Wishcraft* (Ballantine Books, 1979), p. 40-41.

3. *Women of the Olympics, Ladies' Home Journal® Special Collectors Edition,* (1996) Story about Florence Griffith Joyner, "Three Gold Medals in Track, 1988,"p. 95.

4. Mark Starr, "Leap of Faith," *Newsweek* (Aug. 5, 1996), pp. 41-48.

5. Bhagwan Shree Rajneesh is the author of this quote.

6. Jack Canfield and Mark V. Hansen, *Chicken Soup for the Soul* (Deerfield Beach, Florida: Health Communications, Inc., 1993), pp. 253-255.

7. Bud Greenspan, "Great Olympic Moments," *Women of the Olympics, Ladies' Home Journal® Special Collectors Edition* (1996), p. 27.

8. Mark Jurkowitz, "The Good News Couple," *The Boston Globe* (May 14, 1996), pp. 29 & 38.

9. Jack Canfield and Mark Victor Hansen, *The Aladdin Factor* (New York: The Berkley Publishing Group, 1995), p. 76.

10. Lou Ann Walker, "I Am Like You," *Parade Magazine* (Oct 29, 1995), p. 10.

11. Bhagwan Shree Rajneesh is the author of this quote.

12. Barbara Sher with Annie Gottlieb, "How to Get What You Really Want," *Wishcraft* (Ballantine Books, 1979), p. 42.

13. Michelle Green and Lisa Kay Greissinger, "Harlem on His Mind," *People Magazine* (April 10, 1995), pp. 67-68.

14. Laurie Lucas, "Kids Against Crime," *Press-Enterprise*.

15. Les Brown, *Live Your Dreams* (New York: William Morrow, 1992), pp. 59-61.

16. Christine Benlafquih, "Heaven on Earth," *The Holton-Arms School Standard* (Nov. 1995), p.1.

17. Michael Ryan, "That's Just Becky," *Parade Magazine* (Nov. 20, 1994)

18. "The Family That Grows Together," *Amagram* (Sept. 1995), pp. 7-8.

19. Jack Canfield and Mark Victor Hansen, *Chicken Soup for the Soul* (Deerfield Beach, Florida: Health Communications, Inc., 1993), pp. 168-170 and also Jack Canfield, *Self-Esteem and Peak Performance* Audiotape Set, CareerTrack.

20. Bhagwan Shree Rajneesh is the author of this quote.

21. William Plummer and Ron Ridenhour, "Saving Grace," *People*, August 28, 1995 p. 40-41.

22. I first experienced this at Insight Seminars. It also happens at Networking Seminars.

Bibliography
and Suggested Reading

Anderson, Joan Wester, *Where Angels Walk*, Ballantine Books, New York, New York, 1992.

Andrews, Andy, *Storms of Perfection 1, 2,* and *3,* Lightning Crown Publishers, Nashville, Tenn. 1991, 1994, 1996.

Anastasi, Tom, *The Fight-Free Marriage*, Thomas Nelson Publishing, Nashville, TN, 1995

Anastasi, Tom, *Personality Negotiating: Conflict Without Casualty*, Sterling Publishing, New York, New York, 1993.

Anastasi, Tom, *Personality Selling: Selling the Way Customers Want to Buy,* Sterling Publishing, New York, New York, 1992

Bach, Richard, *Illusions*, Dell Publishing, New York, New York, 1977.

Balch, James and Phyliss, *Prescription for Nutritional Healing*, Avery Publishing Group, 1990.

Blanchard, Ken and Johnson, Spencer, *The One Minute Manager*, Berkley Books, New York, New York, 1987.

Brown, Les, *Live Your Dreams*, William Morrow, New York, New York, 1992.

Canfield, Jack and Hansen, Mark Victor, *The Aladdin Factor*, Berkley Books, New York, New York, 1995.

Canfield, Jack and Hansen, Mark Victor, *Chicken Soup for the Soul: 101 Stories to Open the Heart and Rekindle the Spirit,* Health Communications, Inc., Deerfield Beach, Florida, 1993.

Canfield, Jack and Hansen, Mark Victor, *A Second Helping of Chicken Soup for the Soul: 101 More Stories to Open the Heart and Rekindle the Spirit,* Health Communications, Inc., 1995.

Canfield, Jack and Hansen, Mark Victor, *A Third Serving of Chicken Soup for the Soul: 101 More Stories to Open the Heart and Rekindle the Spirit,* Health Communications, Inc., 1996.

Carnegie, Dale, *How to Win Friends and Influence People,* Pocket Books, 1981.

Chambers, Oswald, *My Utmost for His Highest,* Discovery House, Grand Rapids, MI, 1992.

Chilton, David, *The Wealthy Barber,* Ruma Publishing, 1991.

Chopra, Deepak, *The Seven Spiritual Laws of Success,* Amber-Allen Publishing, 1994.

Clason, Richard, *The Richest Man in Babylon,* Penjuin Books, New York, New York,1926, 1955.

Conari Press, *Random Acts of Kindness,* Emeryville, CA, 1993.

Cohen, Alan, *I Had it All the Time,* Alan Cohen Publications, 1995.

Covey, Stephen R., *The 7 Habits of Highly Effective People,* Simon nd Schuster, New York, NY, 1989.

ovey, Stephen R. *First Things First,* Simon and Schuster, New rk, New York, 1994.

Vos, Rich, *Compassionate Capitalism,* Penguin, New York, w York, New York, 1993.

die, Betty, *Embraced by the Light,* Bantam, Doubleday, Dell, w York, New York.

itz, Robert, *The Path of Least Resistance,* DMA, Salem, MA 1984.

ulghum, Robert, *All I Really Need to Know I Learned in Kindergarten,* Random House, Inc., New York, New York 1986.

Gawain, Shakti, *Creative Visualization,* Bantam Books,New York, New York, 1982.

Hay, Louise, *Learning to Love Yourself*, Simon and Schuster, and *Loving Yourself*, audio tape

Hayward, Susan, *A Guide For The Advanced Soul*, In-Tune Books, Crows' Nest, Australia, 1984.

Hayward, Susan, *Begin It Now!*, In Tune Books, Crows' Nest, Australia, 1987.

Hendrix, Harville, *Getting the Love You Want (couples)*, Harper & Row, 1988.

Hill, Napoleon, *Think and Grow Rich*, Ballantine Books, New York, NY, 1937.

Hill, Napoleon and Stone, W. Clement, *Success Through a Positive Mental Attitude*, Prentice Hall, Inc., 1960.

Hulnick, Ron and Mary, *Financial Freedom in 8 Minutes a Day*, Rodale Press, 1994.

Jampolsky, Gerald, *Love Is Letting Go of Fear*, Ten Speed Press.

Jeffers, Susan, Ph.D., *Feel the Fear and Do It Anyway*, Fawcett Columbine Book, New York, NY, 1987.

Jeffreys, Michael, *Success Secrets of the Motivational Superstars*, Prima, 1996.

Jones, Charlie, *"Tremendous," Life is Tremendous*, Tyndale House, Wheaton, IL, 1968.

Jones, Laurie Beth, *Jesus– CEO*, Hyperion Books, New York, New York, 1995.

Levine, Barbara, *Your Body Believes Every Word You Say*, Aslan Publishing, 1991.

Mandino, Og, *The Greatest Miracle In The World*, Bantam, New York, NY, 1975.

McGinnis, Alan Loy, *The Power of Becoming a Tough-Minded Optimist*, 1995

Ornish, Dean, *Eat More, Weigh Less*, HarperCollins Publishers, New York, New York, 1993.

Peale, Dr. Norman Vincent, *The Power of Positive Thinking*, Ballantine Books, New York, NY, 1982.

Peale, Dr. Norman Vincent, *You Can if You Think You Can,* Prentice-Hall, New York, NY, 1974.

Peck, M. Scott, M.D., *The Road Less Traveled,* Simon and Schuster, New York, NY, 1978.

Perez, Rosita, *The Music is You: A Guide to Thinking Less and Feeling More,* Dr. Trudy Knox.

Qubein, Nido, *Achieving Peak Performance,* Bestsellers Publishers, 1995.

Redfield, James, *The Celestine Prophecy,* and *The Tenth Insight,* Warner Books, New York, New York, 1993 and 1996

Robbins, Anthony, *Unlimited Power,* Simon and Schuster, 1986.

Robinson, Margot, *The Peaceful Soul Within,* Kendall/Hunt Publishing, 1995.

Roger, John and McWilliams, Peter, *Life 101,* Prelude Press, Santa Monica, CA, 1992.

Roger, John and McWilliams, Peter, *Wealth 101,* Prelude Press, Santa Monica, CA, 1992.

Schwartz, Dr. David J., *The Magic of Thinking Big,* Simon and Schuster, New York, NY, 1987.

Schuller, Robert H., *Prayer: My Soul's Adventure with God,* Thomas Nelson, Nashville, TN, 1995

Schuller, Robert H., *Power Thoughts,* Harper-Collins Publishers, New York, New York 1993.

Sher, Barbara, with Gottlieb, Annie, *Wishcraft,* Ballantine Books, New York, New York, 1979.

Shula, Don and Blanchard, Ken, *Everyone's a Coach,* Berkley Books, New York, New York, 1995.

Siegal, Bernie, *Love Medicine & Miracles,* Harper & Row Books, New York, New York, 1986.

Sinetar, Marsha, *Do What You Love, the Money Will Follow,* Aslan Publishing, 1991.

Resources

Recommended Music:

Desiree, *I Ain't Movin'*, Sony Music Entertainment, 1994.

Dion, Celine, *Celine Dion*, Epic Records, 1992.

Estefan, Gloria, *Greatest Hits*, Sony Music Entertainment, 1992.

Franks, Mike, *Dragonfly Summer*, Reprise Records, a Time Warner Company, 1993.

Jackson, Michael, *Dangerous*, Epic Records, 1991.

Lion King Soundtrack, Walt Disney Music Company, 1994.

Loggins, Kenny, *Keep The Fire*, CBS/Columbia Records, 1979.

Mr. Holland's Opus Soundtrack, Poly Gram Records, Inc., 1995.

Stansfield, Lisa, *Affection*, bmg eurodisc ltd., 1990.

Taylor, James, *Greatest Hits*, Warner Brothers Records, 1976.

Tuck & Patty, *Tears of Joy*, Windham Hill Records, 1988.

Vangelis, *Chariots of Fire*, Poly Gram Records, Inc., 1981.

Vandross, Luther, *Power of Love*, Sony Music Entertainment, 1991.

Any of the Olympics Collection albums.

Recommended Movies:

Angels in the Outfield, Apollo 13, The Boy Who Could Fly, Field of Dreams, Flashdance, Hook, Jack, The Little Princess, Mr. Holland's Opus, Mrs. Doubtfire, The Never Ending Story, Rudy, The Secret of My Success, Sister Act, Sister Act 2, Vision Quest, Working Girl, Olympics' Collection videos

Miscellaneous Resources

Jack Canfield – for information about Jack Canfield's books, tapes and trainings, please contact: The Canfield Training Group, P.O. Box 30880, Santa Barbara, CA 93130 Call toll free 800-237-8336 or fax 805-563-2945.

Les Brown – For information about Les Brown's seminars and programs, please contact: Les Brown Unlimited, Inc, 2180 Penobscot Building, Detroit, MI 48226 or call toll free 800-733-4226.

Special Programs Mentioned in the Book

CareerTrack – 1775 38th Street, Boulder, Co. 80361. 303-440-7440

Dolphins Plus – Key Largo Florida, 305-451-1993.

Elf Louise – San Antonio, Texas, 210-224-1843

National Speaker's Association – 1500 South Priest Drive, Tempe, AZ, 85281. 602-968-2552

Nightingale-Conant Videos and Audios – 1-800-572-2770

Project Safeguard – Contact Warren Berry, Mastricola Middle School, Merrimack, NH 03054, 603-424-6221

THE "FIRED UP!" CREED

Inside me is the fire of life. That fire is my passion, my life purpose, my mission and my fulfillment. It burns brightly as I pursue my dreams. I get "FIRED UP!" by regularly scheduling what I love to do. I am clear about what I want and I use my vivid imagination. I regularly visualize my dreams as fully realized and I create dreammaps and dream collages to build my fire. As a "FIRED UP!" person, I act "as if" I am already fully living my dream. I dreambuild, connect with the right people and ask for what I want. I am open to receive the wisdom and assistance of others and I express my appreciation for their help. I thank God for giving me my dreams and the ability to make them come true. As a "FIRED UP!" person, I tap into all my resources, take good care of my health, use my time wisely, manage my money effectively and get out of debt. I stay "FIRED UP!" by laughing often and watching humorous and inspirational movies on a regular basis. I listen to uplifting audiotapes daily and attend seminars and workshops often. As a "FIRED UP!" person, I create affirmations for my dreams and support them with action options. I take action on my dream every day. I overcome all obstacles and nothing keeps me from achieving my dreams. As a "FIRED UP!" person, I invite my little kid inside to come out and play and share their creativity and enthusiasm with me. As a "FIRED UP!" person, I keep going, no matter what, doing whatever it takes. I pursue my dreams with passion, persistence and a positive vision of the outcome. I use tools to stay "FIRED UP!" associate with winners and share my story with others. I use every experience as an opportunity to learn and grow. By living my dreams, doing what I love and staying "FIRED UP!" I make a positive difference in the world. I live my dreams fully, and share my heart and gifts with the world.

I AM "FIRED UP!"